Reading for the Moral

SUNY series in Chinese Philosophy and Culture

Roger T. Ames, editor

Reading for the Moral

Exemplarity and the Confucian Moral Imagination
in Seventeenth-Century Chinese Short Fiction

Maria Franca Sibau

Cover art: Illustration of the fourth story in *Exemplary Words. Bieben Erke Pai'an jingqi* edition preserved at the Bibliothèque Nationale in Paris. Reproduction courtesy of the Institute of Chinese Literature and Philosophy, Academia Sinica.

Published by State University of New York Press, Albany

© 2018 State University of New York

All rights reserved

No part of this book may be used or reproduced in any manner whatsoever without written permission. No part of this book may be stored in a retrieval system or transmitted in any form or by any means including electronic, electrostatic, magnetic tape, mechanical, photocopying, recording, or otherwise without the prior permission in writing of the publisher.

For information, contact State University of New York Press, Albany, NY
www.sunypress.edu

Library of Congress Cataloging-in-Publication Data

Names: Sibau, Maria Franca, author.
Title: Reading for the moral : exemplarity and the Confucian moral imagination in seventeenth-century Chinese short fiction / Maria Franca Sibau.
Description: Albany : State University of New York Press, 2018. | Series: SUNY series in Chinese philosophy and culture | Includes bibliographical references and index.
Identifiers: LCCN 2017031612| ISBN 9781438469898 (hardcover) | ISBN 9781438469911 (ebook) | ISBN 9781438469904 (pbk.)
Subjects: LCSH: Chinese fiction—Ming dynasty, 1368–1644—History and criticism. | Chinese fiction—Qing dynasty, 1644–1912—History and criticism. | Literature and morals—China—History—17th century. | Short stories, Chinese—History and criticism. | Ethics in literature.
Classification: LCC PL2436 .S55 2018 | DDC 895.13/4609—dc23
LC record available at https://lccn.loc.gov/2017031612

10 9 8 7 6 5 4 3 2 1

Contents

List of Figures   vii

List of Abbreviations   ix

Acknowledgments   xi

Introduction: Reading for the Moral   1

Chapter 1   Filial Quests   27

Chapter 2   Filial Dilemmas   49

Chapter 3   The Spectrum of Loyalty   83

Chapter 4   Female Exemplarity and the Violence of Virtue   105

Chapter 5   Interchangeable Brothers   127

Chapter 6   Friends in Need and Friends in Deed   139

Concluding Note   159

Appendix   165

Notes   169

Bibliography   207

Index   223

Figures

I.1.1   Page 1 (recto) from Lu Yunlong's preface to the first story in *Exemplary Words*, printed in calligraphic script. Kyujanggak edition.   8

I.1.2   Page 1 (verso) from Lu Yunlong's preface to the first story in *Exemplary Words*, printed in calligraphic script. Kyujanggak edition.   9

I.2.1   Page 2 (recto) from Lu Yunlong's preface to the first story in *Exemplary Words*, printed in calligraphic script. Kyujanggak edition.   10

I.2.2   Page 2 (verso) from Lu Yunlong's preface to the first story in *Exemplary Words*, printed in calligraphic script. Kyujanggak edition.   11

I.3.1   First page of the first story in *Exemplary Words*. Kyujanggak edition.   12

2.1   Illustration of the fourth story in *Exemplary Words* (recto). *Bieben Erke Pai'an jingqi* edition preserved at the Bibliothèque Nationale in Paris.   79

Abbreviations

CHC   Mote, Frederick W., and Denis Twitchett, eds. *The Cambridge History of China*. Vols. 7 and 8: *The Ming Dynasty, 1368–1644*. Part 1 and 2. Cambridge, UK: Cambridge University Press, 1988–1998.

CK   Ling Mengchu 凌濛初. *Pai'an jingqi* 拍案驚奇, edited by Chen Erdong 陳邇冬 and Guo Junjie 郭雋傑. Beijing: Renmin wenxue chubanshe, 1991.

DMB   Goodrich, L. Carrington, and Chao-ying Fang, eds. *Dictionary of Ming Biography 1368–1644*. New York: Columbia University Press, 1976.

ECCP Hummel, Arthur W., ed. *Eminent Chinese of the Ch'ing Period (1644–1912)*. 2 vols. Washington, DC: Government Printing Office, 1943.

EK   Ling Mengchu 凌濛初. *Erke pai'an jingqi* 二刻拍案驚奇, edited by Chen Erdong 陳邇冬 and Guo Junjie 郭雋傑. Beijing: Renmin wenxue chubanshe, 1996.

JSTY Feng Menglong 馮夢龍. *Jingshi tongyan xinzhu quanben* 警世通言新注全本, edited by Wu Shuyin 吳書蔭. Beijing: Beijing shiyue wenyi chubanshe, 1994.

QYZ   Weiyuan zhuren 薇園主人. *Qingye zhong* 清夜鐘. In *Guben xiaoshuo jicheng* 古本小說集成. Ser. 4. Vol. 13. Shanghai: Shanghai guji chubanshe, 1990.

SDT   Tianran chisou 天然癡叟. *Shi diantou* 石點頭, edited by Li Zhongming 李忠明 and Wang Guanshi 王關仕. Taipei: Sanmin shuju, 1998.

XHEJ   Zhou Ji 周楫. *Xihu erji* 西湖二集, edited by Chen Meilin 陳美林. Taipei: Sanmin shuju, 1998.

XSHY   Feng Menglong 馮夢龍. *Xingshi hengyan* 醒世恆言, edited by Gu Xuejie 顧學頡. Beijing: Renmin wenxue chubanshe, 1999.

XSY   Lu Renlong 陸人龍. *Xingshi yan* 型世言, edited by Chan Hing-ho 陳慶浩. 3 vols. Taibei: Zhongyang yanjiuyuan, Zhongguo wen zhe yanjiusuo 中央研究院中國文哲研究所, 1992.

XSYPZ   Lu Renlong 陸人龍. *Xingshi yan pingzhu* 型世言評注, edited by Chan Hing-ho 陳慶浩, Wu Shuyin 吳書蔭 and Wang Ying 王鍈. 2 vols. Beijing: Xinhua chubanshe, 1999.

YSMY   Feng Menglong 馮夢龍. *Yushi mingyan xinzhu quanben* 喻世明言新注全本, edited by Chen Xizhong 陳曦鐘. Beijing: Beijing shiyue wenyi chubanshe, 1994.

Acknowledgments

I would not have been able to finish this book without the help, support, and encouragement of many teachers, mentors, peers, friends, family members, and institutions. I owe an immense debt of gratitude to all the great teachers and advisors I had the good fortune to learn from, especially Mario Sabattini, Magda Abbiati, Maurizio Scarpari, and Marco Ceresa at Venice University, and Richard Strassberg and David Schaberg at UCLA. At Harvard, Wilt L. Idema and Wai-yee Li have been the best possible advisors one could hope for. I owe a special debt to Robert Hegel not only for his exemplary scholarship but also for his compassion and support. During the long years of graduate study, I was fortunate to find formidable cohorts, who have inspired me with their intellectual brilliance and nourished me with warm friendship: Vincent Leung, Xiaoqiao Ling, Qiulei Hu, Yue Hong, Chengjuan Sun, Xiaosu Sun, Allison Miller, Kristin Williams, William Hedberg, and Jeffrey Moser.

I am very grateful to my colleagues at Emory, Juliette Apkarian, Rong Cai, Cheryl Crowley, Julia Bullock, Sun-Chul Kim, Yu Li, Hong Li, Jia-chen (Wendy) Fu, and Eric Reinders for their support, advice, example, and friendship. I have presented portions of chapters at various conferences over the years, including the Association for Asian Studies conferences, the meeting of the Western Branch of the American Oriental Society, the Northeast Modern Languages Association convention, and faculty colloquia at Emory University. I thank the discussants, fellow panelists, and audiences for their insights, feedback, and corrections during those occasions. I was fortunate to be awarded the Emory University Research Committee grant which allowed a semester release from teaching duties and the time to concentrate on the manuscript revision. I am equally grateful for the financial support received from the Center for Faculty Development and Excellence at Emory and the Confucius Institute of Atlanta. Rivi Handler-Spitz generously lent her intellectual acumen and supernaturally sharp eye and offered invaluable suggestions and corrections on a few chapters on short notice, for which I am truly grateful. I also thank Karin Myhre, Amanda Wright, Kevin Corrigan, Marco Ravina, Tonio Andrade, Eric Moore, and Angela Porcarelli for their advice and support at various junctures. Elena Chiu, Eugenio Menegon, Pauli Wai Tashima, Susan H. Bush, Barbara Bisetto, and Alessandro Moretto are to be especially thanked for the steadfast support and friendship over the years (and for bearing with my regrettable tendency to disappear into the woods).

Heartfelt thanks must be given to the Woodruff Library staff at Emory, especially Wang Guo-hua and Marie Hansen for their help acquiring or borrowing sources countless times over the past few years. I am deeply grateful to the anonymous reviewers for their insightful feedback, and to Christopher Ahn for his faith in my project and unflagging support throughout the whole process; working with him and the staff at SUNY Press has been a pleasure. I would also like to thank the Institute of Chinese Literature and Philosophy of the Academia Sinica for graciously granting permission to reprint reproductions of the Kyujanggak edition of *Exemplary Words*. Needless to say, I am solely responsible for all the remaining errors and shortcomings.

I dedicate this book to my family: Enzo Borean, Marisa Rossi, and Clark and Francesco (Schino) Nguyen, with boundless love and gratitude for everything.

Introduction

Reading for the Moral

Be filial to your parents.
Be respectful to your elders.
Live in harmony with your neighbors.
Instruct your sons and grandsons.
Be content with your calling.
Do no evil.

孝順父母, 尊敬長上, 和睦鄉里, 教訓子孫, 各安生理, 毋作非為。

—Ming Taizu, *Sacred Edict in Six Maxims*[1]

Perhaps there is no better way to begin a book about morality and its representation in late Ming vernacular stories than by taking a look at the moral exhortations attributed to its founder, known as the *Sacred Edict in Six Maxims* (*Shengyu liuyu* 聖諭六語). What is striking in Zhu Yuanzhang's bare-bones formulation of Confucian ideology is the emphasis on the hortatory injunctions, or the "do's," rather than the cautionary directive, the lone "don't" in the last maxim.[2] It is no exaggeration to say that many vernacular stories—a best-selling genre of China's long seventeenth century that is most readily associated with popular didacticism—may be read as so many commentaries on the last cautionary maxim, rather than elaborations on the hortatory instructions that precede it. Whereas the last maxim is at once bland and darkly ominous in its refusal to spell out what exactly constitutes evil (*fei wei* 非為), the vernacular stories often thrive in exploring and staging precisely that. What we read about in so many of Feng Menglong's (1574–1645) and Ling Mengchu's (1580–1644) stories are the endlessly intriguing or banal ways in which men and women *do* evil and are consequently punished for it—or, more rarely, find their redemption.

In the modern age, the explicit moral message in these stories has often been dismissed as a perfunctory homage to a rather vague notion of "conventional morality," while the real focus and energy of the narration is supposedly located elsewhere: in the bold exploration of human desire, the frank depiction of sex, or the lurid details of crime stories. Literary critics tend to be fascinated with what they see as subversion rather than order, with transgression rather than conformity. Readers naturally find the colorful villains or the flawed heroes more interesting than the perfectly virtuous but perfectly boring heroes or heroines in didactic stories.[3]

The focus on the darker side of human action and psyche also fits well with what has been the modern dominant narrative of the late Ming, a narrative that has tended to depict it as a period characterized by subjectivity, individualism, and libertarianism.[4] As the narrative goes, starting from the sixteenth century, under the influence of Wang Yangming (1472–1528), scholars and writers began to move away from the dominant Cheng-Zhu school of Neo-Confucianism, which emphasized the accumulation of knowledge and rigid observance of rites and principles, and began to shift toward more individualized approaches to self-cultivation. Wang Yangming's followers, particularly the members of the radical Taizhou school, continued to elaborate and popularize ideas of innate goodness, spontaneous intuition, and genuine expression. Li Zhi (1527–1602) vocally defended the legitimacy of desire and even the pursuit of individual profit. This had profound reverberations in the realm of literature and the arts. In the words of F. W. Mote, during the last century and a half of the Ming dynasty, "expressionism took form in the new poetry and literary essay; eroticism found a place in expression; trends towards abstraction appeared in the graphic arts; social freedoms were championed in radical thought; humor and pathos filled the new dramatic literature of human feelings; and a broadly ironic rhetoric marked the profoundly imaginative reworking of popular themes in the great works of Ming fiction."[5]

For all its merits, this narrative has drawn disproportionate attention toward selected figures and currents (Tang Xianzu, the Taizhou school, the "cult of feelings," etc.), which have been seen as representative of the entire late Ming period. In the literary arena, scholarly attention has been focused on the representations of human feelings, subjectivity, irony, and subversion in fiction and drama, while the undeniable didacticism of many literary works produced in this period has failed to generate a comparable amount of scholarly discussion.[6]

This book focuses on a group of vernacular stories that, by their very nature, complicate the dominant narrative of the late Ming I have just described. The last two decades of the Ming, in particular, saw the publication of a strain of story collections intensely concerned with Confucian moral exempla. Other similarly oriented collections appeared in the aftermath of the Qing conquest. While these collections include a fair number of cautionary tales, they often focus on examples of positive morality, thus reverting our attention toward the first five hortatory maxims in the *Sacred Edict*. The primary texts discussed in this study are *Exemplary Words for the World* (*Xingshi yan* 型世言, 1632) and *Bell in the Still Night* (*Qingye zhong* 清夜鐘, c. 1645), attributed to the Hangzhou brothers Lu Renlong 陸人龍 (fl. first half of seventeenth century) and Lu Yunlong 陸雲龍 (1587–1666),[7] but shared source materials and concerns are also found in *West Lake Stories, Second Collection* (*Xihu erji* 西湖二集, pre-1644) by Zhou Ji 周楫, *Stories of Figures from the Seventy-Two Domains* (*Qishi'er chao renwu yanyi* 七十二朝人物演義, c. 1640), and *Sobering Stone* (*Zuixing shi* 醉醒石) compiled by Gukuangsheng 古狂生 in the early Qing. After Patrick Hanan's seminal article on this group of story collections, which he termed "fiction of moral duty," little scholarly attention has been given to this corpus.[8] While a measure of explicit moral illustration has long been recognized as one of the staple features of the mature vernacular story as codified in Feng Menglong's enormously successful *San Yan* (Three Words), scholars have rarely probed deeply into the ethical dimension of these stories.

The concept of "self-containment" and the struggle between abandon and temperance, which Keith McMahon has singled out as fundamental to the ideological fabric of seventeenth-century fiction in an early study, do not seem to adequately explain the dynamics at work in stories of moral exemplars, particularly those in which the very morality of the hero or heroine is displayed through *excess* and out-of-the-ordinary feats.[9] Timothy Wong's claim that morality is spectacularized for the sake of entertainment is likewise not entirely convincing, in that it tends to trivialize the kind of "superhuman morality" embodied in the stories as ludicrous.[10] Shuhui Yang has grappled with the apparent ideological inconsistencies found in the *San Yan* stories, by arguing that the degree of reliability of Feng's storyteller-narrator is predicated on "the nature of the moral message" he intends to impart to the reader in a given story.[11] Yang seems to assume that the storyteller's voice represents "conventional morality," while Feng's subtle manipulations of that voice may in turn confirm, problematize, or outright subvert the explicit message. Yet it is unclear to what extent Feng's celebrated friendship stories, for instance, where Yang finds a perfect alignment between the conventional storyteller's voice and Feng's own views, represent "conventional morality," a concept that remains elusive and undefined.[12] More recently, Tina Lu has offered penetrating and provocative analyses of a number of vernacular stories, including tales of filial "cannibalism" and tales that dramatize situations in which the five relations are terribly at odds with one another, but her work does not directly or systematically address morality per se.[13]

In contrast with these earlier approaches, this study brings morality into sharper focus, by arguing that the idea of "conventional morality" itself needs to be more rigorously unpacked and historicized. In the remainder of the introduction I will present the provenance of the stories under discussion in this book. I will then examine the key concepts that make up the Confucian moral universe as reflected in the stories: the Five Cardinal Relationships, the concept of retribution (*bao* 報) and its interplay with notions of virtue, the rhetoric of exemplarity, and the spectrum of positions regarding the role of nature vs. nurture in the shaping of the moral hero or heroine. I will also address the crucial role of the commentarial tradition in articulating the ideal readership and envisioning the social function of these narratives.

The Provenance of the Stories

The stories discussed in this book are primarily drawn from two collections, *Exemplary Words for the World* and *Bell in the Still Night*. Both collections have been attributed to the Lu brothers Renlong and Yunlong, although the attribution is more uncertain in the case of *Bell in the Still Night*. Readers interested in a more detailed discussion of the authorship and editions of these texts are referred to the appendix.

Exemplary Words includes forty stories. It is a carefully arranged and organic *collection* of stories. Whereas Western scholarship on the European novella tradition has historically paid much attention to the organization of story collections as *books*—perhaps not surprisingly considering the enormous influence of the *Decameron* and its elaborate architecture at the macro-textual level—it is only in recent times that the organizing principles of Chinese story collections have been studied. One reason may be the absence of a tradition of frame stories and similar devices, with the notable exception of the early Qing collection *Idle Talk under the Bean Arbor* (*Doupeng xianhua* 豆棚閒話). Shuhui Yang has shown how paired stories in *San Yan* often mirror or contrast with each other in significant ways.[14] The pairing device as a structuring principle also operates in *Exemplary Words* stories. For example, Story 3 tells of a filial man who swaps his foolish wife to ransom his mother, while Story 4 is about a filial girl who slices her flesh to save her grandmother. Story 5 tells of a righteous man who kills a lecherous adulteress who happens to be his own lover, while Story 6 portrays a chaste young widow who is driven to commit suicide by the machinations of her corrupt mother-in-law. Further, Stories 4 and 6 are based on historical records, while Stories 3 and 5 are adapted from fictional sources. Clearly these stories have been carefully arranged as pairs and they mirror one another on multiple levels: the gender of the main character, the main virtue illustrated in the story, the fictionality or historicity of the characters and events.

What makes *Exemplary Words* especially appealing for this study is that morality functions as an organizing principle. The collection appears to be neatly organized into two distinct halves. The first twenty stories are devoted to positive examples of moral behavior, while the latter twenty consist mostly of cautionary tales of the kind more commonly found in the *San Yan* and *Er Pai* collections. The last three stories deal with the supernatural, in the form of fox spirits, dragons and oysters, and a gibbon in a vain quest for immortality. The moral impulse is still present in the second half—one could chart the stories as tales of upright officials (*qingguan* 清官), skilled generals (*liangjiang* 良將), and the like—but in these stories the focus is not so much on the exemplarity of the good characters, but rather on the twists and turns of the plot. This book focuses on the stories from the first half.

Bell in the Still Night was published sometime during the Longwu reign (1645–1646) of the short-lived Southern Ming.[15] With the original edition including sixteen stories, it is much more modest in scope than *Exemplary Words*. Like the latter, *Bell in the Still Night* is a thematically organic collection of stories, with a prevalence of stories on loyal ministers. However, the stories do not have an individual preface, nor do they have the abundance of marginal and final commentaries that characterize *Exemplary Words*. The final commentary is limited to a line or two. Some scholars believe that the author of the final commentaries is Lu Renlong, although there is no definitive consensus.[16]

The Lu brothers, whose names are connected in the capacity of compiler and commentator to both *Exemplary Words* and *Bell in the Still Night*, were active in the world of commercial publishing during the last two decades of the Ming. Lu Yunlong, the elder brother, is the better known of the two. Like many others of his generation, he had attempted to pass the civil service examinations several times, without success. He later founded his own publishing house in Qiantang (modern-day Hangzhou), called Zhengxiaoguan 崢霄館 (Lodge of Lofty Clouds), which specialized in poetry and prose anthologies and works of fiction. The output of Zhengxiaoguan appears to have been comparatively modest, but it includes titles such as *Informal Essays by Sixteen Eminent Authors of the August Ming* (*Huang Ming shiliu mingjia xiaopin* 皇明十六名家小品), a best-selling anthology of *xiaopin* (informal essays, or vignettes) by Ming authors, which continues to be widely available, in modern editions, to the present day.

Lu Yunlong's activity as editor, or, more precisely, *pingxuan jia* 評選家 "specialist in producing anthologies with commentary," is noteworthy. Virtually all the books published by Zhengxiaoguan bear his substantial interventions, in the form of prefaces and commentaries. This body of comments provides material that allows us to reconstruct Lu Yunlong's literary sensibility and, more broadly, his cultural allegiances in the turbulent decades preceding the fall of the Ming.[17] Lu Yunlong is also attributed the authorship of *The Story of Wei Zhongxian: A Book of Indictment* (*Wei Zhongxian xiaoshuo chijian shu* 魏忠賢小說斥奸書, 1628), one of the many works written during that period that have been categorized as "instant fiction," or more literally "fiction on current events" (*shishi xiaoshuo* 時事小說).[18] Indeed, Lu Yunlong's activity as both author and editor/publisher bespeaks a clear commitment to contemporary times, ranging from a celebration of the literary giants of the mid and late Ming in his best-selling collection of *xiaopin* (informal essays), to a harsh indictment of the eunuch faction, visible not only in the novel on the notorious Wei Zhongxian but also in the letters and essays included in his *Recent Words by Cuiyuge* (*Cuiyuge Jinyan* 翠娛閣近言) (Cuiyuge, or Hall of Azure Entertainment, was one of Lu Yunlong's sobriquets). Lu Yunlong's stance seems to have been sympathetic to the Donglin party, a loosely organized association of scholar-officials who opposed the eunuch faction and advocated a kind of puritanical Confucianism. He also professed to be a great admirer of the Yuan brothers' Gong'an school, which advocated spontaneity and individual sensibility in poetry.

We have but scant information on Lu Renlong, the younger brother and the compiler of *Exemplary Words*. In 1630 his forty-chapter novel *A Record of Fervent Loyalty in the Liaodong Peninsula* (*Liaohai danzhong lu* 遼海丹忠錄) was published by Zhengxiaoguan, followed in 1632 by *Exemplary Words*. The novel, a piece of "fiction on current events," tells the story of the controversial late Ming general Mao Wenlong 毛文龍 (1576–1629) and his military exploits against Nurhaci (Qing Taizu, 1559–1626) in the Liaodong region.[19] In the novel, Mao is portrayed as a faultless patriot heinously murdered by Yuan Chonghuan 袁崇煥 (1584–1630), although the story ends on a note of hope as Mao's legacy is taken up by his successors. It is conceivable that Lu Renlong's fascination with Mao Wenlong may be partly derived from the fact that Mao also hailed from Hangzhou. Lu Renlong, as mentioned above, was also involved for a number of years in his brother's editorial activity. However, there is a complete silence around Lu Renlong after the year 1635 in the available sources.

Lu Minshu's biography of his father Lu Yunlong alludes to some kind of disagreement among the brothers, after which Lu Renlong withdrew from the publishing house.[20]

Prefaces and Commentaries: Staging the Ideal Readership

Literary analysis that focuses on morality is inevitably concerned with the issue of readers' response—whether actual (rare) or implied. In this sense, the tradition of fiction commentaries, while subject to its own generic conventions, offers precious material for analysis. Among mid-seventeenth-century story collections, *Exemplary Words* is remarkable for its rich and varied paratextual apparatus; but all the story collections discussed in this book have at least one kind of commentary (eyebrow commentaries, which run on the upper register of the page atop the main text, were typical of late Ming editions, while brief tail commentaries seem to be preferred in wartime and early Qing editions).[21] Prefaces and commentaries frequently provide insight into how the actions of contemporary or near-contemporary characters were linked with paradigmatic examples, how specific choices and traits were appraised from a moral standpoint, and what kind of moral lessons readers were supposed to extrapolate from the texts. In this sense, these texts are packaged in a way that not only anticipates but actually stages the enactment of their desired social function.

As noted earlier, the Lu brothers worked as a team in crafting *Exemplary Words*. Lu Renlong was responsible for redacting the text of each story, while Lu Yunlong contributed prefaces and commentaries. Lu Renlong's act of compilation is designated through a variety of terms: *yan* 演 or *yanyi* 演義 (spin out; expound the meaning), *ji* 輯 (compile), *zhuan* 撰 (compose), and *bian* 編 (edit). These terms point to varying degrees of re-elaboration of pre-existing source materials. As for Lu Yunlong, he contributed the prefaces, final commentaries, and in all likelihood, the marginal or "eyebrow" commentaries beneath the variety of pseudonyms under which they appear.[22] Individual story prefaces—an unusual feature among story collections of the time—are clearly separated from the texts of the stories and printed in a variety of calligraphic styles (fig. I.1.1–I.2.2). The commentators' pseudonyms, such as Staunch Man from Yanguan (Yanguan mujiangren 鹽官木強人) in Story 1 (fig. I.3.1), the Hero among Women from Qinhuai (Qinhuai nüzhong zhangfu 秦淮女中丈夫) in Story 6, or the Old Lady who Understands Poetry from Wulin (Wulin jieshi ao 武林解詩媼) in Story 10, are clearly linked with the story content and establish the commentators as model readers who stand in a metonymical relationship with the story.

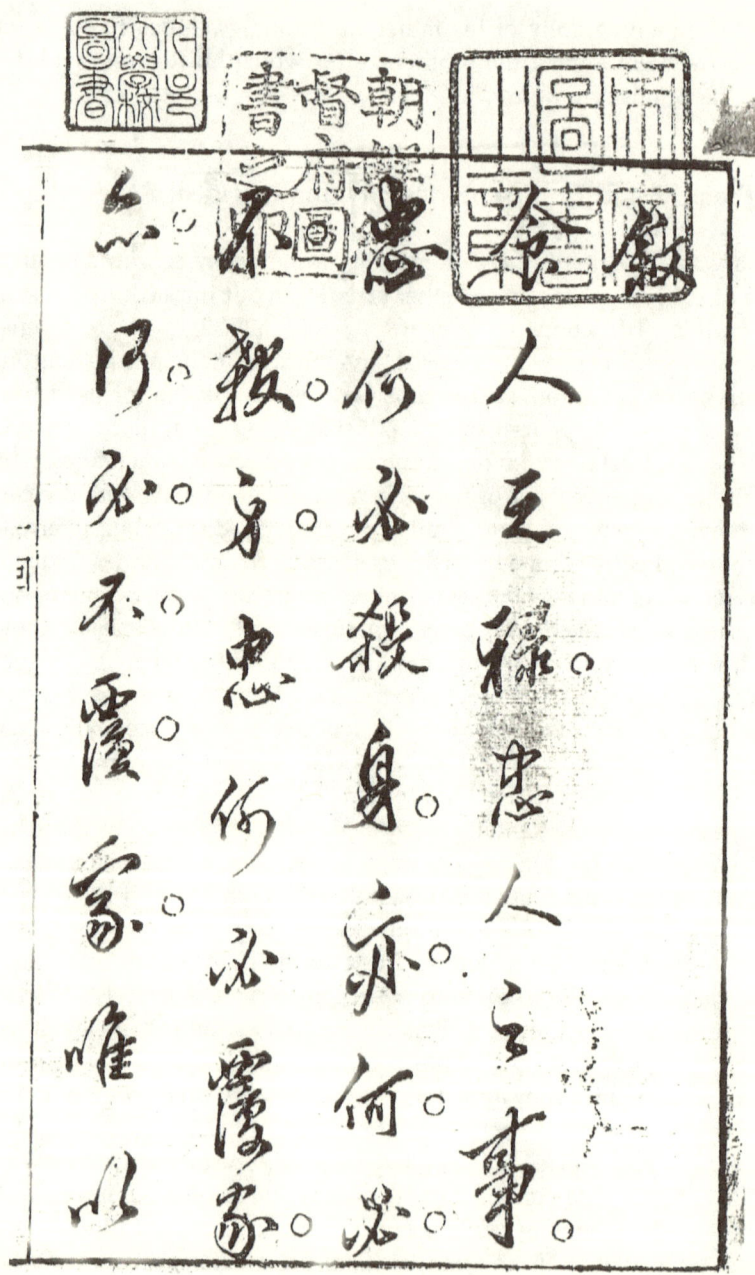

Figure I.1.1. Page 1 (recto) from Lu Yunlong's preface to the first story in *Exemplary Words*, printed in calligraphic script. Kyujanggak edition. Reproduction courtesy of the Institute of Chinese Literature and Philosophy, Academia Sinica.

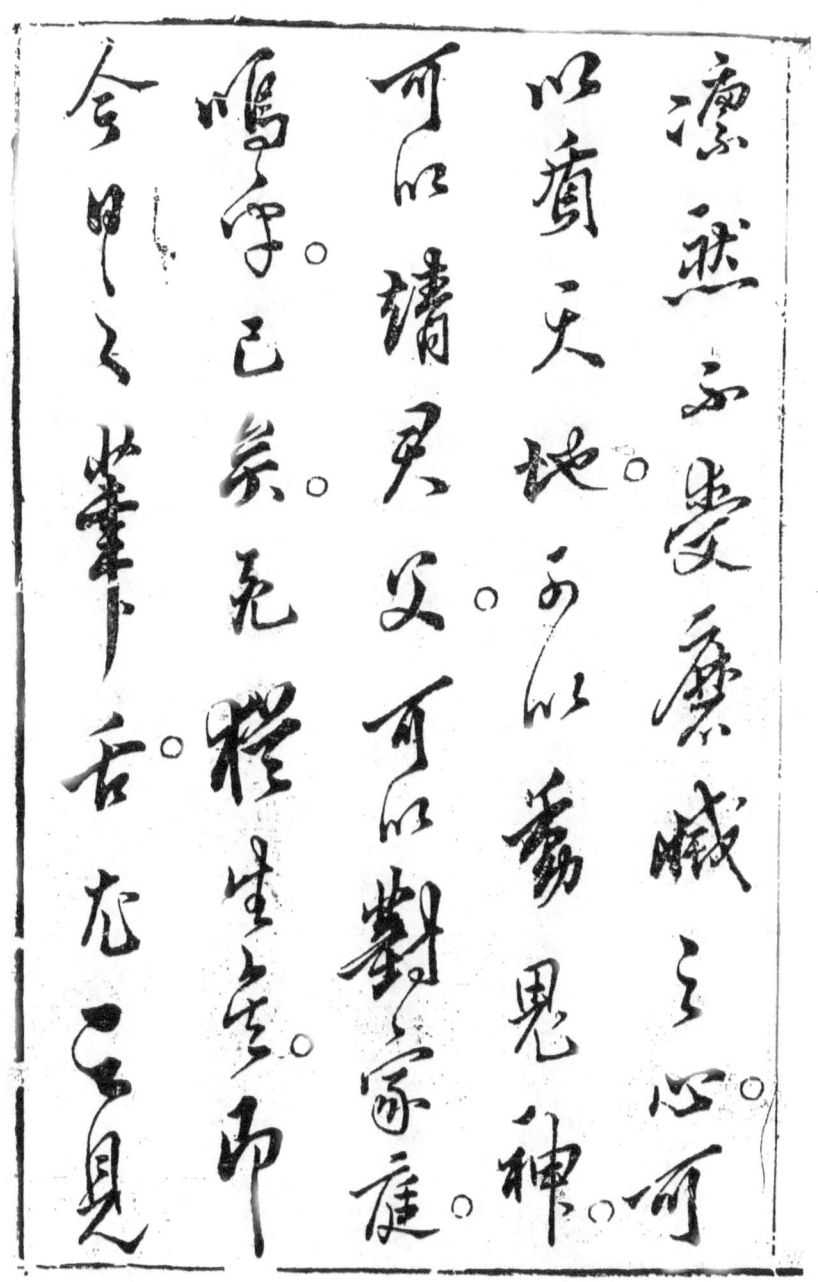

Figure I.1.2. Page 1 (verso) from Lu Yunlong's preface to the first story in *Exemplary Words*, printed in calligraphic script. Kyujanggak edition. Reproduction courtesy of the Institute of Chinese Literature and Philosophy, Academia Sinica.

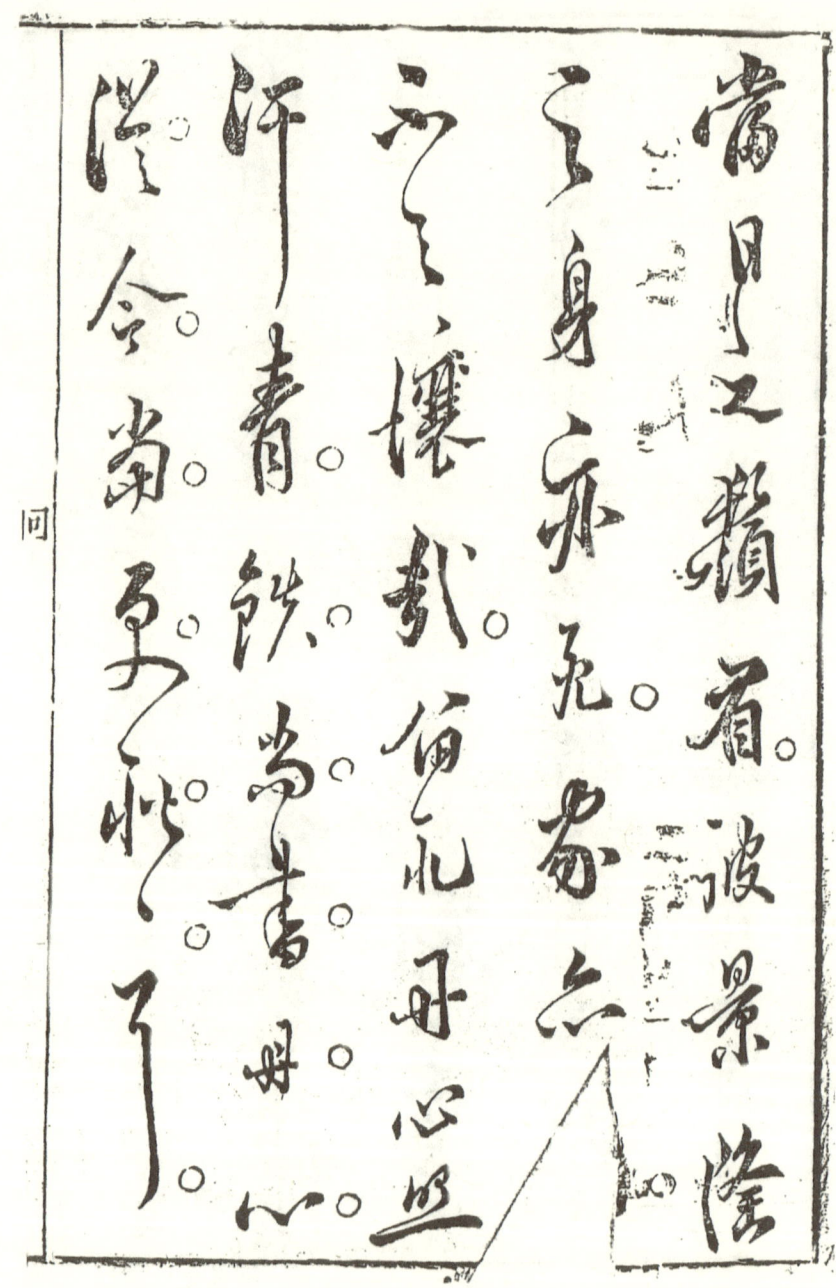

Figure I.2.1. Page 2 (recto) from Lu Yunlong's preface to the first story in *Exemplary Words*, printed in calligraphic script. Kyujanggak edition. Reproduction courtesy of the Institute of Chinese Literature and Philosophy, Academia Sinica.

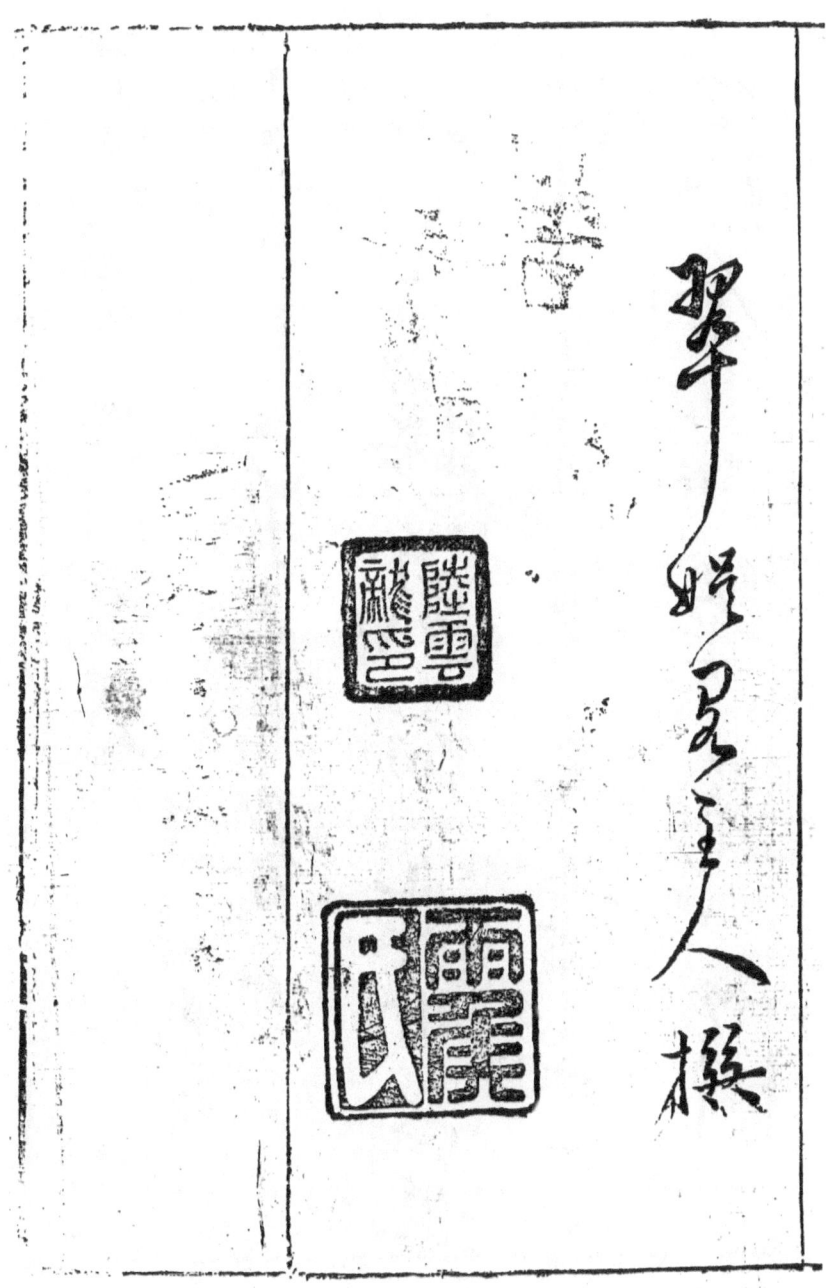

Figure I.2.2. Page 2 (verso) from Lu Yunlong's preface to the first story in *Exemplary Words*, printed in calligraphic script. Kyujanggak edition. Reproduction courtesy of the Institute of Chinese Literature and Philosophy, Academia Sinica.

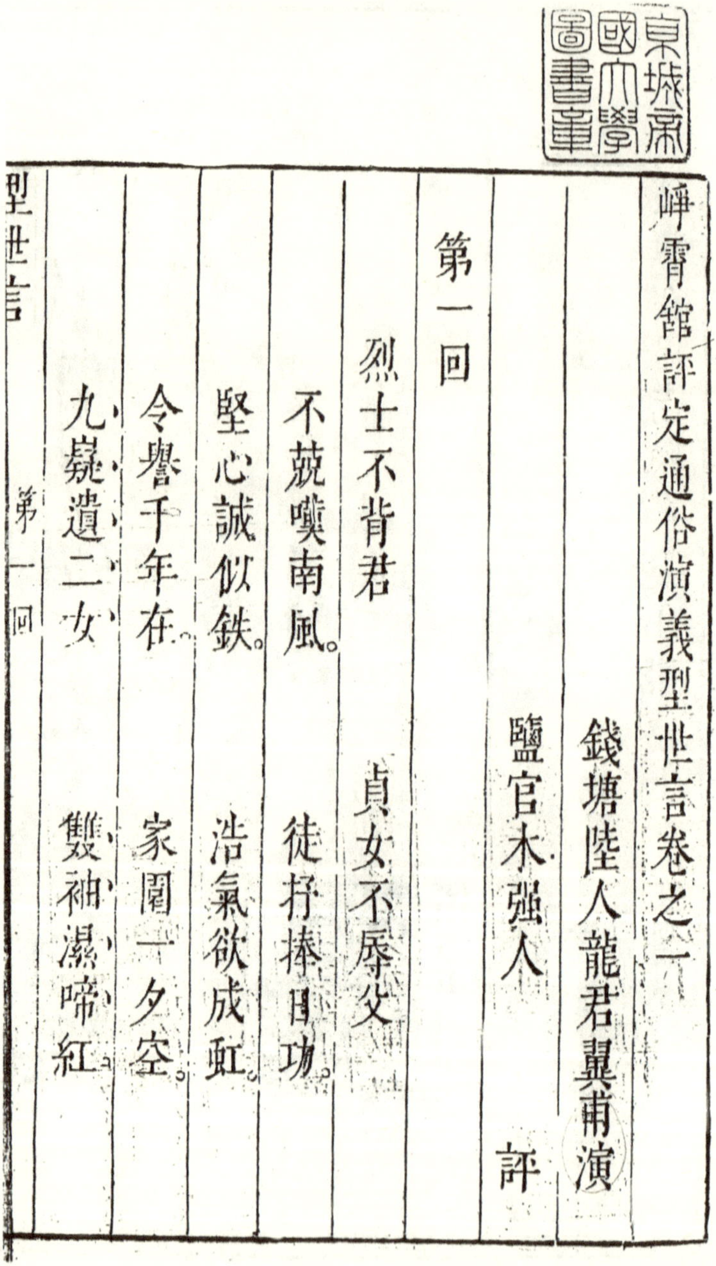

峥霄館評定通俗演義型世言卷之一

錢塘陸人龍君翼甫演

鹽官木強人　　　　評

第一回

烈士不背君　貞女不辱父

不兢嘆南風　徒抒捧日功

堅心誠似鐵　浩氣欲成虹

令譽千年在　家園一夕空

九嶷遺二女　雙袖濕啼紅

Figure I.3.1. First page of the first story in *Exemplary Words*. Kyujanggak edition. Reproduction courtesy of the Institute of Chinese Literature and Philosophy, Academia Sinica.

Scholars have argued that the arrangement of the stories in the collection may also be due to Lu Yunlong.[23] The division of labor is interesting in that the stories themselves are practically devoid of narratorial asides, simulated dialogue with the audience, and the usual formal features of vernacular stories. The narrator's comments are usually confined to the introduction and conclusion of the story. As a result, much of the explicit evaluative comment rests on the commentators' shoulders. This study will pay special attention to the dynamics between these different voices and levels, and their interpretive claims toward the narrative.

Because the copy of *Exemplary Words* rediscovered by Chan Hing-ho at the Kyujanggak Library is missing the first fascicle (*ce*), which must have included one or more prefaces to the collection as a whole, we can only speculate on the kind of rhetorical pronouncements the compiler and/or commentator would have offered there. We can, however, turn to the preface of *Illusion* (*Huanying* 幻影), an anthology that appropriated thirty stories from *Exemplary Words*. The preface is signed by a Mengjue daoren 夢覺道人 (The person of the Way awakened from dreams) and dated 1643.[24]

> After closing the gate, and having nothing better to do, I picked up some tattered volumes, and got hold of one or two unofficial histories. Just as I was about to fall prey to boredom, I chanced upon [these stories], which are for the most part about loyalty, filial piety, chivalrous behavior, and heroism. In the midst there are also a few cases of greed and depravity, treachery and evildoing. Observing how people endure contempt and bear humiliation, until the true circumstances are finally revealed, is sufficient to stir people to a profound awakening. In general, the moral principles governing the bonds between ruler and subject, husband and wife, elder and younger brothers, and between friends should be recognized as true (*zhen* 真), whereas the accidents of high and low status, failure and success, and the cardinal vices of wine, lust, money, and anger, ought to be regarded as illusory (*huan* 幻). One moment is all hustle and bustle, the next turns to emptiness—only shadows of all sorts of good and evil deeds are left behind. These have been widely circulated among the people, until an aficionado has elaborated them [into vernacular stories]. Future generations will be filled with reverence for the noble deeds or moved with indignation at the ugliness and perversity [portrayed in these stories]. Amazing and surprising, are these not all

extraordinary cases? Today, I have especially selected a few of the most outstanding among these stories to be printed, and this is not without significance.

A guest paid a visit and reproached me thus: "This country is currently troubled by so many calamities—if we are not plagued by drought and flooding, then we have to suffer from conflicts and wars. So why don't you draw up a plan to revive [those who are languishing in] ditches and gullies, or perform a meritorious deed to reconstitute our defeated army, instead of vainly babbling about popular tales and unofficial histories and busying yourself with inessential tasks?"

I could not help but sigh as I replied, "Not only do you not know me, but you also do not know what it really means to serve the country! The disorder in the country originates entirely from the fact that people cling ignobly to their life and pursue personal profit, turn their back on king and kin, and flout the principles of virtue and rightness. So in the end it all comes to this grand illusion. Was there ever an army that, not being plagued by internecine strife, failed to fight against enemies on the outside? Today everyone thinks that the army ought to stop [fighting], so that there would be relief from violence and famine. Yet, in the end, they cannot be of any help. Isn't it sad! But since *they* are completely useless, why should they be vexed with *my* babbling? My own plan consists in using this book to bring remedy. If people read it, they will be able to follow the principles, rectify their feelings, and awaken to the truth. They will realize that ruler and father, teacher and friend, each have their own prescribed place, and that wealth and honor, profit and success, each have their greater principle. Therefore, although my narration of past people is at times based upon hearsay, if my stories can edify the crowds, I will truly have fulfilled my innermost desire. Who can say that this is of no use to the world?"

掩關無事，簡點廢帙，得一二野史。煩倦之頃，偶抽閱之，多忠孝俠烈之事。間有貪淫奸宄數條，觀[其含垢]25蒙恥，敗露情狀，亦足發人深醒。總之君臣、父子、夫婦、兄弟、朋友之理道，宜認得真；貴賤、窮達、酒色財氣之情景，須看得幻。當場熱哄，瞬息成虛，止留一善善惡惡影子，為世人所喧傳，好事者之敷演。後世或因芳躅而敬之，或因醜戾而憤之。驚驚愕愕，奇乎不奇乎？今特攝其最奇者數條授梓，非無謂也。

客有過而責余曰:「方今四海多故, 非苦旱潦, 即罹干戈, 何不畫一策以蘇溝壑, 建一功以全覆軍, 而徒曉曉于稗官野史, 作不急之務耶?」予不覺嘆曰:「子非特不知余, 並不知天下事者也！天下之亂, 皆從貪生好利, 背君親, 負德義所至, 變幻如此。焉有兵不訌于內, 而刃不橫于外者乎? 今人孰不以為師旅當息, 凶荒宜拯, 究不得一濟焉。悲夫！既無所濟, 又何煩余之饒舌也? 余策在以此救之, 使人睹之, 可以理順, 可以正情, 可以悟真; 覺君父師友自有定分, 富貴利達自有大義。今者敘說古人, 雖屬影響, 以之喻俗, 實獲我心, 孰謂無補于世哉?」26

The manner in which Mengjue daoren promotes the stories in *Illusion* stands in striking contrast with Feng Menglong's well-known defense of the vernacular story articulated in his preface to *Stories Old and New* (*Gujin xiaoshuo* 古今小說, aka *Yushi mingyan* 喻世明言, 1620), the first installment of the *San Yan*. Feng was primarily preoccupied with defending the vernacular story from the classical tale, and proving its worth alongside canonical genres of literature represented by the classics and histories. "Fiction rises when orthodox historiography is on the wane" 史統散而小說興, he famously wrote.27 Feng Menglong's apology for the act of collecting, redacting, and reading vernacular tales was thus mostly *literary*. Mengjue daoren, on the other hand, defends the legitimacy of vernacular stories not in literary terms, but rather vis-à-vis public service. The compilation of these stories for print is here defended not against other literary pursuits, but rather against social action and concrete endeavors for the benefit of the country—a country which, as the disapproving fictional guest quoted in the preface says, is plagued by unruly armies, drought, flood, and famine, and thus urgently in need of concrete action. Mengjue daoren argues that the moral benefit provided by his stories is more far-reaching than any concrete plans to repair the dams or provide famine relief. While it is not uncommon to find gestures toward the general moral malaise of the time in many story collection prefaces, the preface of *Illusion* is remarkably forceful in its detailed articulation of the country's troubles.

The preface of *Illusion* is by no means unique, though, in emphasizing the ideal social function of vernacular stories, and popular fiction in general. The prefaces of *San Yan*, when read in chronological succession, exhibit a progressive emphasis on moral instruction. The prefaces of *Common Words to Warn the World* (*Jingshi tongyan*, 1624) and *Constant Words to Awaken the World* (*Xingshi hengyan*, 1627) explicitly frame the vernacular stories as uniquely powerful carriers of moral messages—powerful because stories, by means of their accessible language and memorable plots, can move the audience in ways that classics and histories cannot. But much energy in the preface of *Common Words* is still directed toward carefully clearing the literary terrain, so to speak, and exonerating fiction from its potential charges of moral dubiousness—moral dubiousness because fiction deals with events or characters that are false (*yan* 贗). The moral purport of the collection itself is at one point phrased in negative terms: "if there is no offense against decency, no deviation from the teaching of the sages and worthies, and no breach of the morals taught by the classics and histories such as the *Book of Odes* and the *Book of Documents*, why should these [works of fiction] be discarded?" 不害于風化, 不謬于聖賢, 不戾于詩書經史。若此者, 其可廢乎?[28] When it is articulated in positive terms, the moral purport seems to comprise a rather catholic range of ideals, from virile, physical courage to the Mencian spirit of compassion elicited at the sight of a child about to fall in the well, as mentioned in the preface of *Constant Words*. In a broad analogy, Buddhism and Taoism are also cavalierly co-opted and presented as complementary to Confucianism.[29]

The preface of *Illusion*, on the other hand, takes the reader squarely into the world of scholastic Confucianism. Twice are the Five Relationships mentioned, at the beginning and at the end of the piece, and they are presented as the core moral message. Intriguingly, the focus is on the moral and social duty of the superior member in the relationship (father, ruler, teacher), which can perhaps be read as a need to reassert the role of authority figures. In the author's words, not only can literature instruct the masses, it can literally save the world.

Prefaces are self-serving, highly wrought endorsement pieces typically written (or presented as if they were written) by someone other than the author or compiler. The preface of *Illusion* clearly reflects the aims of the editor, whoever he was. Even if all the stories in this anthology are lifted from *Exemplary Words*, they have been radically rearranged, the titular couplets rewritten (with few exceptions) and the individual story prefaces and eyebrow commentaries omitted.[30] In reducing the number of stories from forty to thirty-four, the editor privileged cautionary stories from the second half of *Exemplary Words*, while omitting some of the most striking exemplary tales found in the first half, such as the story of the filial granddaughter Chen Miaozhen who cuts her liver to save her grandmother (*XSY* 4), that of Wang Yuan who travels in search of his father (*XSY* 9), and the story of the young widow who commits suicide with her mother's acquiescence (*XSY* 10). In so doing, the editor reshaped the collection to be more in line with the preference for cautionary examples shown in widely popular collections such as Ling Mengchu's *Two Slaps*.

The tone of the preface of *Bell in the Still Night*, signed by a Weiyuan zhuren 薇園主人 (Master of the Fern Garden; believed to be Lu Yunlong), is considerably more somber than that of *Illusion*. The author describes his contemporaries as constantly bustling about like "ants swarming on rankish meat," a self-deluded mass wallowing in mental and moral confusion. If the preface of *Illusion* took the dichotomous pair truth (*zhen* 真) and illusion (*huan* 幻) as its main trope, the preface of *Bell in the Still Night* turns to the concept of dream (*meng* 夢) and awakening (*xing* 醒) as its central metaphor, which is then developed into the image of "clapper" (*duo* 鐸) and "bell" (*ling* 鈴)—as well as the eponymous alarm bell (*zhong* 鐘)—as tools for "waking up" the befuddled audience and bringing them back to their senses. The audience is envisioned as "the masses" (*da zhong* 大眾), and the social function of fiction is to serve as a tool of moral enlightenment that will awaken the readers to "loyalty and filiality," "sagehood and wisdom."[31]

The Debate on the Five Cardinal Relationships

The Five Cardinal Relationships (*wu lun* 五倫)—the bonds between father and son, ruler and subject, husband and wife, elder and younger brother, and friends—not only constitute the way in which interpersonal relations were understood, but represent the very means through which moral cultivation was performed in traditional Confucian ethics. With each bond is associated a "cardinal virtue," namely, filial piety, loyalty, chastity, brotherly deference, and trustworthy friendship. While it is certainly true that these bonds and their concomitant virtues were continuously invoked throughout imperial Chinese history, contributing to sense of unchanging and stagnant society, it is important to keep in mind that their precise nature, scope, and ranking were far from immutable since the time of their earliest formulations in the *Mencius* and the *Record of Rites* (*Liji*). As Tu Wei-ming has noted, in their original formulation the five relationships were understood as fundamentally reciprocal.[32] One can trace a general evolution toward an increasingly absolutistic understanding of the five bonds and a de-emphasis on the reciprocal, however asymmetrical, obligations pertaining to each (with the exception of friendship).

The five relationships were usually not theorized as discrete relationships, but rather seen as part of an integrated, harmonious whole, where each bond ideally mirrored the others. This homologous or "parallel conception of society," to use Norman Kutcher's phrase, was generally recognized at all levels of society.³³ Yet plays and novels often poignantly dramatize situations where bonds are at odds with one another, for example in the conflict between brotherhood and political loyalty in *The Three Kingdoms,* or between filial piety and conjugal fidelity in *Injustice to Dou E.* In contrast, Ming didactic plays such as *Wulun quan bei* 伍倫全備 (*Five Relationships Perfected and Completed*), showing a perfect fulfillment of all five bonds, were traditionally dismissed as pedantic and lackluster works.³⁴

The late Ming represented an important moment in the evolution of the discourse on the cardinal relationships. If many compilations reaffirmed the traditional sequence (ruler-subject, father-son, husband-wife, elder brother-younger brother, friends),³⁵ some writers began to question and reorder that sequence. In particular, the husband-wife and the friendship relations were given primacy by different authors—or sometimes by the same author in different writings.

The writer who most famously emphasized the husband-wife relation is perhaps Li Zhi, the *enfant maudit* of late Ming philosophy. In his *First Collection by the Pond* (*Chutan ji* 初潭集, 1588), a collection of anecdotes modeled after Liu Yiqing's *New Accounts of the Tales of the World* (*Shishuo xinyu* 世說新語),³⁶ Li Zhi organized the entries according to the five relationships. But instead of following the conventional order, Li adopted a radically re-organized sequence that started with husband and wife and ended with ruler and subject. He explained his reason in the prefaces and in the general introductory essay, titled "On Husband and Wife" (Fufu zonglun 夫婦總論, 1588).³⁷ Quoting from the *Classic of Changes* (*Yijing*), Li Zhi writes:

> Husband and wife are the beginning of human relations.³⁸ It is only after there are husband and wife that father and son can exist. It is only after there are father and son that elder and younger brother can exist. It is only after there are older and younger brother that hierarchical distinctions can exist. Once [the relationship between] husband and wife is correctly established, none among the ten thousand events and ten thousand things will fail to be correctly established. In this way the relationship between husband and wife is the beginning of all things.
>
> 夫婦,人之始也。有夫婦然後有父子,有父子然後有兄弟,有兄弟然後有上下。夫婦正,然後萬事萬物無不出於正矣。夫婦之為物始也如此。³⁹

He also argues that the husband-wife relation is the key to the correct understanding of the Five Constant Norms (*wuchang* 五常):

I say that only if [one understands] the husband and wife relation can he understand the Five Constant Norms. If the Five Constant Norms are discarded, how could there be an alternative foundation for speech and conversation, affairs of the state, and letters and scholarship?

言夫婦則五常可知, 豈有舍五常而別有言語政事文學乎?⁴⁰

The notion that the relation between husband and wife ought to take pride of place among human relations is also often found in fictional narratives, classical and vernacular.⁴¹ It figures importantly in the work of Feng Menglong. In the second preface to *History of Love* (*Qingshi* 情史, ca. 1628–1630), an anthology of classical language tales selected and organized around the topic of love or feelings (*qing*), the compiler affirms the primacy of the husband-wife relation by citing evidence from the full spectrum of the classics.

The teachings in the Six Classics are all founded on feelings [*qing*]: the *Changes* esteem the relationship between husband and wife; the *Odes* opens with the poem "Ospreys"; the *Documents* begins with a passage on the wedding of Yu; the *Rites* pays close attention to the distinction between union completed through engagement or elopement; the *Spring and Autumns* offers a detailed discussion of the marital relations between the Ji and Jiang clans (i.e., between Qi and Lu). Is this not because, since feelings begin with the relation between man and woman, everyone must first start from here, and the Sages must therefore also lead through feelings?

Is this not also the reason why the Sages have led through feelings, so that they would not fall into neglect, and therefore they flow abundantly in the relations between lord and minister, father and son, elder and younger brother, and friends?

六經皆以情教也。《易》尊夫婦,《詩》有《關雎》,《書》序嬪虞之文,《禮》謹聘、奔之別,《春秋》於姬、姜之際詳然言之。豈非以情始於男女, 凡民之所必開者, 聖人亦因而導之, 俾勿作於涼, 於是流注於君臣、父子、兄弟、朋友之間而汪然有餘乎！⁴²

The primacy of the conjugal bond is likewise illustrated in many of Feng's celebrated *San Yan* stories.⁴³

Li Zhi was also a great proponent of the importance of friendship.⁴⁴ Although he placed the "Husband and Wife" section at the beginning of

First Collection, over a third of the book is dedicated to the "Teacher and friend" (*shiyou* 師友) section. Gu Dashao 顧大韶 (1576–?), who edited Li Zhi's writings in a monumental collection, also wrote in no ambiguous terms about the centrality of the friendship bond. Gu Dashao argued that the bond between friends is superior even to that between father and son.[45] According to Gu, friendship should be considered "the mainstay of human relations" 朋友者, 五倫之綱也, and as "a bond that transcends the five relations and completes them" 我所謂朋友, 謂其超五倫者也, 謂其成五倫者.[46] The most hallowed figures of antiquity who are traditionally considered as paragons of the first four bonds (such as Yao and Shun, King Wen and his consorts, the Duke of Zhou) are recast by Gu as supreme examples of friendship. Thus Yao and Shun, King Wen and the Duke of Zhou, King Wen and his virtuous consort are not just paragons of the ruler-minister relation, father-son relation, and husband-wife relation respectively, but rather should be regarded as exemplary friends.[47] By rereading the whole history of Chinese civilization under the lens of friendship, Gu Dashao is in fact advancing a view of friendship as the central axis of moral cultivation, a role traditionally played by filial piety.

How is the debate on the nature and ranking of the five social bonds reflected in the stories that are the object of this study? In many ways, stories in *Exemplary Words* and other collections may be read as a traditionalist reaction against some of the more radical pronouncements in the essays by Li Zhi, Gu Dashao, and others, but also against some of the more daring *San Yan* stories. There is hardly space in their moral universe for a fallen-then-redeemed heroine like Wang Sanqiao in "The Pearl-Sewn Shirt" (*YSMY* 1),[48] or for the kind of moral acrobatics of Zhang Tingxiu (*XSHY* 20), who accumulates as many as three fathers and somehow manages to be filial to all three of them. Loyalty and filial piety loom large in the first half of *Exemplary Words* and in *Bell in the Still Night*. Friendship is exalted and celebrated in Stories 13 and 14 of *Exemplary Words*, for example; but it is carefully reconciled with or subordinated to family duties. One of the stories included in the post-Conquest collection *Sobering Stone*, quoting a passage from the *Record of Rites*, draws a fundamental distinction between the duties of subject toward ruler and son toward parent on one hand, and the obligations toward a lesser kin or a friend on the other. While the former are seen as absolute and unconditional, admitting no exception, the latter are presented as if they should be based upon careful deliberation and exercise of discernment—lest one fall into ridicule, or worse.[49]

The redactors and commentators of vernacular stories seek to bridge the gap between universal principles and particular narratives, carefully located in time and space, and they often engage with the debates surrounding particular practices (e.g., filial slicing, widow suicide, filial revenge, etc.) and the appraisal and reappraisal of historical figures. When read side by side with other genres, such as classical tales, morality books, and works in the genre of *Stories for Daily Learning* (*Riji gushi* 日記故事), the vernacular stories offer rich documentary evidence of the recognized *repertoire* of virtuous behaviors categorized under each relationship that was specific to this historical period—what compilers, publishers, and readers found most compelling and representative for each relationship. Stories found in *Exemplary Words*, in contrast with full-length novels, often focus on one core relationship.[50] Emphasis on a particular relationship may reveal the compiler's orientation, but it also shows that each relationship and attending virtue tended to carry specific structural and narrative implications—in a sense, each relationship accumulated its own body of lore.[51] Further, the decided orientation toward "this dynasty" (*benchao* 本朝) in the choice of exemplars found in some of the classical tale anthologies, biographical collections, and children's primers may be seen as inspiration or part of the same trend (updating moral exemplars, outdoing ancient paragons) as we find in *Exemplary Words*, *Bell in the Still Night*, and other vernacular collections from this period.

Exemplarity, Nature, and Nurture

One of the contentious points in stories of moral exemplars is the role of education, particularly literary education, in the construction of the hero. There is a common rhetoric that equates education with pedantry and a "paralysis of the will" and sees uneducated or poorly educated characters (children, women, peasants) as "naturally" more heroic and resolute. This is not only because with education and worldly experience the subject is deemed to have become corrupted and swayed by considerations of personal interest and fame. The accumulation of education is often blamed for producing a tendency to make excessively minute distinctions, and to argue over trivial matters, thus causing the subject to lose sight of the fundamental values.[52]

However, the heroes or heroines in many *Exemplary Words* stories are portrayed as actively inspired by the models and exemplars of the past. Chen Miaozhen (*XSY* 4) is inspired to perform her first act of flesh slicing by the memory of the stories of filial daughters that her grandmother used to tell her. Wang Shiming (*XSY* 2) devotes his spare time to copying and chanting "aphorisms on loyalty and filial piety" (*zhongxiao geyan* 忠孝格言). Since a tender age, Tang Guimei (*XSY* 6) is inculcated by her father, a village schoolmaster, with virtuous models from *Exemplary Women* and the *Classic of Filial Piety*. Conversely, the unfilial sons and ungrateful daughters of the cautionary tales are often presented as the product of a faulty upbringing, in which the parents are to be blamed.[53]

By emphasizing the role of written texts and stories in the construction of the moral heroes and heroines, the author and commentator are also indirectly congratulating themselves. If ancient exemplars are seen as a "real presence" in the conduct of the main characters, then the characters in these stories too can become a source of inspiration for the actual readers, thus strengthening the claim that writing and consuming fiction is indeed a morally valid activity. It is important to note, however, that the virtuous heroes and heroines of the stories are often not presented as objects for actual emulation, but rather as occasions for rumination. For example, in filial stories the idea of "putting to shame" (*kui, kuisi* 愧, 愧死) those who have their own parents still alive, safe and sound at home, yet fail in their basic duty to nourish them (*yang* 養), is repeated time and again.[54]

Virtue and/as/vs. Retribution

The most common way of depicting virtuous behavior in vernacular stories is to inscribe it in a scheme of karmic retribution (*bao* 報), by showing that virtue never goes unrewarded, just as its violation never goes unpunished. So powerful and ubiquitous is the principle of *bao* that Hanan has described it as the "moral grammar of interaction among men or between men and gods," and he deems it to determine the structure of virtually all stories on moral themes, in spite of the vast differences in emphasis and attitude among individual authors.[55]

The logic of *bao* is also the governing principle in the genre of morality books, and the connection between vernacular stories and morality books has been explored in detail.[56] But while morality books provide lists of actions, they stand in contrast with collections of exempla that teach not by rules and norms but by narrative examples, offering exemplary or counter-exemplary figures whom the reader is invited to admire or condemn. If the logic of *bao* is particularly obvious in stories of "hidden merit" (*yinzhi* 陰騭 or *yinde* 陰德), in which a good deed, typically performed for the sake of a stranger, is spectacularly rewarded (and examples of this story type can be found in both *Exemplary Words* and *Bell in the Still Night*), the "ledgers" mentality (or rather a trivialized version thereof) is also openly ridiculed in a story from *Exemplary Words* (XSY 28).⁵⁷ In the story, a hapless student, Zhang, is swindled by a monk whose service he had sought to obtain a male offspring as well as success in the examinations. Claiming to be a disciple of Li Zhi, the monk uses Yuan Huang, the literatus who had most famously promoted the ledgers method, as a kind of brand-name advertisement to persuade Zhang of both the efficacy of his method and his own disinterestedness. In the tail commentary, the foolishness of scholars who seek career advancement by means of monks' services and prayers is excoriated in no uncertain terms as the epitome of ridicule.⁵⁸

A clear statement of the ambivalent attitude toward the principle of *bao* held by certain vernacular story narrators can be found in "Yao Bozi Is Glorified for His Extreme Filiality" *(XHEJ 6)*, a story included in Zhou Ji's *West Lake Stories, Second Collection* published in the 1640s. In the prologue, the narrator writes that the emphasis on rewards for virtuous (in this case filial) behavior is dictated by the purpose of instructing "the ignorant people":

> The story I am about to tell you now is about the rewards attending those who act filially. Yet, being filial is the basic duty of human beings, so why do we need to talk about rewards? This is because the ignorant people of this world claim that if they act in a filial manner they will not necessarily reap benefits, and conversely, if they act counter to filial piety they will not necessarily be punished, and that is why they dare to act recklessly. They do not realize that the word "filiality" startles heaven and shakes the earth, and it has always been the case that all deities—from the great sages and immortals, to Buddha and the bodhisattvas, from the Jade Emperor, to Laozi, and King Yama—stand in awe of the word "filiality."

> 如今這回說行孝的報應, 但行孝是人的本等, 怎生說到報應上去? 只為世上那一種愚下之民, 說行孝未必有益, 忤逆未必有罪, 所以他敢於放肆。不知那個「孝」字驚天動地, 從來大聖大賢、大佛菩薩、玉皇大帝、太上老君、閻羅天子, 那一個敢不敬重著這一個字?⁵⁹

Zhou Ji's characteristic complacency toward the medium of the vernacular story is apparent in this passage. One is left to wonder who the intended audience is—is it the "ignorant people," the perennially recalcitrant target of the zealous literati's civilizing efforts, or is it rather the more cognizant reader who wonders about the necessity of discussing rewards for filial actions? A similar sentiment is voiced in the tail commentary to the *Exemplary Words* story "The Crook Loses Wife and Money; the Good Man Gains Both Woman and Goods" (*XSY* 25), which remarks how the logic of success or failure is just an expedient—and admittedly crude—means to enlighten the "vulgar people" (*yongren* 庸人).[60]

In spite of the ubiquity of *bao*, however, a rather different way to illustrate virtue appears to be at work in many *Exemplary Words* and *Bell in the Still Night* stories. Stories illustrative of the Five Cardinal Relationships, especially those based on classical language biographies, often obey a different logic, a logic of "virtue as its own reward." The virtuous heroes or heroines are tested through extreme trial, often ending in martyrdom, with no visible reward other than the *aesthetic* celebration of their virtuous deeds. This dichotomy in the representation of virtue and *bao* harks back to the discrepant way in which virtue was conceived since the time of Confucius and Mencius, that is, virtue as performative and ritually determined versus virtue as inner and innate tendency toward the good, the latter of which is not only not susceptible to reward, but would actually be tainted by it. The mode of representing virtue as decoupled from material reward has a long literary pedigree, and is commonly found in literary biographies. It is, however, rather extraneous to the short story genre. I argue that stories in *Exemplary Words* and *Bell in the Still Night* represent a new direction in depicting virtue as its own reward. For example, in "Wang Mian the Exemplary Friend" (*XSY* 14) and "Filial Avenger Wang Shiming" (*XSY* 2) there is no tangible reward awaiting the hero. These stories usually contain a more or less explicit self-celebration of the author, who, while immortalizing the protagonist's deeds, casts himself as a sympathetic and sensitive observer, a *zhiyin* (bosom friend) figure mediating between the story and its readers. This is particularly common in stories of female exemplars, which typically end with a note mentioning the particular literatus (often quite prominent) who rescued the heroine from oblivion and immortalized her in poetry or classical prose. Such sources are then the basis for the vernacular author to spin off his own rendition, which is sometimes deemed superior to the source.[61]

Book Overview

This introduction has provided grounding in the historical and cultural context of the late Ming, introduced the primary texts, and addressed terms and concepts that will inform the discussion in the following chapters, including the discourse on the Five Cardinal Relationships, the rhetoric of exemplarity, the interplay between virtue and retribution (*bao*), the spectrum of positions regarding the role of nature vs. nurture in the shaping of the moral hero or heroine, and the role of the commentarial tradition in articulating the ideal readership and envisioning the social function of these narratives. In the following chapters I will examine the moral dimension of individual stories, thematically organized under the framework of the Five Cardinal Relationships.

The first two chapters explore the representation of filial piety, arguably the quintessential virtue in Confucian ethics. The first chapter, "Filial Quests," begins by discussing the rich discourse of filial piety in the late imperial period. It then focuses on narratives of filial sons who traveled great distances in search of their parents. The second chapter, "Filial Dilemmas," turns to other key motifs that inform fictional representations of filial exemplars in these short stories: filial dilemmas and filial bodies. These stories are brimming with colorful and sometimes gory characters and situations, including a son who defies a maternal injunction to seek a wandering father, a husband who unflinchingly exchanges his wife to ransom his mother, and a girl who slices a piece of her liver to save her bedridden grandmother. Taken together, these stories show how filial piety is subtly yet continuously reconceptualized in response to anxieties about family dismemberment, absence of authority figures, and notions of reciprocity.

More than other cardinal relationships, the bond between ruler and subject is by necessity historically and contextually determined. The third chapter turns to representations of loyal officials, examining the compilers' fascination with two specific moments in recent history, the Jianwen-Yongle transition (1402) and the Ming-Qing transition (1644–1645). As I show in my analysis, the models of loyalty articulated in these stories range from supererogatory embodiments of loyalty (exemplified by martyr figures) to more pragmatic forms of loyalty (as seen in the survivors and younger generations in the wake of problematic succession or dynastic transition).

Unlike tales of filial offspring or loyal ministers, stories that are centered on exemplary heroines almost invariably end with a self-inflicted death. Chapter 4 discusses several stories of faithful maidens, chaste wives, and loyal widows, which are often among the most troubling stories for modern audiences. In spite of the seeming paucity and fixity of situations and motifs in these narratives, the compilers cast the heroines' adherence to ethical imperatives in a new light, by populating the narrative with a crowd of noisy neighbors and onlookers, and by exploring the domestic contexts and repercussions of an extreme choice such as suicide.

Chapter 5 turns to representations of brotherly love, perhaps the least studied of the Five Cardinal Relationships. Stories of exemplary as well as estranged brothers illustrate a deep tension between hierarchical and horizontal conceptions of the fraternal bond in the late imperial time. By characterizing younger and older brothers as mutually replaceable, the stories envision the brotherly bond as closer to a notion of equality than to classic Confucian formulations that emphasize precedence and seniority.

Finally, the sixth chapter focuses on stories of loyal friends, reading them against the backdrop of the lively late Ming discourse on friendship, a discourse that has captured the attention of Western scholarship in the recent decade. While the intellectual debate on friendship tended to portray it as an idealized communion of the souls and to valorize it above and beyond the other cardinal relationships, the fictional representations of exemplary friends found in these stories offer a different picture, by depicting a model of friendship in perfect harmony with the other bonds and by stressing the inescapably material nature of the friendship bond.

The stories discussed in this book often take a critical view of mechanical notions of retribution, countering them with the logic of virtue as its own reward—a logic that can be traced all the way back to Mencius. Conflict between passion and duty is typically resolved in favor of duty—a duty redefined with a palpable sense of urgency. Ultimately, I argue that these largely overlooked stories, far from being tediously moralistic tales, provide a deeper understanding of the cardinal relationships because they explore the inherent tension between what we might call "textbook morality" on one hand and untidy everyday life on the other.

Chapter 1

Filial Quests

In the early sixteenth century, a young man named Wang Yuan 王原 left his mother and newly wedded wife to undertake a long and risky journey in search of his father—a father who had abandoned the family to escape corvée duties while Yuan was still in his swaddling clothes. After several years of wanderings through modern day Hebei, Shandong, and Henan provinces, Yuan eventually discovered his father in a temple, where he had been living as an unordained monk. Having overcome his father's initial reluctance, Yuan returned with him to his hometown and at long last achieved his dream of family reunion. Yuan was later celebrated as a resplendent filial exemplar in the local gazetteer, official and unofficial historical compilations. His story was also adapted multiple times into fiction and drama.

Wang Yuan's tale was one of the most popular "filial quest" narratives—my rendering of the Chinese phrase *wanli xunqin* 萬里尋親 (searching for parents across 10,000 miles)—but his was by no means an isolated case.[1] In the latter part of the seventeenth century, the great Confucian scholar Huang Zongxi 黃宗羲 (1610–1695) wrote, "When one looks at historical biographies, there is no end of tales about sons who face calamity and endure arduous travels and physical hardship, all in search of their parents" 嘗觀史傳, 人子所遭不幸, 間關踣頓, 求父母者不絕書.[2] Huang was commenting—not without a tinge of impatience—on the deluge of filial quest accounts in order to highlight the extraordinary feat of his own ancestor, who went in search of his brother instead. What is not immediately apparent in Huang's statement, however, is that the filial quest was not a motif of great antiquity, but rather a relatively recent phenomenon. In her extensive survey of accounts of filial quest included in Ming and Qing local gazetteers, Taiwanese scholar Lu Miaw-fen has found an overwhelming majority of entries (200 out of 282) dating from the Ming-Qing transition and early Qing dynasty (mid to late seventeenth century).³ Narrative predilections reflected changes in the historical reality. The "filial journey" was first instituted as a category eligible for imperial reward in the early Ming, as established by an edict of the founding Ming emperor.⁴ The glorification of filial journeys continued to the end of the dynasty (and beyond), as documented, for example, in the late Ming compilation *Filial Records* (*Xiaoji* 孝紀, 1639) by Cai Baozhen 蔡保禎, where the filial journey is one of the sixteen categories into which the book organizes its material.⁵ By contrast, earlier records of filial exemplars, such as the medieval accounts discussed by Keith Knapp, do not feature filial journey as a discrete category.⁶

Why did filial quest narratives have such wide appeal at this point in time? What kind of anxieties and tensions are explored, or belied, in these stories? By focusing on the development of the narrative motif of filial quest as seen in two vernacular adaptations of the story of Wang Yuan, this chapter shows how this particular embodiment of the supposedly perennial virtue of "filial piety" reveals broader shifts in moral and intellectual concerns during the seventeenth century. Before doing so, however, we will review the broader coordinates of the discourse on filial piety during the Ming, a discourse in which didactic literature, intellectual debates, imperial policies, and actual practice play significant and often conflicting roles. This will provide the necessary backdrop against which the stories discussed in this and the next chapter can be fully appreciated.

Traditional Discourse of Filial Piety in the Ming

Filial piety (*xiao* 孝) is arguably *the* quintessential virtue in traditional Confucian ethics.⁷ Ubiquitously invoked throughout Chinese premodern history, filial piety not surprisingly became the target of vitriolic condemnation by the May Fourth intellectuals' wholesale assault on Confucianism in the early twentieth century. Yet the traditional discourse of filial piety is riddled with contradictions, and the very notion of filial piety and the way it was enacted through specific practice were far from uniform throughout the centuries.

The notion of filial piety as a "natural" virtue was continuously reiterated. Yet the very existence of texts such as the *Classic of Filial Piety* (*Xiaojing* 孝經) and the *Twenty-Four Filial Exemplars* (*Ershisi xiao* 二

十四孝)—which were among the first texts that children of both sexes encountered in their literary education—lays bare the necessity to inculcate this supposedly natural virtue in the minds of young readers. Filial piety is said to be what sets humans apart from plants and beasts—yet murder committed to avenge one's parent is not only contemplated, but at times even prescribed and officially pardoned. As the *Classic of Filial Piety* famously dictates, sons and daughters should preserve intact the body given to them by their parents—yet many stories of filial exemplars entail bodily sacrifice, which can, for example, take the form of slicing off a piece of flesh (*gegu* 割股) to prepare a life-restoring broth for the dying parent. Moreover, according to the famous Mencian prescription, the greatest violation against filial piety is the failure to produce an heir who can ensure the continuation of the family line—and yet filial exemplars gladly sacrifice their progeny for their parents' survival, or act in such a way as to impair or obliterate their chances of producing heirs.

At the level of official discourse, the Ming inaugurated a renewed emphasis on filial piety. Both the Ming founder and the Yongle emperor purportedly authored didactic texts promoting filial piety, which were explicitly intended for the wider audience. The Ming founder Zhu Yuanzhang promulgated the *Sacred Edict in Six Maxims* (*Shengyu liuyu* 聖諭六語), which opens with an exhortation to "be filial to the parents."[8] He also compiled the *Record of Filial Piety and Parental Benevolence* (*Xiaoci lu* 孝慈錄, 1375), a work in 20 *juan* that Norman Kutcher describes as aimed at restoring "the people and members of the officialdom to the path of filial piety so neglected by his Yuan predecessors."[9]

Lamenting that records of filial exemplars, however numerous, were scattered across countless different sources, the Yongle emperor oversaw the compilation of *True Cases of Filial Piety* (*Xiaoshun shishi* 孝順事實, 1420), which gathered over 200 anecdotes of outstanding filial piety. This work included a preface, as well as final commentaries and poems appended to each entry, all of which were attributed to the emperor himself.[10] The notion of "transference" of filial piety from the father-son relationship to the emperor-minister relationship was given particular emphasis, while the last *juan* was devoted to female filial exemplars. Yongle's *True Cases* was the basis for later expanded and revised compilations, among which is Cai's *Filial Records* mentioned earlier. Yongle's compilation of *True Cases* is not itself without irony. Yongle usurped the throne that was rightfully occupied by Jianwen, the son of his father's legitimate heir, thus disturbing the succession chain supposedly cemented by filial piety. As shown in chapter 3, Yongle also plays a highly ambivalent role in stories of loyalty.

Notions of filiality, paternity, and ancestral rites also lie at the heart of the so-called Great Rite Controversy (*da liyi* 大禮議) that stormed the court in the third decade of the sixteenth century.[11] The controversy saw the opposition between the Jiajing emperor and the great majority of the state bureaucracy over the correct ancestral rites and posthumous designations to be observed by Jiajing himself, who was a cousin of the preceding emperor. The ministers pleaded with the emperor to honor his uncle, the Hongzhi emperor, as his father by way of posthumous adoption, to preserve the integrity of the succession line. The emperor adamantly refused, considering this course of action as most unfilial, and continued to venerate his biological father instead.

The Jiajing emperor's position was aligned (though not by conscious design) with the most innovative developments in mid and late Ming intellectual debates, which sought to redefine filial piety, along with the other cardinal virtues, as based on *qing* 情 (emotion, feelings). The great Neo-Confucian thinker Wang Yangming held that sincerity and earnestness (*chengxin* 誠心), rather than ritual prescription or historical precedents, should dictate the expression of one's filiality. Significantly, he considered the two most widely debated manifestations of filial piety (flesh slicing and filial huts) as neither right nor wrong in and of themselves.[12]

There is also much discussion of the religious connotations of filial piety. Some scholars argue that the sentiment of filiality comes closest to a kind of religious feeling. Central to this religious dimension is the notion of *ganying* 感應 (variously rendered as "sympathetic resonance," or "sympathetic response"), according to which sincere filiality can reach and move the spirits above.[13] This notion is already present in the *Classic of Filial Piety*, and it is abundantly manifested in miracle tales and hagiographical accounts of filial exemplars, from medieval times onward. The religious dimension of filiality, however, is not confined to popular literature and local beliefs and practices. Lu Miaw-fen has studied a current of late Ming exegesis on the *Classic of Filial Piety* that was essentially religious in nature. Filiality was reconceptualized as a kind of "cosmic Spirit" by Yu Chunxi 虞淳熙 (1553–1621) and others.[14]

The late imperial discourse of filial piety was also profoundly influenced by Buddhism. Alan Cole has identified the shift toward the mother-son dyad, as opposed to the traditional emphasis on the father-son relationship, as a major influence of Buddhism. Moreover, the Buddhist discourse on filial piety stresses the importance of joining or donating to the monastic community (*sangha*) as much more effective means than the traditional sacrificial offerings to the spirits of the deceased parents.[15] While Cole's study does not focus on the specific historical development of the Buddhist discourse on filial piety and family in the Ming, some of the vernacular stories discussed below portray Buddhist belief as playing a significant role in the performance of filial acts.

When it comes to popular filial practices, flesh slicing or *gegu* is arguably the most notorious—and often misunderstood.[16] It was usually performed by the son, daughter, or daughter-in-law, as a form of extreme remedy, when all other medicines and prayers had proven ineffective. The practice, though attested with increasing frequency from the Song onward, was subject to vivid debate among the literati, and a matter of controversy for the imperial court as well. The Hongwu emperor prohibited *gegu*, and Xuande refused to grant awards to those who performed it; yet biographies of filial sons and daughters (usually of commoner status) in Ming and Qing local gazetteers and other sources continued to include *gegu* as a staple feature of filial behavior. As shown in the story "A Slice of Liver for Grandma" (*XSY* 4) discussed in chapter 2, the practice of *gegu* is enmeshed in an intricate web of didactic literature, Buddhist beliefs, popular lore, and intellectual debates.

Another contested field of filial behavior is the nature and extent of mourning practices. While at the level of state officialdom the issue of *duoqing* 奪情, "cutting the feeling," that is, shortening the period of filial mourning for reasons of public service, was hotly debated (with Zhang Juzheng as the most eminent case), an abundance of records and anecdotes indicates that at the popular level filial sons distinguished themselves by their exemplary mourning, which typically exceeded ritual prescriptions.[17] Similar to the case of filial slicing, filial mourning practices often intermingled with a variety of local lore and popular religious practices. Side by side with the construction of the filial hut by the deceased parents' grave (*lumu* 廬墓), filial sons would also make lifelong vows of abstinence from meat, or subject themselves to extenuating physical duress in the course of their filial mourning.

Representations of Filial Piety in Vernacular Stories

In spite of its centrality in the Confucian ethical system and the ubiquity with which it is invoked, filial piety is seldom foregrounded as the central theme in vernacular fiction before the eighteenth century.[18] The "stories of moral duty" discussed in this book may be among the earliest examples of fiction showing a sustained concern about filiality.

While filial piety does not figure as a major theme in the first two volumes of *San Yan*, it becomes more prominent in the third. Three stories in *Constant Words to Awaken the World* take filial piety as a central concern, and all three have been attributed by Hanan to Langxian, Feng Menglong's collaborator, who may or may not have been the author of *Rocks Nod Their Heads* (*Shi diantou* 石點頭), a collection discussed below. The eponymous heroine in "Li Yuying Appeals for Justice from Jail" (*XSHY* 27) is a filial daughter.[19] "Zhang Tingxiu Escapes from Death and Saves His Father" (*XSHY* 20), the longest story in the collection, tells of the vicissitudes of Zhang Tingxiu and his brother, who manage to rescue their wrongly accused father. Finally, "Enduring Humiliation, Cai Ruihong Seeks Revenge" (*XSHY* 36) is a variation on the time-honored theme of female revenge, and recounts the odyssey of a woman who undergoes many tribulations before she is eventually able to obtain revenge for her murdered parents.

A distinct characteristic in the *Constant Words* stories is the role assigned to official justice. In both Li Yuying's story and Cai Ruihong's story, the redressing of injustice is entrusted to the state (the local magistrate or the emperor), and not to an individual act of heroism. Another notable feature is the interest in configuring the parent-son relationship not just as a biological one, but rather as a human-made bond. Rather than the nuclear family, it is the extended family with all its permutations that occupies center stage: adoptive fathers and adopted sons and daughters, live-in sons-in-law, and stepmothers. While stepparents and live-in sons-in-law are consistently portrayed as evil and are duly punished at the end, the case of adoptive parents appears more ambivalent. Still, in the story of Zhang Tingxiu, where the two brothers have multiple adoptive parents in addition to their biological parents, the author deftly steers away from potentially conflicting claims. The ending of the story is exemplary in this sense: Zhang Tingxiu and his brother Wenxiu conveniently have three and two sons respectively, so that the family line of each of their adoptive parents can continue, as well as their own biological line.[20] The focus on the adoptive relationships may be read as an echo of the Great Rite Controversy. The perfectly harmonious extended family can be seen as a blatantly fictional fantasy running counter to the grim reality of an irredeemably divided imperial court. By contrast, adoptive offspring are virtually absent from filial piety stories in *Exemplary Words*. These stories tend to focus on biological relationships and on nuclear or stem families.

One also finds a handful of stories about filial piety in Ling Mengchu's *Er Pai*, but these stories focus predominantly on negative examples. In particular, "The Parricide" (*CK* 13) features an extraordinarily callous son solely preoccupied with his wife, while "The Old Tutor" (*EK* 26) presents a teacher whose daughters turn out to be unabashedly ungrateful. Here too, as in *Constant Words*, the figure of the adopted son crops up frequently.[21]

In comparison with *San Yan* and *Er Pai*, filial piety becomes a prominent theme in *Exemplary Words* and other collections of "fiction of moral duty." *Rocks Nod Their Heads*, published around 1627, also engages with the illustration of filial piety in as many as three of fourteen stories (one of the three is about Wang Yuan). Filial piety stories in Zhou Ji's *West Lake Stories, Second Collection* predominantly focus on filial mourning. The main character in "Yao Bozi Is Glorified for His Extreme Filiality" 姚伯子至孝受顯榮 (*XHEJ* 6) goes on a filial quest to retrieve the bones of his parents, killed by bandits during the chaos of the Yuan–Ming transition. He then establishes mourning rites for a whole month each year, since he does not know the exact time of his parents' murder. "Loyalty and Filial Piety Are Assembled in One Family" 忠孝萃一門 (*XHEJ* 31) is also about a filial quest by Wang Shen to retrieve his father's bones, which he was able to locate through a dream.

The Story of Wang Yuan

The remainder of this chapter is devoted to the discussion of two vernacular adaptations of the story of Wang Yuan. The first is the ninth story in *Exemplary Words*, titled "The Filial Quest of Wang Yuan" (original title: "Fleeing from the Local Tyrant the Coward Runs Far Away, Through a Premonitory Dream the Filial Son Meets His Parent" 避豪惡懦夫遠竄, 感夢兆孝子逢親, *XSY* 9). The second is "Wang Benli Searches for His Father at the Far End of the Empire" ("Wang Benli tianya qiufu" 王本立天涯求父, *SDT* 3) (Benli is Wang Yuan's *zi* or courtesy name in this version) and is included in Langxian's *Rocks* collection. There is also a much briefer version of Wang Yuan's story in the prologue of "Loyalty and Filial Piety Are Assembled in One Family" in Zhou Ji's *West Lake Stories*. All three versions are probably derived from a classical language biography of Wang Yuan included in Li Zhi's *Sequel to a Book to Hide* (*Xu Cangshu* 續藏書, 1609).[22] Similar to the vernacular retellings of biographical accounts of heroic women or loyalist martyrs examined in chapters 3 and 4, the vernacular texts discussed here explore the dynamics among family members, as well as the fault lines that are left implicit or glossed over in the classical language accounts.

How to explain the fascination with Wang Yuan and the account of his filial trek? Wang's tale may be seen as archetypal of late imperial filial quest narratives, as Shang Wei and others have suggested.[23] A comparison with the earlier legend of Zhu Shouchang 朱壽昌,[24] canonized as one of the twenty-four filial exemplars, may serve to illustrate the differences between late Ming and earlier narratives of filial quest. According to the legend, Zhu was a Song official who quit his post to search for his mother, a concubine who had been expelled from his family when he was just a little boy, due to the animosity of the principal wife. The first difference between the Song and Ming filial quest is their objects: the biological mother in Zhu Shouchang's case, the father in Wang Yuan's. Indeed, the filial impulse in Zhu's case falls, strictly speaking, beyond the boundaries of ritual duty, since an expelled wife no longer enjoys the same rights of being mourned by her son.[25] The social status of the journeyer is also different: Zhu Shouchang is a member of the official elite, while Wang Yuan comes from a peasant family. Whereas in the earlier tale the official career stands as a direct obstacle to the filial impulse and as such must be sacrificed, no such opposition is staged in Wang Yuan's case.[26] The family/state opposition, while not present as an element of the filial choice, reappears instead as the driving force that dissolves family unity at the beginning: "His father was oppressed by the village corvées," says Li Zhi's biography, and this is presented as the motivation behind the father's decision to flee.[27]

Wang Yuan's story also features the motif of the premonitory dream (as well as its deciphering) as a form of supernatural help, which was absent from Zhu's tale. Such supernatural intervention is traditionally justified according to the theory of *ganying* or "sympathetic resonance," whereby heaven is believed to come to the aid of the earnestly filial son. While the motif was not present in Zhu Shouchang's tale, it is a staple feature of many hagiographical accounts from both the medieval and the late imperial periods.[28]

Of the three vernacular adaptations, the prologue story in "Loyalty and Filial Piety Are Assembled in One Family" is, as expected, the briefest. It is also the one that follows the biographical account most closely, even preserving some of the original phrasing. The main story tells of the vicissitudes of Wang Hui 王禕 (1323–1374), his son Wang Shen 王紳, and his grandson Wang Tu 王稌. (This is a neat reversal of focus with "The Filial Quest of Wang Yuan," where Wang Shen is mentioned in the prologue, while the main story is devoted to Wang Yuan.) Wang Hui and Wang Shen were well-known early Ming figures. The father, an eminent official under Hongwu, was killed by the Mongolian insurgents during a diplomatic mission to Yunnan in 1374. The son went on a filial quest to retrieve his father's bones, which he was able to locate through a dream. The actual identification was made through the traditional method of "dripping blood on the bones," based on the belief that the bones of a consanguineous kin would promptly absorb the blood.[29] The main story may thus be seen as an example of a "Confucian family tale" that celebrates the twin virtues of filial piety and loyalty, as well as the idea of lineage cemented by filial piety, which functions here as a kind of cultural capital handed down from father to son to grandson.[30] This stands in striking contrast with the morally ambiguous father figure in Wang Yuan's story.

Compared to the succinct rendition in *West Lake Stories*, the story of Wang Yuan is greatly expanded in Lu Renlong and Langxian's hands. However, the two stories "The Filial Quest of Wang Yuan" and "Wang Benli Searches for his Father at the Far End of the Empire" are dramatically different. Indeed the comparison between the two gives us the opportunity to delve into the vastly different sensibilities and styles of the two authors. Both authors elaborate on the description of the hardship of the corvée system that prompts the father's desertion at the beginning of the story, as well as on the core motif of the journey. But while the *Rocks* version focuses, as one would expect, on the son's journey, Lu Renlong makes the curious choice of greatly expanding the journey of the father instead, while the journey of the son is dealt with in a relatively hasty way.

In "The Filial Quest of Wang Yuan," the hero's filial deed is presented as superior to earlier examples: Wang Yuan has never even known his father, since the latter had abandoned the family when Yuan was but a baby in swaddling clothes. Nor does Yuan know his whereabouts in the wide empire. This gesture of outdoing earlier examples is at once a narrative device (it is a common way of linking prologue to story proper in later stories) and a cultural trope pervasive in the late Ming—what historian Weijing Lu has termed the Ming's "craving for extremes."[31]

A brief discussion of the story's setting is in order, since Lu Renlong is usually quite faithful to his sources. Compared with the original biography, the *Exemplary Words* version backdates the events by about a century, from the Zhengde era (early sixteenth century) to the Hongwu and Yongle eras (late fourteenth and early fifteenth centuries). This may not be a casual choice, as many Ming accounts viewed the Zhengde era precisely as the beginning of the decay.[32] This consideration may have prompted Lu to situate the exemplar of filial piety in the early phase of the dynasty, thus conforming to the familiar narrative of dynastic decline. At the same time, however, one is left to ponder the implications of situating a rather bleak picture of corruption at the village level at such an early moment in the dynastic history. Another narrative reason for the backdating of the story to the late fourteenth century is that the construction of the capital offers the justification for the particularly onerous amount of corvées and taxes.

Another point of divergence is the geographic location. While the original account situates the story in Wen'an county (modern Hebei), Lu Renlong places it in Anqiu county (Shandong). The reason is laid out in the speech that Wang Xi makes to his wife to justify his decision to flee. Shandong, occupying a key position between the capital region and the sensitive northeastern frontier region, was heavily subjected to draft and levies.[33] The temporal and geographic relocations of the story are thus functional in a narrative where the individual plight is connected with larger domestic and international issues.

The Making of a Filial Son

"A fatherless man—can he still be considered a man?" 人而無父, 何以為人?[34] This quote, attributed to the historical Wang Yuan in Li Zhi's biography, powerfully captures the kind of *horror vacui*, the mortal fear of the absence of relationships, which in the Confucian tradition are seen as the indispensable condition for the enactment of morality. The *Exemplary Words* version does not make much of this and has nothing of the pathos of the original source. The young Wang Yuan's tears when he hears his mother talk about his father are presented as an act of sympathetic mimicry of his mother's own tears. When old enough, Yuan's decision to go in search of his father is also described as stemming from practical concerns. "Father is no merchant, how is he going to make ends meet being away from home? And why should I be sitting idly at home, instead of going to search for him?" he muses.[35] By contrast, the absence of the father takes on deeper, almost existential connotations in Langxian's "Wang Benli Searches for his Father at the Far End of the Empire." Wang's search for his father becomes tantamount to a search for his own identity. He is truly a *selfless* offspring, to use Knapp's phrase.

The story opens by addressing a central issue in the discourse of filial piety, that is, the role of natural inclinations as opposed to nurture in determining filial behavior. On this issue, the narrator explicitly takes the side of nature,[36] except that he then devotes several pages to describing Wang Yuan's education under the pedantic licentiate Bai (Bai *xiucai*). Of his education, the narrator solely focuses on a few encounters with famous texts or passages on filial piety: the "Lu'e" 蓼莪 (Thick Tarragon) poem from the *Book of Odes*,³⁷ the passages from the *Analects* where Ziyou and Zixia inquire about filial piety (which prompt a long explanation from Bai), and the *Classic of Filial Piety*. Even the legend of Tian Heng's loyal retainers from the *Book of Han*, while not about filial piety, is read by the fourteen-year-old Wang Yuan as an inspiration for filial behavior, and it triggers his resolution to search for his missing father with the same unwavering devotion that Tian Heng's 500 retainers displayed by taking their lives for their leader. (Tian Heng also serves in an important role later in the narrative, by leading Wang Benli to find his father.) By providing the reader with an account of the *Bildung* of the filial hero in which his *nature* is stirred through strategic *textual encounters*—as well as opportune explanations from the teacher—Langxian cleverly deals with the paradox of nature versus nurture in the construction of filial piety.

Wang Yuan's progressive realization of the implications of his father's absence almost takes on the contours of existential angst. Even after he has set out on his journey, the landscape he traverses is populated with filial landmarks (such as the shrine of the filial exemplar Min Ziqian) and filial personages. The public splendors of the magistrate whose parents are showered with honors cannot but be contrasted with his own private misery. There could not be a starker contrast with the carefree enjoyment of natural scenery experienced by his father at the beginning of his journey.³⁸

But not everything is what it seems. In one of the most memorable episodes of the story, while Wang Yuan the filial son sighs at the all-encompassing power of filiality that reaches even to a eunuch, we the readers are told the ugly truth behind Eunuch Li's display of filiality. It turns out that the eunuch's real mother is a decrepit old lady whose desiccated looks are enough to cause her son's revulsion when she is brought in front of him. He unceremoniously disposes of her. The old lady, stranded far away from her hometown, conveniently dies soon afterward. The magistrate in charge of finding the eunuch's mother then gets the cue. He selects a plump and comely former courtesan and sends her to the eunuch. The eunuch showers her with exemplary filial devotions, and after she passes away, he sees to her burial and performs all required mourning rituals.³⁹

This episode can be read as a parody of Zhu Shouchang's story: Eunuch Li does not travel at all, but rather sends his underlings to complete the mission; he does not discard his official position in favor of family affects, but rather uses the latter as a means to enhance his official status and reputation. In a more serious vein, the episode of Eunuch Li can also be read as a harsh criticism of those who too easily transfer their familial or social duties toward more convenient or opportune subjects; as such, it may be read as an indirect reflection of the Great Rite Controversy of the Jiajing reign.

It is noteworthy that the true state of affairs about Eunuch Li is revealed in a lengthy aside to the reader, while the filial exemplar remains blithely oblivious to the awful truth. How are we to interpret this episode, as well as other moments in the narrative where there is a sharp discontinuity between the point of view of the character Wang Yuan and that of the narrator? How are we to reconcile exemplary illustration on one hand and satiric exposé on the other?

One of the passages that best illuminates the differences in the characterization of the filial son in the two stories is found in the description of the journey's inception.

This is how the journey starts in Lu Renlong's "The Filial Quest of Wang Yuan":

> Wang Yuan thought that since his father had left without money, he could not have gone too far away. Hence he first went to each county in his home prefecture [Qingzhou]: Yidu, Linzi, Boxing, Gaoyuan, Le'an, Shouguang, Changle, Linqu, Zhucheng, Mengyin, Juzhou, Yishui, Rizhao. In each place, he first went to the city and then to the countryside. He searched everywhere he would see signs of human habitation. He then thought to himself: "If father had met his good chance and become rich or noble, he would have returned for sure. Since he has not sent any news, it must be that he has fallen into dire straits." Therefore he searched everywhere among monks and diviners, low-class coolies and beggars in the villages. After searching for several months, he could not find the slightest trace. He then continued his search into the other prefectures in Shandong: Jinan, Yanzhou, Dongchang, Laizhou. He was deceived countless times by people who told him that there was such and such a person that resembled him, and once he had reached the place [that was indicated to him] amidst countless tribulations, it turned out to be a false lead. Still, he did not harbor the slightest resentment.

> 想道他父親身畔無錢，不能遠去，故此先在本府益都、臨淄、博興、高苑、樂安、壽光、昌樂、臨朐、諸城、蒙陰、莒州、沂水、日照各縣，先到城市，後到鄉村，人烟湊集的處在，無不尋到。又想道：「父親若是有個機緣，或富或貴，一定回來。如今久無音信，畢竟是淪落了。」故

此僧道、星卜、下及傭工、乞丐裡邊,都去尋訪。訪了幾月,不見踪跡,又向本省濟南、兖州、東昌、萊州各府抓尋。也不知被人哄了幾次,聽他說來有些相似,及至千辛萬苦尋去,却又不是。他並沒個怨悔的心。[40]

And here is the counterpart passage in Langxian's "Wang Benli Searches for His Father at the Far End of the Empire":

Wang Xun had not left behind a single trace, so it was like looking for a needle in the ocean, how could he possibly scoop it out? And so, how come Wang Yuan was only traveling towards the east? The reason is that he had done some careful preparation. He had bought a route book of the empire, which he had studied carefully until he had familiarized himself with the routes in all four directions. He had also inquired broadly on the agreeability of the local customs of each region. First of all, he considered that his father was a farmer. Now, on the road to the northern capital were barren and cold lands, and moreover lately there had been reports of bandits, so he concluded that his father would not have taken that direction. As for the road to Shanxi on the west, it was cramped and perilous, with mountains and rivers difficult to cross, so he conjectured that his father would not have gone there either. So in the end he thought that his father must have gone on the eastbound road towards Shandong, where the customs and climate were comparable to those of their home village, and where the people were simple and honest. Second, he was set on the idea that east was where the sun rises, where the whole cosmos manifested itself, and where all the dark and desolate places under heaven became brilliant and shining. "Can it be that this goal of looking for my father I've set for myself, which leaves me in darkness and dream-like confusion, is not going to eventually find sudden illumination?" Therefore, he only traveled eastward. – Gentle reader, consider this thought of his: can we not say that he was a truly filial son, and an outright foolish man?"

這王珣蹤跡無方,分明大海一針,何從撈摸?那王原只望東行,卻是何故?原來他平日留心,買了一本天下路程圖,把東西南北的道路,都細細看熟,又博訪了四方風土相宜。一來諒著父親是田莊出身,北去京師一路,地土苦寒,更兼近來時有風警,決然不往。西去山西一路,道路間關,山川險阻,也未必到彼。惟東去山東一路,風氣與故鄉相仿,人情也都樸厚,多分避到這個所在。二來心裡立個意見, 以為東方日出, 萬象昭明, 普天幽沉闇昧之地, 都蒙照鑒, 難道我一點思父的心跡, 如昏如夢, 沒有豁然的道理? 所以只望東行。看官你道這個念頭, 叫不得真真孝子, 實實癡人。⁴¹

Wang Yuan in the *Exemplary Words* story proceeds by methodically searching through each city in Qingzhou and neighboring prefectures, following progressively expanding circuits. He may be temporarily led astray by false leads, but even after he realizes the truth, he does not care, and continues his search unperturbedly and systematically. By contrast, Wang Yuan in the *Rocks* version sets on his eastbound journey armed with an odd combination of topographical knowledge and supernatural inspiration. He remains entirely oblivious to the reality behind the various Eunuch Lis of the world. His actions are systematically exaggerated compared with the original biography. Not only does he start inquiring about his father at an early age, he is also unbearably tormented by his absence; he leaves his bride not after one month, but after a day; his journey lasts twelve years; after his father declares his unwillingness to return home, he immediately proceeds to smash his head on the ground.

However, I argue that it would be misguided to read Langxian's ironical stance toward his character as a sign of subversive intent toward the moral message the character stands for, as some critics have suggested.⁴² What the narrator may be suggesting is that it takes someone as single-mindedly consumed by filial fervor as Wang Yuan to perform such an act of filial prowess, and that the line between sincere naïveté and monomaniac obsession in performing exemplary virtue may be very thin indeed. Blindness and insight are shown as inextricably linked. By pronouncing Wang Yuan an "outright foolish man," the author is using the term *chi* 癡, which in the late Ming is closely linked with the discourse of *qing* (passion, feelings, emotions), in which (to put it in greatly simplified terms) aspects of the human psyche such as passion, sentiment, madness, and obsession (which were traditionally looked at with suspicion if not outright censure) are newly valorized as the only authentic source of the self, including one's moral self. What the author is doing here, in other words, is bridging the gap between passion and duty, obsession and ritual obligation.

The Fleeing Father

One of the key tropes of many filial exemplar tales is that the paternal or parental authority is held above scrutiny. It is a paradoxical situation:

not only are vicious fathers and mothers not explicitly criticized, they are actually turned into potent foils against which the filial heroism of the son can be better displayed and celebrated: the more vicious the parent, the more heroic the child's virtue. Shun's tale of tribulations and narrow escapes from his father's and other family members' repeated attempts to murder him may be seen as the archetype. Sure enough, some tales may include a moment of final redemption, in which the despicable parent is shown as repentant, but that is far from being a required element. In filial quest stories, the parent's absence—whether voluntary or involuntary—is of course the precondition for the story to happen in the first place. But it is not without significance that with the evolution of this motif, we often see stories that focus on absent *fathers* who leave of their own accord, rather than out of external calamity (warfare, bandits). The fact that it is the father rather than the mother (as in the Zhu Shouchang tale or the other major filial quest legend, the Buddhist saga of Mulian in search of his mother) is significant, and may be read as the reaffirmation of Confucian ritual orthodoxy. In Zhu Shouchang's tale, the bond between Zhu and his biological mother, a concubine who had been expelled from the family, may be seen as purely affective in that it falls beyond ritual regulations and mourning degrees. The opposite is true in Wang Yuan's story, which features a purely ritual relationship. After all, Wang Yuan had never truly met his father.

While the biographical accounts avoid explicit evaluation or even elaboration of the father's character, the vernacular stories explicitly or implicitly problematize this figure. The vernacular stories, in other words, stage a kind of cognitive dissonance between textbook notions that "there are no bad parents in the world" (*tianxia wu bushi zhi fumu* 天下無不是之父母) and the reality of often-delinquent fathers. In the *Exemplary Words* version, the father is unceremoniously called a *nuofu* 懦夫, a coward, weakling, or spineless figure, and he is generally depicted as an inept husband and paterfamilias. Both *Exemplary Words* and *Rocks* versions greatly expand on the first part of the story that depicts the hardships of a poor villager—something that has been duly noted by both premodern commentators and modern scholars (*huaben* had been a predominantly *urban* genre, and this kind of excursion into the nitty-gritty details and miseries of daily life in the countryside is a rare treat).[43]

The *Exemplary Words* story takes particular care in grounding the narrative in the sociopolitical reality. Lu Renlong lists the three misfortunes—bad weather, bad officials, bad village head—that can befall a small landowner like Wang Xi (the father's name in the *Exemplary Words* version). He also refers to a variety of malpractices. These are listed but not glossed, as Langxian would probably have done—the reader's familiarity with these malpractices is simply assumed. The blame is attributed not to the system, but to its representatives, in particular the village head—even if that person is clearly a stock character whose name, Cui Ke 崔科, is homonymous with his role, *cuike* 催科 ("urge tax payment"). Indeed, at the end of the story, with Cui Ke's death, all problems seem to be solved. His successor not only does not persecute the returned Wang Xi, but he immediately recommends Wang Yuan's exemplary deed to the authorities for official reward. While the *Exemplary Words* version tends to depict the father as a victim of the system, Langxian locates the main source of the problem in the father himself: he is described as weak and naive, and *therefore* an easy target.

While the depiction of the father's tribulations at the village has elicited commentators' and scholars' interest and praise, what to make of the narrative of the father's journey, with its picaresque set of adventures? Once the father leaves home, there is no preestablished social role for him—a potentially exhilarating narrative situation for the writer. In the *Exemplary Words* story the father goes through various peregrinations before ending in the monastery. In spite of labeling him a "coward" in the titular couplet, Lu Renlong ends up portraying him as a figure in search of a social role, though his search ends in a temporary escape from society. The obvious literary precedent for this narrative situation is provided by the Liangshan heroes in *Water Margin* (*Shuihu zhuan* 水滸傳). In his farewell speech to his wife, Wang Xi claims to have been forced to escape in a way that is reminiscent of certain scenes in the novel.[44] But the narrator does not embrace the *Water Margin* model. Indeed, one can detect his uneasiness in dealing with this free-floating figure outside of the family—the narrator seems here to be struggling to re-invent a role for him.

The father's wanderings across the empire are also used as a pretext to weave in larger historical events such as a lost battle in the (otherwise victorious) Mongolian campaign led by the famous general Feng Sheng 馮勝 in 1386–87. But like Pierre Bezukhov wandering in the fields in the battle of Borodino in *War and Peace*, Wang Xi is the unwitting witness of a debacle, in a war he has stumbled on and does not understand. For the one who has deserted the family, the opportunity to make himself useful for the country is ultimately denied. There is no gain to be had either, as the ill-gotten money Wang Xun collects from the corpses lying around on the battlefield is quickly stolen from him.

The recognition scene is a revealing moment in the father's characterization in the two stories. While Langxian's version follows the common mold in that the recognition works in one direction only (it is the son who must repeatedly recognize the father, by means of a physical description of somatic features),[45] in "The Filial Quest of Wang Yuan" much weight is given to the father's recognition of the tokens carried by the son—some items of clothing given to him by his mother.

> [The abbot] Mahā-maitrī asked: "Why are you crying?" He replied: "This gown looks just like the one I used to wear back at home, and this skirt is just like the one worn by my wife. That's why I am crying." Mahā-maitrī asked: "How can you tell they are the same?" "I remember that when I was back at home this gown tore on the front, and so I went to buy a piece of blue cloth to mend it. Now the patch has blended in with the older fabric. Also, since we did not have blue thread, we used white thread to stitch it together. Then, I thought it didn't look right, so I dyed it with black dye—now black and white have blended. And since there were one or two inches of fabric left, my wife used it to make a waistband for her skirt—and here it is, on this skirt. I cannot help being filled with sadness by looking at these clothes."

> 大慈道:「道者緣何淚下?」那道人道:「這道袍恰似貧道家中穿的, 這裙恰是山妻的, 故此淚下。」 大慈道:「你仔麼這等認得定?」 那道者道:「記得在家時, 這件道袍胸前破壞了。 貧道去買尺青布來補。今日胸前新舊宛然。又因没青線, 把白線縫了。貧道覺得不好, 上面把墨塗了, 如今黑白相間。又還有一二寸, 老妻把來接了裙腰, 現在裙上。 不由人不覩物淒然。」[46]

The commentator remarks on this amazing act of recognition: "His wife Deng-shi [sic] simply said that he would have recognized the old clothes, but who would have expected that Wang Xi was filled with sadness and despondency, and that each inch of fabric was invested with a memory of his past life?" 鄧氏只說他認得舊物, 那知王喜滿肚皮窮愁, 寸寸都是心事所寄.[47] By inverting the direction of the recognition, Lu Renlong gives the father the chance to reject his role as simply a passive, inert object of recognition. He becomes the agent of recognition in his turn, thus effectively regaining his place in the secular family. At the same time, his ties to the monastic family are invalidated. By recognizing not only the clothes, but also each seam and each discoloration on them, the father shows that he has not forgotten the value of shared domestic life, as well as the hardship that caused him to flee from the village in the first place. One of the items is Huo-shi's skirt, the very skirt that had been pawned to gather the money to bribe Cui Ke at the beginning of the story.

The alternative world of the monastery is seen as a simple, temporary substitution for the family in both Langxian's and Lu Renlong's versions. Particularly in the *Rocks* story, it is clear that Wang Xun lives in the temple because it can assure his material survival. The monastic community can provide the nurture (*yang* 養) that ought to be the duty of his son and that he has renounced by abandoning the family; though it is ironic that Wang Xun is entrusted with the menial tasks, fetching water and tending to the fire, that are also called *yi* 役, the same term as the corvée duties from which he had initially escaped. However, the sincerity of the father's decision to leave home and join the monastic community (*chujia* 出家) is given more weight in "The Filial Quest of Wang Yuan." While Wang Xun in Langxian's version is only preoccupied with how he will face his wife, Wang Xi is worried about facing not just his wife but the whole village. He is also afraid to relinquish the monastic community and lifestyle that he had earnestly espoused. The abbot comes up with the witty (and somewhat facile) solution, which is not questioned by either father or son, that it is possible to be a monk even within the family (也有個在家出家的).[48]

The ideal of reunion is predicated here on physically sharing the same enclosed space (and the idea of enclosure is also graphically represented by the Chinese characters for "reunion" *tuanyuan* 團圓). It is a rather claustrophilic ideal: the father *must* go back home, and resume his life with his family under the same roof; it is not sufficient that the son has found him safe and sound and contentedly spending his days at the monastery.

The Abandoned Mother

In his version of the story, Langxian develops the mother into a memorable character. Zhang-shi is characterized as one of those lively, outspoken, and strong-willed women who are so often paired with comparatively spineless male characters in popular fiction from this period. The role of the mother in this story also illustrates how filial quest narratives evolved through time. In some earlier narratives (such as the story of Zhou Yu and his son Zhou Ruilong as dramatized in the *chuanqi* play *Zhou Yu Instructs His Son; Searching for the Parent / Zhou Yu jiao zi xun qin ji* 周羽教子尋親記), it is the mother who reveals to the son what happened to the father, and it is she who orders the son to quit his office and go in search of the father.⁴⁹ The crucial change in the Wang Yuan story is the self-appointed mission, and the ensuing tension with the mother. Among the adaptations of Wang Yuan's story, it is Langxian's version that most thoroughly explores this tension. This is how Zhang-shi reacts after hearing her boy's proposition to go and search for his father:

> Zhang-shi said, "A fine filial heart, a fine will indeed! There's just one thing: you know that you have a father—but do you realize that you have a mother, too?"
>
> Wang Yuan replied, "Mother, you 'carried me with great pains in your belly for ten months,' and you 'labored to breastfeed me for three years,' all the way to now. From the top of my head to the bottom of my feet, there is nothing that I have not received from you! How can I not know that I have a mother?"
>
> Zhang-shi said, "There you go again! Now, let's please forget about this business of carrying you in my belly and breastfeeding you. When your father walked out of the door, you were barely one year old. I had to support the family, while caring for you, little devil! Even if we were able to avoid the corvée duties, I was still worried that 'if one sits down idly, one will eat up a whole mountain.' Because of this, I did not spare efforts but labored restlessly day and night."

> 張氏道：「好孝心, 好志氣。只是你既曉得有爹, 可曉得 有娘麼?」王原道：「母親十月懷胎之苦, 三年乳哺之勞, 以 至今日, 自頂及踵, 無一非受之於母親, 如何不曉得有娘?」張氏道：「可又來。且莫說懷胎乳哺的勞苦, 只你父親出門時, 你才週歲, 我一則要支持門戶, 二來要照管你這冤家。雖然脫卸差役, 還恐坐吃山空。為此不惜身命, 日夜辛勤。」⁵⁰

In contrast with her son's bookish and abstract understanding of the "care debt" he owes her (to use Keith Knapp's phrase)—which in his mind is reduced to the pains of labors and breastfeeding—his mother replies with a long tirade on the years of strenuous work and constant worries she has undergone in raising her son all by herself. The author stages here an opposition between textbook Confucianism on one hand and lived life on the other.

Unable to dissuade her son from his plan to leave in search of his father, Zhang-shi finally concedes: "So be it! The dragon sires a dragon, the phoenix begets a phoenix. It's no surprise that a father who couldn't care less about the family and went begging his way around the world would have a son who doesn't care for his mother and will drift about and [end up] in the gutter." (龍, 龍！龍生龍, 鳳生鳳。有那不思家乞丐天涯的父親, 定然生這不顧母流落溝渠的兒子。⁵¹) While in the original biography and in the other vernacular adaptations the reward of the filial son takes the form of copious male progeny (scrupulously enumerated: six male sons, fifteen grandsons, twenty-two great-grandsons, etc.), this element is not even mentioned in "The Filial Quest of Wang Yuan." Rather, his reward comes in the guise of political employment, according to the famous adage that concludes the story: "one should seek a loyal minister in the home of a filial son" 求忠臣必于孝子之門.⁵² Lu Renlong and his brother are fervent subscribers to what Norman Kutcher terms the "parallel conception of society."⁵³ Much stress is given here to the political implications of filial piety.

In sum, while Langxian's filial hero is animated by a kind of filial piety that borders on single-minded obsession and foolishness, like many of the characters in his stories, Lu Renlong endows Wang Yuan with the traits of a comparatively lucid, if less striking and memorable, moral exemplar. By developing the character of the father (though not entirely successfully, as we have seen above), the motivation of Wang Yuan's filial journey becomes less abstract in the eye of the reader. The filial hero's reward lies in the official career he enjoys after he has brought his father back home—not in the large progeny bestowed on him by both historical sources and Langxian's version. All in all, Lu Renlong strives to reframe the story of Wang Yuan and his father into a larger social and historical context. In the universe of *Exemplary Words*, the ultimate achievement of the filial son is his ability to serve as a (presumably) exemplary officeholder. We will see this motif appearing also in Wang Shiming's story, discussed in the following chapter.⁵⁴

∾

The episode of Filial Guo (Guo xiaozi 郭孝子) included in the eighteenth-century novel *The Unofficial History of the Scholars* (*Rulin waishi* 儒林外史) can be considered at once the glorious culmination and the most devastating critique of the trope of the filial son in quest of his father.⁵⁵ The episode can be read as a reworking of the hagiographical conventions found in previous accounts of filial sons. While in previous accounts the aid is often supernatural (in the form of premonitory dreams, apparitions of gods, and the like) while the dangers may be hyperbolic but are usually grounded in reality, in Filial Guo's tale the opposite is true.

It is the circle of virtuous Nanjing literati who had taken part in the construction of the Taibo temple who finance Filial Guo's trip. On the other hand, the dangers and obstacles take the guise of tigers and weird animals and monsters (*guai dongxi* 怪東西), thus likening this part of the journey to a scary ride at Luna Park. One of these monsters turns out to be a setup by a man reduced to dire straits: he has his wife made up as a scary ghost hanging from a tree, thus luring passers-by into a trap so that he can rob them. Filial Guo, true to his nature, morally redeems the man and even passes his martial skills on to him. The "transformative" power of the filial son toward the bandits is also a common motif of hagiographical accounts.

Unlike other accounts, Filial Guo seems to enjoy a reputation as a filial son throughout the empire (hence his name); the narrator labels him as such, without using his given name. His journey is invested with a publicly recognized meaning, in spite of his constant reticence in revealing the extent of his mission (to protect his father's reputation, he cannot easily reveal why he has deserted his family). In other words, Filial Guo enjoys an iconic status both within the narrative and at a meta-diegetic level.

As Shang Wei has noted, Filial Guo does everything that Wang Yuan does, but things go awry, since his father refuses to recognize him.[56] In fact Filial Guo does much more than Wang Yuan: not only does he search for his father for twenty years amid countless vicissitudes, but after his father refuses to recognize him, he takes up residence by his father's temple to provide for him, and after he has exhausted his funds, he sells himself out as a hired laborer (another stock motif in filial accounts). In the end, Guo tirelessly brings back his father's bones to bury them in his hometown. The tragedy is of course that the object of Guo's devotion refuses to acknowledge him as his son, precipitating Guo into the identity abyss that Wang Yuan in the *Rocks* story had only approached. Hence the supererogatory adherence to ritual duty and to a father who does not recognize him is Filial Guo's only anchor to his own sense of self, however paradoxical that may sound. The case of Filial Guo also constitutes a radicalization of the juxtaposition between family duty and sociopolitical duty, since Guo's father Wang Hui is a rebel who joined the rebellion of the prince of Ning.

∼

Filial quest tales might have appealed to the late Ming authors and collectors of stories of filial exemplars for a number of reasons—not least of which is the inherently appealing narrative potential of journey itself. These texts reveal a heightened sense of anxiety over the dismemberment of family units—something that would become all the more resonant in the turmoil of the Ming-Qing transition. They may also be read allegorically as ruminations on the absence of an authority figure. They push readers to interrogate themselves on what it means to be filial *without a father*. There are disquieting intimations of the lack of worth of the parental figure. Through the character of the son, who is gently derided as a "fool," the texts (especially the *Rocks* version) stage a kind of cognitive dissonance between morality textbook notions that "there are no bad parents in the world" and the grim reality of undeniably delinquent fathers. The two versions of Wang Yuan's story are vastly different in terms of narrative craft—but from the ideological point of view, they both attempt to achieve a similar goal, that is, to bridge the rarefied, stylized world of *imitatio* with the everyday world of *mimesis*, to help the reader make sense of the terse and distant biographical account in literary language.[57] Humanizing the father is one strategy; turning the son into a passionate hero is another. For all the gentle teasing of the son as a "foolish" man, it is *his* vision that triumphs in the end. The dissimilarities between these two versions thus expose the complexity and range often occluded by the term "didactic."

Chapter 2

Filial Dilemmas

While the filial quest narratives discussed in the previous chapter end with the physical reconstitution of the ideal family togetherness (*tuanyuan* 團圓), this very togetherness functions as a catalyst for family conflicts and dilemmas in the stories discussed in this chapter. I use the term "dilemma" to indicate a situation in which a choice must be made between two unpalatable options, but without the implication, common in the modern usage, of inner torment. There is rarely any indication that the heroes and heroines themselves are agonizing over the right course of action; rather, the spectrum of moral choices is externalized and dramatized in what I call the "discursive frame." The type of moral dilemma staged in the stories—a conflict between filial duty and the obligations associated with other family bonds—may be traced back to the early medieval accounts of filial offspring. The most famous example is perhaps Guo Ju 郭巨, later canonized as one of the twenty-four filial exemplars. As the legend goes, Guo Ju, whose family was very poor, was ready to bury his son alive to ensure his mother's survival. But as he proceeded to dig the grave, Guo found a golden casket buried in the ground, with his name written on it, and so his little son's life was spared.[1] Keith Knapp reads this kind of plot as a "feminization" of filial dilemmas, noting that the authors of medieval filial accounts often put "male protagonists in story lines that in the past were solely associated with women," such as stories in which the hero must sacrifice his own children to save those of a sibling, or get rid of his child or wife for the sake of his parent.[2]

Similar to medieval hagiographies of filial exemplars, late Ming vernacular stories tackle issues that fall into what may be termed moral casuistry: to whom should one give priority, father or son? Mother or wife? Mother-in-law or husband? Father or adoptive father? One remarkable story, "Cui Jian the Filial Boy" (QYZ 7), stages a conflict of duty toward father vs. mother, from the perspective of a twelve-year-old boy. What the stories tend to avoid is the opposition between filial piety and political loyalty, between domestic and public morality. The notable exception is the story of Wang Shiming, which presents a clash between private morality and public duty; but even there, such opposition pertains to the incongruity between moral code and legal system, rather than to potentially contradictory demands within the Five Cardinal Relationships.

In contrast with early medieval accounts, late Ming stories offer a more nuanced representation of family dynamics. The filial sons and daughters facing a moral dilemma may be every bit as unperturbed and determined as their medieval counterparts, but they are no longer acting in a virtual social vacuum.[3] The solution to the dilemma often involves an exchange, as in "Mother Comes First" (XSY 3), or a murder, either in the form of revenge or the more rare case of preemptive murder as in "Cui Jian the Filial Boy." The dilemma also calls forth self-sacrifice and death, as discussed in the last section.

Stark Choices

"Mother Comes First" (original title: "A Shrewish Wife with a Trick Gets Rid of Her Widowed Mother-in-Law, A Filial Son Brings Back His Old Mother Alive" 悍婦計去孀姑, 孝子生還老母, XSY 3) deals with the perennial motif of the animosity between mother and daughter-in-law, with the son caught in the middle. It tells of a Suzhou merchant, Zhou Yulun 周于倫 (a name that could read as "solicitous toward human bonds"), whose wife Qian Zhangzhu 錢掌珠 and mother Sheng-shi 盛氏 do not get along. During one of Yulun's frequent trading trips, the wife, instigated by the neighbors, tricks her mother-in-law into getting married to a man from out of town. When Yulun comes back, he searches for his mother in vain, until he fortuitously runs into her during one of his business trips. With a trick, he swaps his mother with his wife, and happily brings the mother back home.

The plot of this story is admittedly contrived. This is one of the few stories in *Exemplary Words* that are based on a fictional source, a classical language tale by Song Maocheng 宋楙澄 (1569–after 1620) titled "The Filial Son from Suzhou" (Wuzhong xiaozi 吳中孝子).[4] Song was also the author of "The Pearl Vest" (Zhushan 珠衫) and "The Faithless Lover"

(Fuqing nong zhuan 負情儂傳), which served as sources for two of the most celebrated *San Yan* tales.[5] "The Filial Son from Suzhou" comes right before "The Pearl Vest" in Song's collection and shares with it the theme of wife-swapping and consequent retribution.

This story dramatizes the conflict between mother and wife, and the choice that the hero is forced to make between the two. The idea that filial piety declines when one gets married and has children is encapsulated in an old adage quoted in the prologue: "Filial piety decreases with the appearance of wife and children" 孝衰於妻子.[6] In this formulation, wives and children are configured as antagonistic to the caring and love that a son owes his parents.[7] The son's choice, in a fashion reminiscent of Guo Ju's tale, is posited in absolute and unnaturally simplified terms: Zhou Yulun must choose between his mother and his wife; he cannot mediate between them, and he cannot have both. But unlike in Guo Ju's tale, no golden casket miraculously appears as deus ex machina to save the day.

In contrast with Guo Ju's tale, in this story the filial act is steeped in a culture of economic transaction and monetary exchange. In her discussion of Song Maocheng's tale, the source for this story, Tina Lu has pointed out that the particulars of the exchange between mother and wife are "commercial enough to be troubling."[8] Even more than Song's tale, "Mother Comes First" presents the choice between mother and wife in the stark terms of a commercial transaction. This story could be subtitled "Filial piety in the age of trade and monetization." One of the liveliest moments is the exchange scene. Mother and wife are both assessed as items of merchandise by prying male eyes. Both are given a price: the mother is worth ten taels, the wife fifty or seventy taels. And let's not forget that Zhou Yulun is a merchant himself. When he trades his wife for his mother, he shrewdly points out to Zhang Erlang, Zhang Bida's son, that he is letting him have the better deal:

> "I give you one in exchange for another, and I give you a young one in exchange for an old one. How can this not be a good deal for you?" Zhang Erlang nodded in agreement and said: "Indeed, you're right." And so he called for Zhou's mother to come out, while at the same time he sent a servant to the boat to take a look at Zhou's wife. [. . .] In a short while, the servant came back and discreetly reported to Zhang Erlang: "She's good looking alright. She's worth a good fifty or seventy *taels*." Erlang was greatly pleased, but pretending to have second thoughts he said: "While here, your mother has been hard-working and congenial, and she

got along very well with the whole family. But I don't know how this newcomer will be. I'm afraid it would be difficult to make this exchange." After Yulun had pleaded with him several times, Erlang finally said: "Well, things being what they are, go ahead and write me a marriage certificate."

「一個換一個, 小的換老的, 有甚不便宜?」章二郎點頭道:「倒也是。」一邊叫他母親出來, 一邊着人看船中婦人何如。[. . .] 須臾看的人悄地回覆二郎道:「且是標緻, 值五七十兩。」二郎滿心歡喜, 假意道「令堂在這廂, 且是勤謹和氣, 一家相得。來的不知何如? 恐難換。」于倫再三懇求, 二郎道:「這等且寫了婚書。」⁹

It matters little that the transaction is unprofitable for the son: it is a transaction nonetheless, and a transaction that the son completes successfully by manipulating the other party through financial considerations. The filial act is here inextricably intertwined with considerations of profit and loss. What is left unaccounted for in the grittiness of the exchange is that it is not just about an old crone being exchanged for a young beauty, of course, but about a mother being exchanged for a wife—*for both parties*. The message of the story, spelled out in the prologue, is that, paraphrasing Zhai Zhong's 祭仲 wife's pronouncement in the *Zuozhuan*, "any woman can be your wife, but only one can be your mother" 人盡妻也, 母一而已.¹⁰ Wives and husbands are replaceable; mothers and fathers are not. Yet, for one man who trades in his wife to get back his mother, there is another man who replaces a nanny (who could be seen as a mother figure) with a wife. For this reason, it is very tempting to read this tale oedipally. The story goes into uneasy territory, and the transaction skirts ideas of incest. Tina Lu has noted that the issue of the two women's chastity is dealt with as neatly as possible in the classical tale.¹¹ In the tale, the man from out of town who purchases Zhou's mother is simply looking for a nanny. The fate of Zhou's wife in the new household is likewise left undetermined. But in "Mother Comes First," Zhang Bida is, more credibly, looking for a "mate" (*lao ban'er* 老伴兒), and Sheng-shi is sold to him as a concubine. It is only after Sheng-shi threatens to commit suicide that the marriage is "commuted" to an employment as nanny for the man's grandson. On the other hand, Zhangzhu is clearly traded in as a sexual partner for the man's son, complete with a written "marriage certificate" given from Zhou Yulun to Zhang Erlang.

The exemplarity of the hero and the exemplary message of the story as a whole are cast in an ambiguous light through the counterpoint of dissonant voices (the commentators, the narrator, and the characters in the narrative). Lauded in the preface and tail commentary as a filial paragon cleverly acting in most unusual circumstances, Zhou Yulun is by his own account not to be upheld as a model. Moreover, the wife Zhangzhu is portrayed in an unexpectedly sympathetic light.

The story is framed as a tale of an exemplary son who is able to make the best of an extremely unusual situation, a point made in both preface and tail commentary. The preface sententiously laments how conjugal infatuation all too often usurps the primacy of filial devotion. How easy it is for men to forget about parental love, and how hard to sever the feelings between husband and wife! The author concludes that Zhou Yulun is truly worthy of being upheld as an exemplar for the present generation, because he combines steadfast morality with the sagacity needed to handle complex situations. This way, Yulun is hailed as an eponymous hero in the collection as a whole. "Devising a wondrous plan stems from one's original inventiveness, so there is no need to follow the steps of the ancients. Someone who is able to uphold the natural family bonds by means of a circuitous scheme [such as the hero of this story] can truly set an example for the present era." 運奇謀於獨創, 何必襲跡古人。 完天倫於委蛇, 真可樹型今世.[12]

In the first of two tail commentaries, Lu Yunlong mentions two other filial exemplars from Suzhou who were noted for entertaining their mother with boisterous songs (*kuangge yumu* 狂歌娛母). The commentator remarks that while their devotion to their mother could be compared to that of Lao Lai (the filial paragon who dressed in multicolored toddler's clothes despite being in his seventies just so he could amuse his aging parents), Zhou Yulun's ability to "handle his predicament in such a tactful way" remains unrivaled.[13] Echoing what he already stated in the preface, Lu exalts the hero of the story as a filial paragon to be upheld *in the present age*. We have here a reiteration of the familiar argument, echoed in many other stories, which stresses the necessity to combine moral rectitude with cleverness and practical insight—the anxiety with which the latter is repeatedly emphasized betrays the commentator's concern with the dangerous times of the present era. The second tail commentary, signed by the Extreme-Natured One 至性人, returns to the uncommon nature of the story, but also emphasizes the deleterious role of the meddling neighbors, urging the readers to take this story as a lesson on the importance of keeping away from bad neighbors. Thus the two commentaries complement each other in drawing the readers' attention to the exemplary significance of the story on one hand (Yulun as an appropriate filial paragon for the modern age) and its cautionary function on the other (Beware of your neighbors!).

Yet in spite of the purportedly unambiguous moral message in the preface and tail commentaries, the story prologue and the characterization of both wife and husband shed a more ambivalent light on the moral adjudications. The prologue begins by warning the reader against bad wives, a category elaborated in a rich inventory:

> There are wives who, coming from a rich and powerful family, look down upon their parents-in-law; wives who are quick at gobbling food but lazy at doing the housework, and do not get along with the parents-in-law; wives who are greedy and petty, and who begrudge spending money to provide for the parents-in-law; wives who, having sisters and brothers-in-law, suspect that the parents-in-law are biased and unfair, and so they don't let a single day pass without gossiping and complaining in the husband's ears.
>
> 或是恃家中富貴, 驕傲公姑; 或是勤喫懶做, 與公姑不合; 或鄙嗇愛小, 嫌憎公姑費他供養; 或有小姑小叔, 疑心公姑護短偏愛。無日不向丈夫耳根絮絮。[14]

In spite of the superficially misogynistic stance, however, the narrator ultimately places the greatest responsibility on the husband's discernment, or lack thereof:

> If the husband is somebody who has a firm discernment, he will take [his wife's complaints and naggings] as so much wind in the ears, and he will instead reprimand her by reminding her of the true principles. He will tell her that "there is no such thing as a bad parent"; and even admitting that some parents-in-law may have small oversteps, one should still grin and bear it—and in this way he may gradually transform and morally enlighten his wife.
>
> 那有主意的男子, 只當風過耳邊, 還把道理去責他, 道沒有個不是的父母, 縱使公姑有些過情, 也要逆來順受, 也可漸漸化轉婦人。[15]

In the prologue to another story, "Injustice to Tang Guimei" (*XSY* 6), the narrator launches into a peroration on the injustice suffered by daughters-in-law, which reads like a mirror image of the invective against bad daughters-in-law in "Mother Comes First" (even as he admits that there are all kinds of bad daughters-in-law, too). He concludes:

In one case, the mother-in-law has a stubborn mouth, in the other the daughter-in-law has a stubborn ear; it comes to a point that even the son cannot aspire to fulfill a reputation as filial son. This is indeed the kind of situation that everyone wishes not to happen, and yet happens all the time.

這便是婆婆口頑, 媳婦耳頑, 弄得連兒子也不得有孝順的名, 真是人家不願有的事, 却也是常有的事。16

In other words, the narrator does not unilaterally condemn one side over the other in the eternal struggle between mother and daughter-in-law. All parties involved have their roles and responsibilities. The narrator also emphasizes that everyday reality is indeed very far from the ideal of domestic harmony typically found in edifying stories.

In the story itself, the wife is portrayed in a surprisingly sympathetic light in the narrative—and, conversely, the hero himself is not without blame. The mutual incomprehension and petty bickering between mother and daughter-in-law are portrayed with realism and humor. This story greatly elaborates on the characterization and relationship between the two female characters. In the classical tale, the daughter is tersely characterized—the information provided by the author is purely functional to the plot. We know that she is "young and beautiful" from the description the husband gives to the merchant. We presume that she is clever and ruthless based on her action, though no explicit judgment is made of her. Likewise, the mother is only described in her physical appearance—not yet forty, neat and tidy in appearance—because this detail is functional to the plot. Whereas the classical tale laconically states "mother and daughter-in-law did not get along" (qi yu gu bu xiang neng 妻與姑不相能), Lu Renlong shows how and why this happens.17

As with the characterization of the corrupt mother-in-law in "Injustice to Tang Guimei," where the narrator details her background and analyzes the circumstances that led to her adulteries, "Mother Comes First" gives a rather sympathetic portrait of the daughter-in-law. As her given name suggests, Zhangzhu ("pearl in hand," a common metaphor for the beloved daughter) is the product of a faulty upbringing. Motherless since tender age, she is raised by a doting father who spoils her in every possible way. (Ironically, Zhou Yulun's own upbringing is described in very similar terms—he is doted on by his widowed mother every bit as much as Zhangzhu). The interlineal commentary is also often sympathetic to Zhangzhu, praising the astute way she handles business while the husband is away. On the other hand, the mother Sheng-shi is depicted as austere and strict, but also narrow-minded and petty. It is she who convinces Zhou Yulun to take up trading to earn supplemental income—a decision that is fiercely but vainly opposed by Zhangzhu.[18] The clash between mother and daughter-in-law can be characterized as a textbook case of "personality conflict," with no facile distinction between villain and victim.

Where the vernacular story departs most strikingly from its classical source is in the role assigned to the meddling neighbors—instantiations of those pernicious *sangu liupo* 三姑六婆 (three aunties and six grannies) who are the source of trouble and objects of the narrator's scorn in countless tales. While the classical tale casts the matchmaker simply as a helper to the scheming wife, Lu Renlong gives life and voice to the bad neighbors Yang Sansao 楊三嫂 and Li Erniang 李二娘, and he turns the matchmaker-neighbor Xu *po* 徐婆 into the architect of the plan to trick Sheng-shi into getting on the boat with Zhang Bida—thus turning her into a figure similar to Granny Xue in "The Pearl-Sewn Shirt."

Just as the sympathetic characterization of Zhangzhu in the first part of the story complicates the story's exemplary message, the ending also casts a dark shadow. Zhou Yulun's story proves that wives are indeed replaceable, unlike mothers. But when the village constable proposes to recommend him for an official reward as a filial son, Zhou adamantly refuses, protesting: "I may be a filial son, but I am no loyal husband." 是孝子, 不是義夫.[19]

A Chinese scholar has suggested as the probable source for this story a tale titled "Jin Chao" 金潮 by the noted playwright Xu Fuzuo 徐復祚 (fl. late sixteenth century).[20] While Song Maocheng's tale is most likely the proximate source, Xu Fuzuo's tale makes for an interesting parallel version. This tale amplifies the exemplary import of the story through an accumulation of filial topoi. At the beginning of the story, Jin Chao performs *gegu* for his ailing father. When his father dies, he cries tears of blood and performs exemplary mourning by living in a shed at the side of the father's grave for three years. When he finds out that his mother has disappeared, he is inconsolable and embarks on a filial quest by assuming the guise of a Daoist going round to collect funds for his monastery. Lastly, he has a dream that reveals to him his mother's whereabouts. Jin Chao's wife is depicted as a virago who bullies her mother-in-law, and is moreover guilty of carrying an adulterous relationship. Conversely, the mother is cast as the hapless victim, who fears her daughter-in-law and does not dare disobey her orders. The story ends with the son "repenting" and promising to his mother that he will never again leave his house in pursuit of business. He marries another woman who is filial and devoted. In spite of the additions at the beginning and end, the plot of "Jin Chao" is more linear than that of "The Filial Son from Suzhou." The author is less interested in describing the stratagem used by the male protagonist to get his wife on the boat. All in all, Xu Fuzuo's version is a black-and-white and rather suffocating exemplary tale.

Filial Murderers

Two stories of filial murder will be discussed in this section, both featuring a son committing murder to preempt or to avenge the murder of one parent. The first story, titled "Cui Jian the Filial Boy" (original title: "Brandishing a Dagger He Gets Rid of the Harpy, The Imperial Edict Gives Special Consideration to His Filial Intention" 挺刃终除鴞悍, 皇綸特鑒孝衷, QYZ 7) is remarkable on many counts. This story stages an unusual choice between father and mother, which leads to the murder of the father's concubine. Its hero, Cui Jian, is a twelve-year-old boy (13 sui). Although hagiographical tales of filial piety often cast young boys as protagonists, this is rarely the case in vernacular stories. The interpersonal dynamics between wife, husband, and concubine are depicted with considerable psychological realism. Cui Jian's predicament is presented in a way that comes closer to a kind of interiorized dilemma than any of the stories we have encountered so far.

In this story, Cui You 崔佑, the boy's father, becomes infatuated with the courtesan Wei Luan 魏鸞, with whom he spends all his time and money, thus provoking the ire of his wife, Wang-shi. Cui You later decides to take Wei Luan as a concubine. As expected, a domestic inferno ensues. One day, during a quarrel, Wei Luan slaps Wang-shi in the face and threatens to deploy the husband against her. Wang-shi, deeply humiliated, decides to commit suicide. Luckily, Cui Jian walks in as she is about to hang herself. The boy flies into a rage and stabs the concubine to death. He then runs away, but retraces his steps soon after, realizing that if he walks away the responsibility of the crime will fall onto his mother. As anticipated, when Cui Jian gets back his father is already dragging his mother to court, amid a crowd of neighbors. The boy immediately declares that he is the culprit. No one believes him at first, but after he reveals the location of the weapon with which the crime had been committed (a Korean dagger that his father had given him) he is finally believed. The local magistrate sends his case for review to his superiors, who unanimously concur on the boy's innocence. The story ends with the Jiajing emperor pardoning the boy.

"Cui Jian the Filial Boy" is based on an actual court case recorded by Wu Guifang 吳桂芳 (1521–1578), who was involved in the resolution of the case. Wu Guifang is explicitly mentioned and his final commentary is even quoted verbatim at the end of the story. Wu's record is found in various sources, including Li Zhi's *Sequel to a Book to Hide* and Jiao Hong's 焦竑 (1541–1620) *Record of Outstanding Figures of the [Ming] Dynasty* (*Guochao xianzheng lu* 國朝獻徵錄, 1616).[21] The case is also briefly recorded in a short entry in Shen Defu's 沈德符 (1578–1642) well-known *biji* compilation *Private Gleanings of the Wanli Era* (*Wanli yehuo bian* 萬曆野獲編, 1606).[22] In Shen's version, the story is framed by a Tang anecdote on Yan Wu 嚴武 and Yan Tingzhi 嚴挺之, which recounts a similar case of a boy who raised his hand against the father's favorite concubine. Shen Defu concludes by drawing a comparison between the Tang precedent and the Ming case: "Although Yan Wu was only a little boy, he came from a powerful family, so he must have been familiar with examples of integrity and heroism. On the contrary, Jian was an ignorant boy from the back alleys, who was stirred to action out of utmost sincerity, so his deed is even harder [to accomplish]." 武雖嬰孺, 然世家胄, 允熟聞節烈。鑒閭巷無知。發於至誠, 較更難矣。[23]

The Yan Wu anecdote reappears in the prologue of the vernacular story, following a familiar rhetorical move in which a modern exemplar outdoes the ancient. To enhance this effect, the narrator deliberately changes the ending of the Tang anecdote by having Yan Wu beat the concubine on the head with a cane, but without killing her. However, while Shen's attitude toward education and family background is implicitly positive (so that the lack of education only makes it harder, hence more praiseworthy, to act in a virtuous way), Lu Renlong looks at education with more skepticism. In the prologue he launches into a defense of children's spontaneity and lack of education-induced inhibitions—perhaps echoing Li Zhi's famous essay "On the Child-like Mind." The narrator deploys the familiar argument against the hackneyed ways of pedants who simply stick to the rites of "greeting the parents and serving them food" 問安視膳, and he praises instead the simple-minded, "uncontaminated" people, as represented by the boy Cui Jian.[24]

In the story the young protagonist faces an unusual moral choice: he must decide whether to side with his mother or father. In contrast with the original source, the vernacular story gives an ambivalent characterization of the boy's mother, Wang-shi.

"Now, Cui You was actually an old hand at whoring; he would make several visits [to the brothel] each month. Wang-shi, on the other hand, was a generalissimo among jealous women, and no month would pass without her making a few scenes."

這崔佑原也是箇嫖婆娘的透手兒。一月也嘗走幾次。這王氏也是箇喫醋元帥,一月也鬧幾場。[25]

The author captures the relationship between husband and wife with remarkable psychological realism. The wife's jealousy and outspokenness (the traditional target of misogynistic satire) are seen here as mutually intertwined with the husband's philandering.

> Cui You knew that his wife would raise a rumpus, so he drank his fill outside before going back home. Then he left some cash on the table, while he himself went to sleep and snored away on the *kang*, still fully dressed. Wang-shi said: "Great! Now that you have exerted yourself at other people's house, you come home to sleep!" Cui Jian said: "It's alright, let it be. Father is already asleep, don't wake him up." But Wang-shi, seeing that he was sleeping, got even angrier. She screamed and yelled the whole night.

那崔佑也曉得妻子要急力拐姑他,先在外邊喫下一包子酒。把些錢丟在桌上,自己鼻鼾的炕上和衣睡了。王氏道:「好,別人家辛苦了,來自己家將息!」崔鑑道:「罷,父親睡了,不要攪他睡頭。」那王氏見他睡越惱了,整整吵了一夜。[26]

Wang-shi's angry outbursts have no other effect than estranging her husband even more. The text depicts with realism the crescendo of animosity between husband and wife. The domestic fights also entail the breaking of pots and bowls, which causes poor Cui Jian to be "so frightened that he did not know where to hide, vainly trying to persuade both parties." 嘗把個崔鑑驚得沒處藏身,東勸不是,西勸不是.[27]

One day Lao Zhou, the store assistant, reveals to Wang-shi that her husband has been spending his days and nights with Wei Luan and his two hangers-on in the room above the store (which is in a different location from the house). Moreover, he tells her that her son knew about this.

> When Wang-shi heard this, she became furious. She said, "I have raised him until now, and here he is, just like his father: both are cheating and deceiving me, who am as [helpless as] a legless crab! Wait till he comes back . . ." Lao Zhou said,

"How can he make his father fight against his mother? Both of you are his parents. This really is in an impossible situation for him."

> 王氏聽了大惱, 道:「養得他大, 他父子兩個欺瞞我這沒腳蟹, 待他回來!」 這老周道:「他叫爹娘相打, 兩邊親也, 是沒奈何。」 28

When Cui Jian returns from school, his mother confronts him:

> Wang-shi said: "And so you obey your father and deceive your mother!" Cui Jian said: "I actually was afraid that you and father would get angry, that's why I didn't tell you." Wang-shi first of all proceeded to give him a beating.

> 王氏道:「你聽父親, 瞞母親?」 崔鑑道:「我實怕父親, 母親兩下淘氣, 故不說。」王氏先將來打上一頓。29

Later, when confronting her husband and Wei Luan, Wang-shi gives a textbook performance as a virago, "roaring like the Hedong lioness," unleashing a stream of curses, and trying to pull out her rival's hair. By characterizing the mother as an ambivalent figure, and the situation as one where no one is entirely innocent, the narrator turns the boy's dilemma into a more poignant one. As can be inferred from the excerpted passages, the boy at first seeks to diffuse the tension. He vainly tries to talk his parents into reason (in one quatrain he is compared to an unheeded loyal minister),30 then he tries to cover up his father's misdeeds. Rather than the prose, it is in the intercalated quatrains that the narrator represents the boy's predicament in the first part of the story.

It is only when the mother becomes, or rather casts herself as, *the* victim that the boy is finally forced to take sides.

> But just as she was getting ready to hang herself, in walked Cui Jian, who had just come back from school. When he saw his mother's disheveled hair, he asked, "Mother, what is going on now?" His mother replied, "I've lived here for fifteen years. We were getting along just fine, me and my husband. But now this slut has come between us and she has made him beat and curse me! Just now, I gave her a piece of my mind since I could not stand it anymore, and that slut has cursed at me and beaten me. She even said that she will get my husband to give me a beating. Might as well just die here, since I cannot kick

her out of the house! Son, make sure to study hard and earn a good name on my behalf, and avenge me!" Cui Jian said, "Enough, mother. Please be patient. When father comes back, I will explain everything to him, and see if he comes to his senses. Don't do this!" At that time, Cui Jian was only twelve, so what could he know about gain and loss? He thought, "My father used to be a decent man. This is all the doing of that whore, who has undone our family. Now she even dares to raise her hands against my mother. There's nothing else for me to do but kill this whore to relieve mother's anger."

正待上吊, 却值崔鑑自學中來, 見娘披頭散髮的, 道:「母親, 又是甚緣故?」王氏道:「我在此十五年, 夫妻好端端的, 被這淫婦來挑撥得不打就罵。適才氣不憤, 說得一聲, 淫婦也來罵我、打我, 還要叫漢子擺布我。我只死了, 叫他走不開!兒, 你可學好, 替咱爭口氣!與咱報仇!」崔鑑道:「罷, 母親還耐心, 父親家來, 咱也說個明白, 看他回心不回心。不要如此。」此時崔鑑才十三歲, 孩子家知甚利害?他想道:「我父親原是好的, 只為這浪淫婦, 攪得不成人家。他又敢打我母親, 我只杀了這浪淫婦, 出了母親氣罷。」³¹

In contrast with the ambivalent characterization of the wife, the courtesan turned concubine Wei Luan is depicted as outright malicious, without a single redeeming trait. In the fight scenes with Wang-shi, however, she is just a shrewish woman who outdoes another shrew. In the end, she becomes the scapegoat. She is condemned as the concubine who did not know to keep her place, and brought misery upon herself. As for Cui You, the husband, he is absolved on the basis of his son's exemplary filiality. His womanizing at the beginning of the story is explained as part of the general lasciviousness of the citizens of the capital region. And at the end, he is simply cast as a spineless man who does not have a mind of his own (原只是沒帳人).³²

In the story, filial murder is officially condoned. The rhetorical strategy of the narrator is worth considering. On the one hand, the boy's murderous act is justified as stemming from irrepressible rage at the humiliation and threat inflicted on the boy's mother. On the other hand, the boy is praised for acting most *wisely*. In going against his father's interest, he has opted for the lesser evil: "killing the prostitute and thus going against his father was a minor offense, while killing the prostitute in order to save his mother was for a greater cause. He demonstrated [that he possessed] both wisdom and virtue." 殺娼忤父之失小, 殺娼全母之事大, 智德又備矣.³³

As Maram Epstein has shown in her study of eighteenth-century court cases of filially motivated homicides, the construction of the defendant's action as motivated by filial concerns was one of the most powerful tools to portray him sympathetically. Often such sympathetic portraiture led to a mitigation of the original sentence.[34] The cases reviewed by Epstein are all, with one exception, about sons whose murderous acts are construed not as actions but *reactions* to the family dramas they are caught in. Cui Jian's behavior is described in similar terms to that of the defendants involved in the Qing court cases. Much emphasis is laid on the gradual accumulation of tension, and rising level of provocation. The homicidal raptus is presented as a form of sudden and uncontrollable rage. Moreover, almost no time elapses between the decision to kill the concubine (as described in the passage quoted above) and its execution. The legal and moral justification of the homicide thus rests on a tenuous balance of impulse and morally calculated predetermination.

If in Cui Jian's story the tension between private morality and legal code is resolved by way of imperial pardon,[35] "Wang Shiming the Filial Avenger" (original title: "A Thousand Pieces of Gold Cannot Make Up for His Father's Murder, His Death Is a Misguided Application of the Imperial Law" 千金不易父仇, 一死曲伸國法, *XSY* 2) paints a very different picture. This story tackles the problem of filial revenge and its justification from moral, ritual, and legal perspectives. The story is based on a sixteenth-century case that had a wide resonance, and was recorded in a number of historical accounts and local gazetteers.[36] The place is Jinhua county 金華, Zhejiang province, where, as the narrator tells us, people are known for their "litigiousness and belligerence."[37] Wang Liang 王良 is killed by his rich and prevaricating nephew Wang Jun 王俊 in the course of a fight over a construction project initiated by Wang Jun on a plot of land which is their shared property. Wang Liang's widow and his son Wang Shiming 王世名 plan to report Wang Jun to the authorities and obtain revenge, but the clan representatives and villagers convince them to accept a private settlement instead. The terms of the settlement require that the offender Wang Jun pay for the funeral expenses and provide for the needs of the widow and the orphan. Wang Shiming seems to acquiesce. However, he insists on paying for the father's funeral expenses. After the prescribed mourning period is over, Shiming gets married and within a year his wife bears a son.

Six years after Wang Liang's murder, the moment has finally come for Shiming to execute his revenge: one night, he kills Wang Jun while he is walking back home, drunk. He then turns himself in to the local authorities for punishment. The magistrates reviewing his case concur on the necessity to perform an autopsy on the father's body to prove that he had been murdered: this would be the only way to obtain a pardon, or at least a mitigation of the sentence. But Shiming adamantly refuses. When the magistrate insists on carrying out the autopsy, Shiming dashes his head on the *yamen* steps, but he is rescued. He then starves himself to death.

Filial revenge poses a tremendous problem in that it brings to the forefront a tension between the contrasting claims of ritual duty and legal code. Ancient classics such as the *Record of Rites* and the Gongyang commentary to the *Chunqiu* prescribe that a son whose father has been killed should take revenge, as encapsulated in the maxim that a filial son "cannot tolerate to share the same heaven [as his father's murderer]" (*bu gong dai tian* 不共戴天).[38] On the other hand, imperial law normally prohibits murder for the sake of social order, while striving to centralize and monopolize the dispensing of punishments. In practice, because of the deeply rooted sense of vengeance as a moral imperative, filial murder was always considered as a sui generis crime that could be officially condoned under certain circumstances. Such circumstances became more and more minutely defined in late imperial times.

The story of Wang Shiming articulates three distinct and competing views of justice and order. First, there is the idea of justice as ritual duty, which calls for revenge as the only solution to the disequilibrium caused by the murder of Wang Liang. This ideal is upheld by Shiming (if only tacitly at first), and the clan elders Wang Dao and Wang Du, but it is also widely shared by the villagers (the "public opinion"). Second, there is the idea of justice as represented by the imperial law and the public authorities. This demands that the offender, Wang Jun, be reported to the authorities, who should alone take charge of dispensing the punishment. There is finally a substandard version of justice that might be termed "convenient arbitration," done within the family clan. This solution—upheld by the mediators and embraced by Wang Shiming's mother—is not only seen as morally unacceptable by those who support the notion of justice as ritual duty, but it is repudiated by the law. Private settlements for homicide (*sihe* 私和), particularly those in which money was involved, were considered a serious offense under Ming law.[39] Nonetheless, this is the solution that is argued for most colorfully in the text, and this is where Lu Renlong's vernacular version departs most conspicuously from the historical account.

A trio of colorful village mediators, Shan Bang, Tu Li, and Wei Gong, manage to convince Shiming and his mother to accept a private settlement instead of reporting the crime to the authorities. These characters are obviously fictional and all bear names that could be read allegorically: Shan Bang 單邦 as *shan bang* 善幫, "good at meddling"; Tu Li 屠利 as *tu li* 圖利, "crave for profit"; and Wei Gong 魏拱 as *weigong* 圍攻, "attack from all sides." The idea is that the mediators do not act out of altruism but rather volunteer to make a profit for themselves, as they expect to be financially rewarded by both parties for their services. The trio of mediators puts forth a twofold argument, which encompasses two mutually paradoxical realities of the late Ming legal system: its malfunction *and* its procedural sophistication. On one hand, they argue that lawsuits are extremely long and costly enterprises with no guarantee of successful outcome. On the other, the proper legal procedure in handling this murder case would require a scrupulously performed autopsy. This is referred to with terminological precision by the village mediators (who are apparently well versed in forensic medicine), to Shiming's great horror:[40]

> "And then there is the autopsy. If the corpse were still fresh as it was when he died, it would have been fine, but in this hot weather the flesh rotted away in no time, so it will be necessary to perform the 'scraping of the bones.' They will strip away all the flesh from the bones. Isn't this going to be dreadful?" When Shiming heard these words, tears crisscrossed his face. Seeing that he could be moved by this argument, Wei Gong pressed on: "Yes, without autopsy they cannot [prove that it is homicide and] hold anyone accountable for his life. And this isn't done just once. There is also the 'steaming the bones' method!"[41] When mother and son heard it, they cried so hard that their tears rolled down the floor.

> 「況且到那檢驗時，如今初死還好，天色熱，不久潰爛，就要剔骨檢，筋肉盡行割去，你道慘不慘?」世名聽到此，兩淚交流。魏拱見他，曉得他可以此動，道:「不檢不償，也不止一次，還要蒸骨檢哩。」母子二人聽得哭得滿地滾去。[42]

Faced with these arguments, the clan elders, who are generally depicted as morally upright, are left speechless. Wang Dao concurs that "the two of you, mother and son, should really gauge your strength carefully. I am afraid that you have neither the means nor the skills to engage in a lawsuit." 你們母子也要自度力量，怕沒有打官司家事、打官司手段. And Wang Du follows suit: "Ever since ancient times, to forgive others is *not* a foolish thing. You go ahead and decide for yourselves." 自古饒人不是痴，你也自做主意.[43]

Autopsy is not always demonized in vernacular stories from this period. In the story "Fratricide in the Rear Garden" (QYZ 8) (discussed in chapter 5), it is the dutiful son who asks the magistrate to perform an autopsy on his father's body to prove that he had been murdered. And it is the magistrate who, being in collusion with one of the murderers, tries to persuade the son not to exhume the body, saying that this would be unfilial. The son objects that not doing an autopsy would be even more unfilial. However, it turns out that the body of the father has remained miraculously intact after eighteen years, and it shows clear evidence of injuries with a simple ocular examination, thus making the recourse to the gruesome practice of "steaming the bones" unnecessary.[44]

The characterization of Wang Shiming encompasses paradoxical elements. As in many narratives of filial revenge, Shiming displays a number of *xia* 俠 (knight-errant) traits. The story opens with a lyric to "Red Fills the River" ("Man jiang hong" 滿江紅), a tune typically associated with virile valor à la Yue Fei. The lyric describes the hero nervously tapping his sword and impatiently waiting to carry out his revenge. In the first part of the story, Shiming shares with many *xia* avengers the fate of being surrounded by the incomprehension and contempt of the "common people." During the six years between the murder of his father and the revenge, everyone in the village, from the clan elders down to his fellow students (with the sole exception of his teacher), despises him for his lack of nerve (*rounuo* 柔懦) and for accepting the money from his father's murderer. But in contrast with *xia* figures, Shiming is very much bound by his social role, and scrupulously discharges his duties: he is a devoted son to his mother, he makes sure to get married and produce a heir before enacting his revenge, and he immediately turns himself in to the public authority after he has carried out his revenge. This is a contradiction already latent in the very idea of the *filial* avenger. As noted by James Liu in his classic study on the subject, *xia* figures typically honor justice and personal loyalty above filial duty and family loyalty.[45] However, in the case of the filial avenger the same *xia* qualities of courage, contempt for wealth, and defiance of the law are mustered in service of the very values that the classic *xia* would ignore. Shiming is, in this sense, a Confucian *xia*.

Another element that sets Wang Shiming apart from the usual filial avengers is his emotional condition. Roland Altenburger has discussed the filial avengers' seemingly paradoxical mixture of emotionality and rationality, passion and calculus.[46] On one hand, the revenge impulse is seen as grounded in strong emotions, particularly anger, and described as natural, spontaneous, and irrepressible. On the other, the postponement of the revenge for years or decades, and the often elaborate preparations accompanying it, presuppose not just premeditation and careful planning, but the containment and suppression of anger over an incredibly prolonged period of time. All this leads to what Altenburger dubs the "syndrome of coldness," that is, the characterization of the avenger's emotional and mental condition as dominated by frigidity and aloofness. Shiming does not quite fit this portrait. He is depicted in strongly emotional terms: he cries copiously throughout the story, he often chants sadly and in a deeply moving manner, and at other times he is suddenly filled with indignation.[47] Perhaps the only scene where Shiming fits into the aura of coldness that, according to Altenburger, characterizes the *xia* avenger is in the episode in which he buys the dagger from a local ironsmith[48]—but the episode is quite comical, thus deflating whatever aura of coldness Shiming might have had.

"Wang Shiming the Filial Avenger" can be read as a subtle critique of the folly of applying a draconian law. Yet the characterization of the filial hero is not without a measure of ambiguity. Shiming and the adamant magistrates who handle his case (the Jinhua magistrate Wang in particular) can be seen as mirrorlike figures of each other: the filial son obeys an absolute moral imperative, while the magistrates advocate an absolute adherence to the letter of the law.

One can detect a metamorphosis in Shiming's characterization halfway through the story. After the revenge, Shiming is portrayed as what James Liu would have called a "supermoral" hero, since he not only does not expect to be saved, but *refuses* to be saved.[49] Magistrates Wang and Chen, after Shiming's first suicide attempt, propose to go in person to the higher authorities to plead for him. However, Shiming rebukes them: "This is against the law! If you discard the law, there is no ruler. I am perfectly ready to die and be done with, and I have no need for the two of you to engage in subtle maneuvering on my behalf!" 這也非法, 非法無君。我只辦了一死, 便不消這兩縣尊為我周旋委婉。[50] The first part of this line is lifted from Zhang Fengyi's biography of Wang Shiming, which is the source of this story, while the last sentence is Lu Renlong's addition. Later on, when his clan members and classmates try to persuade him to yield to the well-intentioned magistrates, Shiming replies, "I absolutely do not want people's sympathy, and absolutely refuse to bear the name of murderer while I am in this world!" These are the last words he pronounces in the text. The interlineal commentator bursts in, "this is too much!" (*tai guo* 太過).[51]

Ironically, subtlety and tactfulness are in fact the very qualities that the commentator approvingly attributes to Wang Shiming's own conduct during the six years in which he delayed his revenge. In the preface,

Lu Yunlong writes: "His determination to get a revenge did not waver through the years and moreover it was buried deep in his heart and was not revealed. In the end his father's murderer was cut down while his own family line was preserved. I am afraid that those who are impetuous lack this kind of subtlety, while those who are too calculative find it difficult to muster this kind of courage and determination." 報仇之心歷久不移, 復深沈不露, 卒親仇殲而親嗣全, 恐激烈者無此委婉, 深算者又難此勇斷也.[52]

The narrator, too, at the end of the prologue, praises Shiming for being a brilliant strategist (*da jingwei ren* 大經緯人).[53] In other words, in the first half of the story Shiming displays tact, expediency, even deceit—combined with the *xia* qualities discussed above. After he has turned himself in to the magistrate, however, he becomes an adamant stickler for ritual propriety. It is the *combination* of the two aspects that the commentator admires and highlights as the core of the protagonists' heroism. The narrator nonetheless expresses regret at Wang Shiming's death. What he laments is not so much the sacrifice of a filial son, but rather the death of a potential loyal subject who could have been put to service for the country. As we have seen in "The Filial Quest of Wang Yuan," the narrator concludes the story by reminding his readers of the *political* value of filial piety. Conversely, the passage quoted from Zhang Fengyi's biography highlights the value of martyrdom as token of individual expression: "But perhaps it was heaven's will not to spare the death of this filial son, just so that he could fulfill his innermost ambition, and display his filiality?" 抑天意不惜孝子一死, 以達其志, 以彰其孝哉.[54]

The burden of responsibility for Shiming's death is squarely placed on the magistrates. They are seen as ineffective in spite of their good intentions. While Shiming, in the passage quoted above, rebuffs them for engaging in "subtle maneuvering," the narrator and interlineal commentator criticize them for failing to do just that. Magistrate Wang in particular is depicted as blatantly tactless when he dubs Shiming's father's remains "long desiccated bones" 已枯之骨—and the interlineal commentator is quick to note that "this will just speed up his death!" 正速其死.[55] Later, the commentator castigates the two magistrates for being "inept as ignorant crones" (*poqi* 婆氣).[56] In the tail commentary, Lu Yunlong also expresses regret that the magistrates were unable to handle the case with the necessary discernment, in spite of their uprightness 經而不權, 不能無憾于二令.[57]

But what exactly would "expediency" or "discretion" (*quan*) have entailed here? The narrator does lay out an alternative course of action: the money paid by Wang Jun, which Shiming had so scrupulously preserved, could have been used as evidence against Wang Jun. So attached is the narrator to this line of action that he spells it out no less than three times in the text: first, as an hypothetical digression placed right after the text of magistrate Wang's verdict: "if only there was somebody in the prefectural office that had some influence, who said . . .";[58] second, as a suggestion to magistrate Wang made by the local scholars and licentiates (they even propose to use Wang Jun's money as indemnity for his—Wang Jun's—death);[59] and lastly, in the passage from Zhang Fengyi quoted at the end of the story. Curiously, no mention is made of, and no further role is given to, the witnesses and negotiators of the private settlement, even though Shiming explicitly mentions the clan elders as witnesses in his written self-accusation. Likewise, no mention is made of Wang Jun's own family members.[60]

Wang Shiming's story is also the subject of another vernacular adaptation, "Against Autopsy" in Ling Mengchu's *Slapping the Table in Amazement, Second Collection* (*EK* 31). If we consider that both collections were published in the same year (1632), in Suzhou by Shangyou tang and Hangzhou by Zhengxiao guan respectively, this overlapping of material may be read as evidence of that shortage of "primary materials" in the wake of the publication of *San Yan* lamented by Ling Mengchu in the preface to his first story collection of 1628. We can also conjecture that there might have been some competition of sorts between Ling's and Lu's collections.[61]

Whereas "Filial Avenger Wang Shiming" is framed in the prologue as an exemplary tale in which the hero avenges his father's murder with courage and cleverness in an age of legal malpractice, Ling Mengchu opens his story with a satirical piece on the subject of autopsy. The reader is informed that the practice of autopsy is so fraught with corruption that it can be used to yield whatever verdict is decided beforehand. Moreover, the prologue story is a cautionary tale that illustrates the disastrous consequences of performing autopsy. The meddlesome clan member who reports the murder of Chen Fusheng 陳福生 and instigates the performing of autopsy on the victim's corpse is driven to an early death by the ghost of Fusheng's disfigured corpse. The magistrate who deals with the case is portrayed as a ruthless figure who delights in performing autopsy and handling murder cases, "the patriarch of family-wreckers" 是個拆人家的祖師;[62] and he too ends up with no gain. By focusing on the single practice, or rather malpractice, of autopsy, and by introducing the element of *bao* (retribution) in the form of gruesome punishment attending those who instigate its performing in the prologue story, "Against Autopsy" is thus framed as a tale in which the hero's firmness about defending his father's corpse at all cost becomes more anchored to practical concerns.

The *xia* elements in Wang Shiming's characterization are further elaborated in Ling's version. Shiming does not simply kill his father's murderer, but he severs his head, wraps it up in his clothes (for lack of the customary leather bag, one can surmise), and brings it back home to show his mother; he then takes it to his father's grave, and, lastly, he carries it with him to the magistrate when he goes to denounce himself. In the end, Shiming dies by dashing his head on the steps, spilling out his brains. All in all, Wang Shiming becomes a much more theatrical character in Ling's story. Furthermore, "Against Autopsy" gives a more prominent role to Yu-shi 俞氏, Shiming's wife (as foreshadowed by the original story title: "The Filial Son Does Not Allow Autopsy [on his father's corpse] Till the End, The Chaste Wife Lingers on to Be Buried Together with Her Husband" 行孝子到底不簡尸, 殉節婦留待雙出柩).[63] Yu-shi is described as the only one who sees through Shiming's true feelings during the years in which he "endures humiliation," and she vows to him that she will follow him in his death. Although Shiming seems to belittle her vow, she promises to show him that "if he can be a filial son, she can equally be a chaste wife." True to her word, after Shiming dies, she postpones the burial of her husband for three years, a decision that puzzles everyone. After three years, she commits suicide by starving herself to death, just like her husband had done. She is then buried together with him, and praised by everyone as a heroic wife.

There is a clear sense of competition, a "contest of virtues" as it were.[64] By contrast, in the *Exemplary Words* version, Shiming's wife is not even given a name. At the end of the story, the narrator briefly notes that "she stayed loyal to her husband and did not remarry, and she urged her orphaned son to study hard and make a name for himself."[65] Here, there is not the slightest hint at competition between the husband and the wife; while the wife is certainly virtuous, she remains quietly so.

Filiality and the (Female) Body

The stories discussed thus far have dealt with male filial exemplars. Late imperial discourse on female exemplarity tends to focus sharply on the virtue of chastity. When filial piety enters the picture, it is most often combined with, and subordinated to, chastity—while the conflicting demands entailed by the two can be dramatized and turned into the source of tragedy, as seen for example in the story of Tang Guimei (discussed in chapter 4). A female equivalent of Zhou Yulun, who declared himself to be a "filial son, but not a loyal husband" 是孝子, 不是義夫, is simply unconceivable. The discourse on female filiality is further complicated by the fact that the kind of rhetoric usually deployed in the case of the father-son relationship—a rhetoric that constructs filial piety as "natural," and focuses on the repayment of the "debt of care" children owe their parents—cannot be easily replicated when filial devotion is transferred from consanguinity to affinity (i.e., from biological parents to in-laws), as in the case of daughters-in-law who are usually the heroines in filial piety narratives. At the same time, however, precisely because filial devotion to parents-in-law cannot be constructed as natural, it becomes all the more arduous to accomplish, and all the more appealing to the late Ming "craving for extremes," to quote Weijing Lu's phrase.[66]

One of the memorable stories of female filial piety in Lu Renlong's collection does not feature the familiar figure of the exemplary daughter-in-law but rather focuses on the ordeals of a young granddaughter. The story, titled "A Slice of Liver for Grandma" (original title: "A Single Heart Moves the Gods from Afar, One Slice of Liver Instantly Revives Grandmother" 寸心遠格神明, 片肝頓蘇祖母, *XSY* 4), offers a polyphonic representation of flesh slicing (*gegu*) which indicates that if the practice sounds highly problematic to our modern sensibility, it was far from being univocally understood even in premodern times. Its heroine Chen Miaozhen is a girl of thirteen (fourteen *sui*, by Chinese count), only slightly older than the protagonist of "Cui Jian the Filial Boy." Miaozhen's father has died early on, while her mother has remarried, leaving her to the care of her loving grandmother, Lin-shi. When her grandmother falls gravely ill, Miaozhen cuts her flesh not just once but twice, first on her arm, then on her liver, to save her. She succeeds the second time. After her grandmother has passed away a few years later, Miaozhen becomes a nun. The second half of the story tells of the girl's ordeals in two nunneries, which turn out to be very different from the holy retreats that she had hoped for. Miaozhen however manages to extricate herself from the lurid traffics going on at both places, and retreats to her own hermitage which she builds by the grandmother's grave.

The story is based on a literary source, "The Biography Inscribed on a Stele of Filial Girl Chen from Lishui" (*Lishui Chen xiaonü zhuan bei* 麗水陳孝女傳碑) by the eminent early Ming literatus Song Lian 宋濂 (1310–1381).[67] While following the original biography quite closely, Lu Renlong has also amplified the text by adding episodes on Miaozhen's mother's early widowhood and remarriage, and Miaozhen's vicissitudes in the monasteries after her grandmother's death.

The story discussed in the previous section tells of how Wang Shiming dies to avoid the desecration of his father's corpse. In that story, there is much discussion of the bodies of the father and the son. Shiming boldly declares to his mother that "It was my father who engendered this body of mine, and today I am in return going to die for him." 兒子這身是父生的, 今日還為父死.[68] (The role of the mother is often defined as the one who nurtures and rears, rather than the one who gives life, as in the oft-quoted poem "Lu'e" from the *Book of Odes*).[69] However, the sacrifice of the son is put in strikingly different terms by magistrate Wang: "Why should you be stubbornly attached to those long desiccated bones, instead of saving your life, which may be put to use?" 仔麼苦惜那已枯之骨, 不免你有用之身.[70] The contraposition between the "long desiccated bones" and the "useful body" points to the problematic nature of the exchange of the son's body for his father's.

There seems to be something quintessentially corporeal about filial piety. Thus, the late Ming thinker Gu Dashao 顧大韶 (b. 1576) differentiated between filial piety and friendship in his radical reevaluation of the five normative bonds: "Your father is someone to whom you owe your body [*shen*] as a son, while a friend is someone to whom you owe your heart [*xin*]. The body, if it does not die prematurely, can live no longer than one hundred years. When it dies, the father and son relationship will cease to exist. However, the heart is something that lasts forever, and it will never die." 父子以身屬者也, 朋友以心屬者也。人之身或殤或夭, 上壽百年而死矣。既死矣, 烏在其為父子哉? 若夫心則亙千古而不死者也.[71]

Gu Dashao's purpose in this essay is to reevaluate friendship above and beyond filial piety as the central axis of moral life. But his point that the essence of the filial bond lies in the body, however provocative his conclusion may be, would have found general consensus in premodern China. If the body is seen as the central locus of filial piety (its origin, substance, and end), it is then not surprising that a practice like *gegu* should have been construed as one of its supreme manifestations.

In her book *Accidental Incest, Filial Cannibalism and Other Peculiar Encounters in Late Imperial Chinese Literature*, Tina Lu addresses the unsettling nature of *gegu* and other patterns of bodily exchange often entailed in filial narratives, which she suggestively calls "arithmetic of filial piety": the son's life span is shortened to augment that of the father, the daughter's body is diminished to resuscitate the mother-in-law, the wife or child can be exchanged for the mother (as we have seen in Zhou Yulun's story), and so forth.[72] Yet the story of Miaozhen seems to both presume and resist such ruthless logic of exchange. It suggests a different way of reading *gegu*, one that calls into question the mechanics of these filial transactions, the neatness of this kind of "arithmetic."

The story opens with an apology of *gegu*, whose polemic tone is an unmistakable indication that the practice was far from being uniformly understood and accepted. It is a twofold apology. First, the narrator addresses the official government's view of the practice:

> Those who have performed the act of slicing off flesh from their thigh to save their parents' life may be praised as filial, but they do not receive public recognition from the administration. This is based on the court's humane policy, as it fears that public recognition may establish a popular custom. While the life of the parent is not yet saved, the life of the child is already lost—this policy is based on the court's love for the common people. However, when the act of slicing off flesh from one's thigh proceeds from deepest sincerity, how would people still care about public recognition if they don't even care about their own life? Indeed, those who are truly filial would still cut flesh from their thigh even if there were no public recognition at all, while those who are not filial would refuse to part with the tiniest particle of their body even if public recognition were offered to them day in and day out.

> 嘗聞割股救親的, 雖得稱為孝, 不得旌表, 這是朝廷仁政, 恐旌表習以成風, 親命未全, 子生已喪, 乃是愛民之心。但割股出人子一段至誠, 他身命不顧, 還顧甚旌表? 果然至孝的, 就是不旌表也要割股; 不孝的, 就是日日旌表, 他自愛惜自己身體。73

Here, as elsewhere, the narrator expresses skepticism toward the use of official awards to encourage or validate virtuous acts. In the case of honorific plaques conferred to chaste wives, he criticizes the award system for its partiality.74 Here he defends the court's policy for not offering rewards to those who perform *gegu* while emphasizing the purity and disinterestedness of the filial act. The claim that *gegu* stems from "deepest sincerity" (*zhicheng* 至誠) is much strengthened indeed if there is no material reward in sight.

Lu Yunlong echoes his brother's argument in the preface, and emphasizes the aspect of exemplarity. He likens Chen Miaozhen to Li Mi 李密 (224–ca. 287), the Western Jin author of the famed "Memorial Expressing My Feelings" (*Chenqing biao* 陳情表), in which he declined to serve the Jin ruler on account of having to support his aging grandmother. In fact, Lu Yunlong argues that Chen Miaozhen's filiality should be considered superior to Li Mi's, since it does not stem from consideration of reciprocation, but is entirely pure in its motives.75

The prologue then turns to the intellectual arguments against the practice of *gegu*. The narrator proceeds by refuting the doctrinal and intellectual arguments deployed by critics, particularly the idea that *gegu* appears to violate the most fundamental tenet that requires children to preserve intact the body they received from their parents, as prescribed in the *Classic of Filial Piety*.[76] This is how Lu Renlong responds to this argument:

> Now you also have that sort of pedant who will argue that to cut flesh from the thigh is tantamount to damaging the body given by one's parents. These pedants don't realize that if you can save your parent's life in this way, you may have damaged your body, but it still would be the same as if it were intact. Only those who preserve their body for an improper cause would adduce the notion of "protecting one's body," while those who sacrifice their body for the sake of loyalty and filiality would not mention this at all. If one would stick to this opinion, then loyalty and filial piety would be equally unfitting [reasons to sacrifice one's body].[77] For instance, those who serve as officials on occasion may die on the battlefields at the frontier, with their heads being chopped off, their throat slit; or they may lose their life remonstrating with the emperor, their bones smashed, their body pulverized—yet, according to the above-mentioned pedants, all these exemplary deaths ought to be considered inappropriate.
>
> 又有一種迂腐的, 倒说道:「割股虧親之體。」不知若能全親之生, 雖虧也與全無異。保身為置身不義之说, 不為那以身殉忠孝的說。若執這個意見, 忠孝一般。比如為官的或是身死疆場, 斷頭刎頸; 或是身死諫諍, 糜骨碎身。 這也都是不該的了。[78]

The narrator argues against the detractors of *gegu* (whom he unceremoniously dismisses as "pedants")[79] by establishing a parallel between filial piety and loyalty. In this he echoes the words of Song Lian, on whose biography of filial girl Chen the short story is based. In the final commentary to the biography, Song had noted: "Loyalty and filial piety are one and the same. The ground is covered with the livers and brains of loyal subjects, yet nobody has ever considered it wrong. Why then do they single out filial sons and cast doubt upon their actions?" 夫忠孝無二道。忠臣肝腦塗地, 世未嘗指以為非, 顧獨於孝子而疑之耶。[80]

By establishing a parallel between loyalty and filial piety, Lu Renlong, like Song Lian, brings to the forefront the notion of "transference" between the two. This is encapsulated in the formulation from the *Classic of Filial Piety*: "It is only because exemplary persons serve their parents with filial piety that this same feeling can be extended to their lord as loyalty" (*junzi zhi shi qin xiao, gu zhong ke yi yu jun* 君子之事親孝, 故忠可移於君).[81] Here, however, the usual logic/chronologic direction is reversed: instead of extending from filial piety to loyalty, the reader is invited to proceed the other way around, that is, to apply the unquestioned spirit of self-sacrifice associated with loyalty back into the sphere of the family.[82]

While *gegu* as a practice cannot but be considered disturbing to our modern sensibility, a description of the practice offered by a seventeenth-century Jesuit provides a useful corrective and a tool to historicize our understanding. In his monumental history of the Society of Jesus, the Italian Jesuit father Daniello Bartoli (1608–1685) wrote, on the subject of filial piety among the Chinese:

> There is no account of a country, as far as my knowledge goes, in which the natural debt that children owe their parents is repaid in love, in reverence, and in all kinds of action that can be performed for their sake, so entirely as it is peculiar to the Chinese people. We have heard that even some young people who were engaged in strenuous manual labor had made a vow to observe the strictest fast every day until their death [. . .]. Some of them did so to show the fresh pain of recent loss [of their parent], some others so that their penance would go towards the salvation of the father's soul. And there were yet others who bit off with their teeth two or three pieces of fresh flesh from their arms, in order to mix it and dissolve it together with the medicine that they prepare to cure their sick father or mother. I do not know the true reason for this act: whether it is because they believe that their flesh naturally has the property to cure their parents, or rather in order to show that they would gladly give away their own life if that would be necessary remedy for their parents' survival. And one can see every day new and wondrously ingenious such tokens of deep love.[83]

Even though Bartoli's description of the specific way in which *gegu* was performed may not be entirely accurate, he describes the practice with curiosity and marvel, seeing it as just one of the many "new and wondrously ingenious tokens of the deep [literally: visceral] love" that children have for their parents (*nuove, e mirabilmente ingegnose . . . pruove di sviscerato amore*). Part of the reason why Bartoli may have regarded the practice of *gegu* as not all that foreign lies arguably in the familiarity with ascetic practices that called for extreme forms of bodily mortification in the Christian tradition. Like other Jesuit fathers, Bartoli acutely perceived filial piety as the closest Chinese correspondent to religious fervor in the West. Accordingly, he does not condemn *gegu* as a bestial abomination or as a cannibalistic act.[84] Instead, he ponders the reasons behind the act: Does this stem out of a *literal* belief in the therapeutic property of the child's flesh? Or is the act rather to be understood as having a metonymic valence, a *symbolic* significance, whereby the piece of the child's flesh is offered as a token for the whole body (*shen* 身), hence life (also *shen*), which the devoted child would gladly surrender for the benefit of the parent?

By emphasizing the sincerity of the motive instead of the efficacy or official recognition, both Lu Renlong and Lu Yunlong provide an answer to Bartoli's question that veers decidedly toward the symbolic plane. But at the diegetic level, the literal (physical) power and presence of the body cannot be so easily obliterated. The titular couplet, "A Single Heart Moves the Gods from Afar, One Slice of Liver Instantly Revives Grandmother" 寸心遠格神明, 片肝頓蘇祖, points to the same kind of disjunction between literal and metaphorical valence, not without a measure of crass irony: Miaozhen's *heart* moves the gods above, while her *liver* saves her grandmother from dying. Lu Renlong questions the configuration of filial bodily sacrifice as a precisely quantifiable exchange, both at the level of the family (with the parent's life being saved or prolonged) and at the level of the state (with the awarding of official honors). Among the people who performed *gegu* mentioned in the prologue (presumably all historical), the narrator includes also a case in which the filial sacrifice did *not* work and in which both parent and son perished.[85] Through this example, the narrator suggests that the validity of the practice of "filial slicing" is not based on its efficacy, nor on its official recognition, but rather on its motive alone.

For all the protestation that the point about *gegu* is not its efficacy but rather its motive, Chen Miaozhen's is a story of success—the girl does succeed in saving her grandmother's life the second time around. Success, however, is soon followed by a host of material entanglements deprecated by the narrator in the beginning. Local reputation (which could become amplified into nationwide fame if the filial deed happened to be picked up by the brush of a famous literatus such as Song Lian) automatically generates tangible economic and social benefits—or at least a privileged access to these. After Miaozhen has performed *gegu*, she instantly becomes the "hottest marriage prospect" in town. The neighbors propose to file her case to obtain a plaque.[86] Needless to say, Miaozhen adamantly refuses both marriage and honors. But even after she has retired from the mundane world by becoming a nun, she finds herself being exploited as a "living Buddha," and as a "new princess Miaoshan" by ruthless nuns who are seeking to attract patrons and donations.[87]

The actual narration of the *gegu* acts in the story takes on a different angle from the prologue. Miaozhen's first attempt at saving her grandmother is described in the following passage:

> Her grandmother's illness got worse with each passing day, and Miaozhen racked her brains but didn't know what to do. Then she remembered that her grandmother had told her a story about someone who had saved her parent by cutting flesh from the thigh. So she got up bright and early, went down to the kitchen, picked up a kitchen knife, lightly pinched the flesh on her left arm to draw it up, bit firmly into it, and cut with all her strength. Fresh blood gushed forth from the wound and so she quickly bandaged her arm with a piece of cloth, and put the piece of flesh she had cut in an earthen pot. She prepared a porridge with it, which she intended to take to her grandmother.

> 只是病日沈重，妙珍想來無策。因記得祖母嘗說有個割股救親的，他便起了一個早，走到廚下，拿了一把廚刀，輕輕把左臂上肉撮起一塊，把口咬定，狠狠的將來割下。只見鮮血迸流，他便把塊布來拴了，將割下肉放在一個沙礶內熬成粥湯，要拿把祖母。[88]

The role of education and familiarity with past exemplars is presented as positive and inspiring, not spirit-numbing. Earlier in the story we are told that Miaozhen's grandmother was from an educated family, and that she instructed her granddaughter by means of exemplary stories of filial children, chaste wives, good-natured sisters-in-law, and the like. From this repository of stories, Miaozhen draws inspiration to perform her act. There is no indication of interior dilemma in the mind of Miaozhen as to what the right course of action should be, nor is there any description of physical pain: the blood gushing forth does not seem to come with suffering or faltering in the determination of the young heroine.

But Miaozhen's first attempt at slicing her flesh is framed by way of a comic insertion. Immediately following the passage above, a nosy neighbor simply named Auntie Zou (Zou *mama*) abruptly enters the scene:

It so happened that a neighbor, Auntie Zou, came by to borrow some fire. When she saw that Miaozhen was cutting off her flesh, she was startled and said, "Greatest force can't even force one to do this! How can she not fear the pain?" She pushed through the gate and walked in. She saw that Miaozhen had already bandaged her arm and put that piece of flesh in the porridge. Suddenly she realized, "You want to save your grandmother by cutting off a piece of flesh? That there are such filial persons in the world! You are still so young and yet have such a good heart! Nothing like that damned son of mine, who has lived in vain for more than thirty years. If I want him to buy some tofu he acts as if I were asking him to cut a piece of flesh from his body, and I'm lucky if he does not curse at me or beat me up!"

適值一個鄰人鄒媽媽, 他來討火種, 張見他在那裡割肉, 失驚道:「勒殺不在這裡勒的, 怎這等疼也不怕?」 推門進來, 見他已拴了臂膊, 把那塊肉丟在粥裡, 猛然道:「你是割肉救婆婆麼? 天下有這等孝順的, 一點點年紀有這樣好心! 似我那天殺的, 枉活了三十多歲, 要他買塊豆腐, 就是割他身上肉一般, 不打罵我也好了!」[89]

The elevated tone in the narration of Miaozhen's sacrifice of flesh is here comically juxtaposed to the grim everyday reality of stingy sons who are loath to buy even a piece of tofu for their parent. The marginal commentary, signed by a Female Historian of Kuocang, comments on Auntie Zou's "stupendous stupidity" (*chi de miao*! 癡得妙) while at the same time praising the realism of her characterization (*dianzhui ye hao* 點綴也好).[90]

To make matters worse, when the outspoken Auntie Zou tells Lin-shi about her granddaughter's act, Lin-shi is crushed by the news and sinks back into her former illness. The secrecy of the act of *gegu* is one of the required attributes for its successful outcome, but as the vernacular author is very well aware, privacy may not have been such an easy thing to achieve in a densely populated village in Ming dynasty Zhejiang.

A look at scholarship on Renaissance and Baroque literature in Europe may offer a useful reading lens to analyze this episode. French literature scholar François Rigolot has drawn a useful distinction between *imitatio* and *mimesis* in Renaissance writing. The former refers to the practice of "uplifting reading of ancient exemplars," as part of "sacrosanct recourse to inherited cultural models." *Mimesis*, on the other hand, gestures to "the actual experience of the real world in reaction to scholastic insularity," which "greatly problematized the reception of ancient models."[91] The tension between these two impulses contributed to what has been called the "crisis of exemplarity" in the transition between the medieval and early modern periods, when the hallowed models of tradition were questioned and problematized.[92] In this perspective, what we see in the episode of Miaozhen's first act of filial slicing is an intriguing blurring of boundaries between the realistic, everyday *mimesis* and the stylized, rarefied world of *imitatio*. On one hand, we have the kitchen knife, the concrete succession of actions, the bandaging, the everyday reality of Auntie Zou and her stingy son; on the other, we have the girl's serene composure, the suspension or erasure of physical pain. It takes a few moments for Auntie Zou to understand what is happening as she looks in, to decode or translate the sequence of disturbing actions she has just witnessed as an act of *gegu*. In this sense, I argue, the narrator seeks at once to dramatize and to bridge the gap between *mimesis* and *imitatio*.

The second time Miaozhen attempts to save her grandmother, by performing the even more astounding deed of slicing a piece of her liver, the tone of the narration veers decidedly toward the miraculous and the hagiographical. Here the vernacular story follows closely the classical Chinese account. At her wits' end on what to do after her grandmother has relapsed into her former illness, Miaozhen dreams of a Taoist immortal who instructs her on cutting a piece of her liver to save her grandmother. The following day after performing ablutions and praying to the gods, she proceeds.

> When she undressed, she saw a bright red line like a thread on her left side. As she applied the knife to that red line, her skin split and her flesh came apart. She suffered no pain and no blood appeared, but she could not see her liver. Miaozhen again addressed heaven after a double bow, saying, "I cannot find my liver. I fear this is because of my insufficient filial piety. So I pray the gods to direct me. I promise to be a nun for the rest of my life to repay this favor of Heaven!" At the very moment she made her bows, moving up and down, her liver popped out, and Miaozhen hastily cut off a piece.

遂解衣，看左脅下紅紅一縷如線，妙珍就紅處用刀割之，皮破肉裂，了不疼痛。血不出，却不見肝。妙珍又向天再拜道：「妙珍忱孝不至，不能得肝，還祈神明指示，願終身為尼，焚修以報天恩」正拜下去，一俯一仰，忽然肝突出來。妙珍連忙將來割下一塊。[93]

Figure 2.1. Illustration of the fourth story in *Exemplary Words* (recto). *Bieben Erke Pai'an jingqi* edition preserved at the Bibliothèque Nationale in Paris. Reproduction courtesy of the Institute of Chinese Literature and Philosophy, Academia Sinica.

80   Reading for the Moral

Once again, the act of *gegu* is described in a very matter-of-fact and even graphic fashion; but here there is no comic scene to diffuse the tension. On the contrary, the scene is concluded by way of a simple quatrain that comments on the extraordinary nature of the event just described.

The story of Miaozhen, then, shows a fascinating intersection of literary, intellectual, religious, and popular elements. While the preface and the prologue frame the story in the somewhat abstract terms of the intellectual debate on *gegu*, the story itself dwells on vividly realistic details of everyday life, as well as supernatural elements. The interplay between these various levels creates a complex picture of the practice of *gegu* at the end of the Ming. The story of Miaozhen also offers a window to probe into the issue of filiality and the female body. If there is one common trait in the representation of female filiality in vernacular stories, it is the conspicuous role played by the body. Female filial piety seems to be always predicated on more or less extreme bodily sacrifice: performing *gegu*, breastfeeding of the parent or parent-in-law, selling oneself and thus losing one's chastity (as in the story of Wang Cuiqiao, *XSY* 7), or committing suicide in the name of filiality. (Miaozhen's decision not to marry is also tantamount to committing social suicide). This aligns with Keith Knapp's observation about the necessity for daughters "to go the extra mile to prove their filiality," but the obsession with the body as the locus of female filial devotion seems to be peculiar to the late imperial narratives.[94] Reading this story side by side with its paired story, "Mother Comes First," may serve to illustrate this point. While male filial piety can take the form of swapping one's wife to ransom one's mother, female filial piety inevitably entails the sacrifice of one's own flesh and blood.[95] While the practice of *gegu* was by no means exclusively performed by women, its incidence in both historiographical and fictional (including dramatic) narratives of female filial exemplars is much higher than in narratives featuring male characters.[96] Both filial piety and the paramount feminine virtue of chastity may be said to focus on the body as the locus of virtue. However, there seems to be a curious asymmetry in the valence of integrity: while chastity is predicated on the preservation of the body's integrity, filial piety often entails a loss of it.

∽

The filial piety stories discussed in this chapter frame filial piety not just as a domestic virtue restricted to the dyad parent-child, but rather as a preeminently *social* value. The filial hero is not simply praised by the narrator and commentator as a devoted son, but also as a "loyal subject"—whether actual or potential. Moreover, the actions of the filial character are often scrutinized and discussed by a crowd of observers. Social and official validation, however, do not take the form of official honors or resolution of conflict in the courtroom. If anything, these stories tend to display a skepticism toward the power of the judge to reestablish family harmony, or the impartiality of the official awards, which are too often bestowed on rich families alone. The story of Wang Shiming is especially striking because it features a clash between a *morally upright* magistrate, who wishes to zealously follow the standard procedures to ascertain the culpability of the offenders, and an *exemplary filial* son who is, quite literally, dead set on defending his father's corpse. This ambivalent attitude toward the judicial system sets apart these stories from Feng Menglong's *Constant Words* and other collections. Furthermore, these stories are not readily subsumed within the usual scheme of karmic retribution. Filiality is not couched in the terms of miraculous rewards or frightening punishment attending those who violate it, as in the *West Lake* stories. In spite of the emphasis on exchange, transactions, revenge, and requital, there is also the idea that virtue is ultimately its own reward.

Chapter 3

The Spectrum of Loyalty

Among the Five Cardinal Relationships, the bond between ruler and subject seems to be by necessity the most grounded in historical contingency. The specific historical circumstances, identity, and (at least implicitly) moral attributes of the ruler, and even the precise modality of the subject's death, appear to be crucial factors in determining the meaning and substance of loyalty (*zhong* 忠). Yet within the discourse of loyalty we also find a current that deemphasizes the precise historical context in favor of an essentialized ideal of the loyal minister (*zhongchen* 忠臣). This is the logic that made possible, for instance, the official recognition, during the Qianlong period, of Ming loyalists who perished while resisting the Qing conquest, and the concomitant condemnation of the turncoats (*er chen* 貳臣, or twice-serving officials) who submitted to the Manchu invaders.[1] It is not so much an act of empathy in which the victor imaginatively places himself in the position of the vanquished, as it is a decoupling and abstraction of the notion of loyalty from its historical frame of reference.

The choice between service and reclusion, engagement and withdrawal, compliance and dissent, particularly in times of political and moral decline, has been debated practically since the dawn of Chinese history. From early on we see the formation of a repertoire of models, ranging from intransigent eremitism to unconditional service, no matter how corrupt or unworthy the ruler was. In a similar way to other bonds in the canonical quintet, the ruler-subject bond, originally conceptualized as a mutual pact predicated on "benevolence" (*ren* 仁) on the part of the ruler and "loyalty" on the part of the minister, became increasingly focused on the duties of the subject alone.[2] Further, although the ruler-subject bond was acknowledged as man-made (and as such, at least to a certain extent susceptible to choice), the family metaphor—a rhetorical move that recasts man-made bonds as bonds of consanguinity—was pervasively applied.

The analogy between father and ruler, son and subject, and the notion of transference between filial devotion and political loyalty are customarily presented as a corollary of the Five Cardinal Relationships system. In times of upheaval, however, the question arises of which bond should be given priority—whether filial obligation or political duty. The dilemma, encapsulated in the proverb "loyalty and filial piety cannot both be fulfilled" (*zhongxiao bu neng liang quan* 忠孝不能兩全), has been richly explored in fiction and drama, as the great modern scholar Qian Zhongshu has noted.[3] Yet this very problematic is, by and large, carefully avoided in the stories discussed in this chapter. The implication, carried over in the actual usage of the proverb, that political loyalty must, if regrettably, take precedence over family duty, does not seem to be a compelling scenario. Rather, in these stories family ties, far from being an obstacle to the fulfillment of political duty, are represented as being in harmony with it. Stories of loyal ministers and martyrs are thus expanded into family tales.

Intriguingly, stories of loyal subjects in *Exemplary Words* and *Bell in the Still Night* are clustered around two crucial moments in Ming history: the Jianwen-Yongle transition in the early fifteenth century and the Ming fall of 1644.[4] But while the *Exemplary Words* stories entertained a range of possible models of loyalty and ways to negotiate one's position as a political subject, the spectrum narrowed dramatically by the time *Bell in the Still Night* was published.

Tales of Martyrs and Survivors

Two stories that celebrate historical figures of loyal ministers in *Exemplary Words* present different models of loyalty that hint at a complex discourse lying just beneath the surface. Both "Tie Xuan and His Daughters" (full title: "The Martyr Does Not Betray His Ruler, Faithful Maidens Do Not Bring Disgrace on Their Father" 烈士不背君, 貞女不辱父, *XSY* 1) and "Cheng Ji and the Jianwen Emperor" (full title: "The One Who Vowed to Acquire Wisdom Obtained It in the End, The One Who Pledged Loyalty Loyal Became" 矢智終成智, 盟忠自得忠, *XSY* 8) are set during a particularly troublesome period in the recent dynastic past, the Jianwen-

Yongle transition. Both stories offer the readers examples of loyalty that range from idealistic intransigence to pragmatic activism, with a decided preference for the latter.

A well-known moment in early Ming history, the Jianwen-Yongle transition saw Zhu Di's (Yongle) usurpation of the throne that was rightfully occupied by his nephew, Zhu Yunwen (Jianwen).[5] Yongle's usurpation was accompanied by much violence and remained a hotly debated topic throughout the dynasty, in spite of Yongle's multifarious attempts to legitimate his accession, including a systematic revision or erasure of the official records pertaining to the Jianwen reign.[6] Sanctions against the relatives and associates of the Jianwen loyalists were partially lifted later in the fifteenth century. But it was not until 1595, during the Wanli era, that the Jianwen reign title was officially restored and his loyal ministers publicly commemorated as martyrs.[7] Meanwhile, at the popular level, stories and legends continued to proliferate which depicted Yongle as the "evil uncle" and Jianwen as a virtuous but ill-advised ruler who met a tragic end. Scholars have noted that the resurfacing and proliferation of stories and legends sympathetic to Jianwen and hostile to Yongle during the late Ming occurred in tandem with a renewed interest in the value and meaning of loyalty.[8] One may think that there remained a sharp bifurcation between imperially commissioned versions of the "veritable records" (*shilu* 實錄, the detailed chronological accounts that covered all important events under each reign) on one hand and popular, and even willfully counterfactual, accounts that circulated underground on the other, and that the two continued to develop in parallel and in antithesis with one another. In fact, we see also a convergence and compromise between the two narratives. The story of Tie Xuan is an intriguing example of such convergence.

One problem with rehabilitating Jianwen and his loyal ministers was of course that such rehabilitation inevitably cast a shadow on Yongle's legitimacy, and by extension all the subsequent Ming emperors, inasmuch as they were Yongle's descendants. As Hok-Lam Chan has noted, one of the strategies to cope with such a dilemma (deployed for instance in private historical writings sympathetic to Jianwen) was the use of the term "vacating the throne" (*xunguo* 遜國) to describe Jianwen's supposedly voluntary abdication of the throne, which was then filled by Yongle in his absence.[9] The narrator in the story of Tie Xuan shows a similar concern with celebrating the Jianwen loyalists—but in a selective way—while at the same time he carefully avoids casting doubts on Yongle's legitimacy. In spite of all this rhetorical maneuvering and verbal acrobatics, however, Yongle still comes out as a highly ambiguous character, whose metamorphosis from rebellious prince into sage ruler happens in just a few paragraphs.

Of the hundreds of Jianwen martyrs, arguably none held a stronger grip on the popular imagination than Fang Xiaoru 方孝孺 (1357–1402).[10] Yet Lu Renlong did not select Fang, but rather opted for lesser-known figures such as Tie Xuan 鐵鉉 (1366–1402) and Cheng Ji 程濟 (fl. late fourteenth–early fifteenth centuries). Tie fought against Yongle, then Prince of Yan, and was eventually executed, while Cheng assisted the deposed emperor-turned-monk in the popular version of the legend according to which Jianwen survived a fire in the palace. Both Tie Xuan and Cheng Ji may be seen as models of a more martial and activist version of loyalty.[11]

Being placed as the first story, "Tie Xuan and His Daughters" arguably carries a special weight in the economy of the collection as a whole. The story tells of how Tie Xuan, the governor of Shandong, valiantly defends the city of Jinan against the attack launched by the Prince of Yan. In spite of his strenuous efforts, Tie is defeated, arrested, and brought to the capital for punishment together with his family. During the trip, the scholar Gao Xianning 高賢寧, Tie's protégé, kidnaps Tie's youngest son and entrusts him to an old farmer in Shanyang (a locality in modern Jiangsu). The Prince of Yan, now formally installed as the Yongle emperor, orders that Tie Xuan be executed, Tie's parents be banished to the far south, his older son be sent to Yunnan in military exile, and his two daughters be sent to the brothel. In spite of their misfortune, however, the two girls scrupulously observe the mourning period for their father and manage to preserve their chastity. News of their deeds eventually reach the ears of Yongle, who, impressed by their virtuous conduct, allows them to leave the brothel and marry Gao Xianning. The family is eventually reunited and relocates to Shanyang, where Tie Xuan's younger son and his foster family live.

In the prologue, the narrator begins by addressing the potential conflict between loyalty to one's ruler and familial ties—only to end with a gallery of famous loyalist martyrs whose wives and children proved as brave and firm when ending their own lives. In between, he lists several historical figures, who are meant to provide a spectrum of possible attitudes in the choice between loyalty and betrayal and the reaction of the family members. We have, for instance, a father as worthy as his son (Xu Kui 許逵), a vacillating father enlightened by his son (Sun Sui 孫燧), a daughter worthier than her father (Hu Guang 胡廣), and a well-meaning father corrupted by his children (Li Shishi 李士實).[12] On one hand, the conjunction of loyalty and familial ties may be seen as a vernacularization of the otherwise "high mimetic" nature of a story in which all characters are famous historical personages. We have here an interaction of what Patrick Hanan has termed the "grand-scale" and "small-scale" historical fiction.[13] The generals, ministers, and advisors mentioned in the prologue are not presented exclusively in their public personae, but rather in a domestic moment, in a revelatory glimpse as they interact with their sons, daughters, wives, and fathers. On the other hand, the domestic sphere is itself elevated and turned into a locus of moral discourse with repercussions on the national level. The battle over virtue or opportunism is fought within the domestic walls before being brought into the public sphere.

All the characters mentioned in the prologue are drawn from two specific historical moments: the Jianwen-Yongle transition and the rebellion of the Prince of Ning 寧王 (Zhu Chenhao 朱宸濠) that occurred about a century later, during Zhengde's reign in the early sixteenth century. The scope and final outcome of the two rebellions could not have been more different: while the rebellion of the Prince of Ning was disposed of within a matter of weeks, the rebellion of the Prince of Yan had a tremendous impact on the subsequent dynastic history, as seen earlier. Yet in spite of the wide dissimilarities in the import of the two rebellions, the narrator makes no distinction in terms of who the object of loyalty should be in each case, that is, the reigning emperor. While the bizarre personality of the Zhengde emperor ("by far the most colorful if not the most appealing of the Ming monarchs," as Ray Huang vividly put it)[14] could theoretically be seen as problematic, the case of the Jianwen emperor is much more complicated. In "Tie Xuan and His Daughters," there is no doubt that Jianwen's ministers owe their loyalty to him; yet Yongle is unequivocally called a wise ruler, and the fact that he took over the empire is presented as a matter of fate.

As the narrator emphasizes at the end of the prologue, it is precisely during the Jianwen-Yongle transition that the most luminous exemplars of loyalty appeared: Fang Xiaoru, Wang Shuying 王叔英, Huang Guan 黃觀, Hu Run 胡閏, and others.[15] These officials (and the archetypal loyalist martyr Fang Xiaoru in particular) were famous for their unswerving loyalty to Jianwen, but even more so for the enormous number of "collateral victims" who were involved in the punishment. It is recorded that a staggering 870 people were executed or committed suicide as a consequence of their association with Fang Xiaoru. In the case of Hu Run, 217 family members suffered punishment.[16] Many more cases are recorded.

We have here the ideal embodiment of the loyal subject: not only is the minister loyal unto death, but his whole family follows suit. Family members, far from being a source of conflict or a potential obstacle to the loyal subject's self-sacrifice, become at times the very enforcers or models for such heroic behavior. Indeed, according to some records the wives, sons, or daughters of Fang Xiaoru, Wang Shuying, Huang Guan, and Hu Run committed suicide together with, or even before, their husbands or fathers. For example, Huang Guan's wife and daughter drowned themselves in the river when the Prince of Yan entered the capital, a few days before Huang Guan himself committed suicide in the same fashion. This idea of virtue as a family tradition and as a legacy that continues across generations echoes with the promotion of "Confucian family tales" through various media and genres during the seventeenth century, as discussed by Ying Zhang in her recent study.[17]

In "Tie Xuan and His Daughters," the story proper does not directly address the question of what constitutes loyalty. Rather, we must turn to the commentarial level to find some explicit reflections on this question. The opening words of the preface, penned by Lu Yunlong, posit the problem in strikingly simple terms: "Be loyal to the one who feeds you" 食人之祿，忠人之事.[18] Loyalty here is understood as a matter of reciprocity. However, Lu Yunlong continues by observing that loyalty does not necessarily require self-immolation, or the destruction of one's family.[19] Indeed, as Lu argues, Li Jinglong 李景隆, the inept commander-in-chief of the army raised against the Prince of Yan, also died and his family was also implicated in his downfall.[20] Yet he differed greatly from the loyalist martyrs. Lu Yunlong concludes the preface by stressing the role of the written records, and more specifically vernacular stories, in recreating and consigning the heroism of the virtuous characters to eternal fame. There is a vivid sense of mission in reevaluating characters of recent history, in rehabilitating those whom the writer sees as "the good guys," while exposing those who are seen as "the bad guys." The polemic tone testifies to the fact that such evaluations were far from undisputed, and that many of the figures from the Jianwen-Yongle transition, such as Li Jinglong, Xie Jin, and Hu Guang, continued to be intensely debated over two centuries later.

The tail commentary, also signed by Lu Yunlong, echoes the argument in the preface. It contains a strikingly harsh appraisal of Fang Xiaoru, Huang Zicheng 黃子澄 (d. 1402), and Qi Tai 齊泰 (d. 1402), the three highest officials under Jianwen.

> During the "expunged period,"[21] the Academician Expositor-in-waiting Fang Xiaoru was in charge of the civil administration, but proved to be impractical and unfit. Qi Tai, the Minister [of

War], and Huang Zicheng, the Vice-Minister, were in charge of the military affairs, but turned out to be quarrelsome and incapable of devising strategies. This state of affairs was enough to rouse the dormant dragon Chengzu to soar high over the capital region. Qi Tai and Huang Zicheng were meritorious subjects of Chengzu, and principal culprits toward Jianwen. But [Tie Xuan] repeatedly attempted to resist the Prince's army, exhausting all his strategic wit to serve the country. [His was a case in which] "human effort could not prevail over predestined fate." He became a martyr for the cause of greater justice. As for Gao Xianning, he composed an essay [indicting Yongle]. Moreover he was not formally employed. His deeds are manifested in the historical records. The poems of the two Tie daughters have also been transmitted. Hence they are fit to be recorded together [with those of Tie Xuan and Gao Xianning] to be offered as exemplars for the world. It is not known whether their offspring were able to survive. But all in all, people are indeed glad to hear that the good and the loyal were able to have offspring at all.

革除之際, 方侍講經文而迂疏無當; 齊尚書, 黃少卿緯武而速衅寡謀, 適足發成祖之蟄, 高飛帝畿。齊、黃, 成祖之功臣, 建文君之罪首也。若屢抗王師, 殫謀報國, 人不能勝天, 卒以死殉, 是為公。而高賢寧之作論, 又不食祿, 見之史冊。鐵氏二女之詩, 見之傳聞。固宜合紀之, 以為世型也。至夫後之能全與否, 事尚未可知。總之, 忠良有後, 固亦人所快聞耳。[22]

Lu Yunlong sees giving bad advice and being impractical and pedantic as serious flaws, tantamount to betrayal (as more explicitly stated in the case of Qi Tai and Huang Zicheng). *Yushu* 迂疏, which I translated as "being impractical," refers here to Fang, whose policies aimed at restoring archaic institutions often inspired by the *Rituals of Zhou* (*Zhouli*), an ancient classic in which Fang was an expert.[23] The poor political advice given by Fang, Huang, and Qi, was used as a justification (or pretext) for the Prince of Yan's decision to "clear away disaster" (*jingnan* 靖難)—the euphemistic phrase used retroactively to refer to Zhu Di's rebellion in official accounts.[24] But Fang Xiaoru's "impracticality" may well extend beyond his antiquarian approach to governance to include the manner in which he died. Whether fictitious or not, the dramatic exchange between Fang and the Yongle emperor was recorded in a number of sources. In this episode, Fang refused to submit to Yongle's requests, and he showed defiance at the emperor's threat to execute his relatives and associates up to the ninth degree, by saying that it would not matter to him even if the punishment would extend to the tenth degree.[25] Fang's conduct on that occasion was judged by many as ultra-idealistic at best, reckless at worst.

Lu Yunlong, like more famously Huang Zongxi half a century later, rejects the notion that loyalty is univocally or mechanically proven by the circumstances of one's death or the extent of one's martyrdom—a view that Huang criticizes as typical of vulgar men (*yongren* 庸人).[26] But while Huang argues that Fang Xiaoru's death together with the destruction of his extended family are a proof of Yongle's unspeakable brutality rather than Fang's loyalty,[27] Lu Yunlong suggests that Fang's grim end may have been at least partially the result of his fatal flaws, impracticality and bookishness.

It is not surprising, then, that Lu Renlong did not chose a famous martyr such as Fang Xiaoru as central hero of his story. In fact, the story is also not primarily concerned with Tie Xuan, whose strenuous fight against Yongle is described in just a few pages (seventeen out of sixty pages in the woodblock edition). And while Tie Xuan dies a martyr's death, Lu Renlong does not linger on the scene of his execution. This contrasts with the lavish description of this event in many historical sources.[28] Rather, this story is about the survivors. While the heroism of Tie Xuan, in spite (or because) of his tragic end, ranks high in the firmament of heroes, the main bulk of the narrative space is devoted to the story of Gao Xianning and the Tie daughters. Gao and the younger of the Tie daughters seem to embody a more pragmatic form of loyalty. Gao writes an indictment against the Prince of Yan, and refuses to serve him (having been a stipendiary student under Jianwen, he cannot then accept to be "fed" by Yongle), but he does not directly oppose or verbally repudiate him, as Tie Xuan had done.

In the story's only direct exchange between Gao Xianning and Yongle, Gao displays superb diplomatic skills. After Tie Xuan's execution, Gao has gathered his remains, at the risk of incurring the new emperor's anger. As feared, he is captured by the guards and brought in front of the emperor:

> Chengzu asked: "Who are you? How dare you bury the remains of an executed criminal?" Gao answered: "I am Xianning, a scholar from Jiyang. I once had the honor of being selected for promotion by Tie Xuan. Now, having heard of his death, and thinking of our brief acquaintance, I ventured to think that while Your Majesty has executed a criminal, as a matter

of course, I, for my part, could bury a bosom friend—but little did I imagine that the local constable would be so quick in arresting me." Chengzu said: "Are you not that same scholar Gao Xianning from Jiyang who wrote the *Essay on the Duke of Zhou who Served King Cheng*?" "I am indeed," assented Gao. Chengzu exclaimed: "You certainly have guts! You are just a student, not a hired official. You've got nothing to do with that pack of traitors. You've written the essay to urge me to stop the war, showing your concern and love for the country and the people. You deserve to be appointed as Supervising Secretary." Gao replied: "I'm afraid that I suffered from a shock when I was arrested, and have consequently developed heart palpitations, which make it impossible for me to be employed."

成祖問:「你甚人? 敢來收葬罪人骸骨!」高秀才道:「賢寧濟陽學生員, 曾蒙鐵鉉賞拔, 今聞其死, 念有一日之知, 竊謂陛下自誅罪人, 臣自葬知己, 不謂地方遽行擒捉。」成祖道:「你不是做《周公輔成王論》的濟陽學生員高賢寧麼?」高秀才應道:「是。」成祖道:「好個大膽秀才! 你是書生, 不是用 事官員, 與奸黨不同。 作《論》是諷我息兵, 有愛國恤民的意思, 可授給事中。」高秀才道:「 賢寧自被擒受驚, 得患怔忡, 不堪任職。」[29]

Gao's response is a little masterpiece in the art of compromise and diplomacy. He manages to preserve all virtues intact, as well as his own life. Both the narrator and the interlineal commentator praise Gao Xianning as a Cheng Ying-程嬰 like figure. Cheng Ying was the loyal retainer who ensured the survival of the orphan of Zhao under disguised identity in the popular legend.[30] In particular, the interlineal commentary stresses the superiority of Cheng Ying over Gongsun Chujiu 公孫杵臼, the retired official who pretended to have sheltered the infant and committed suicide immediately afterward.[31] The moral achievement of the survivor is praised over that of the martyr.

What is also notable in the above quoted passage is Yongle's characterization. He is shown here as an enlightened ruler who is able to appreciate Gao's talents.[32] Paradoxically, it is by recognizing as meritorious the man who indicted him that Yongle transforms from villainous usurper into a sage ruler.

If Gao Xianning may be said to embody a more pragmatic notion of loyalty that lies at the opposite end of the spectrum from the idealistic position of Fang Xiaoru, Tie Xuan's daughters articulate a similar tension between idealistic (contemplative) and pragmatic (active) notions of chastity. The younger Tie girl consistently takes the lead, while the elder seems to be constrained into a more rigid and impractical notion of virtue:

> Miss Tie said to her younger sister: "We've been holding on to life here only because we were hoping to find a way to reunite with our grandparents, exiled in the far south, and with our brother, who is serving in the army in the north. Who would have thought that we would be humiliated so? We might as well die and be over with. That way at least we can preserve our reputation intact." The younger Miss Tie replied: "'Only twisted roots and gnarling branches allow one to test the sharpness of one's blade.'[33] This is the moment to show everyone that we cannot be tempted with riches and luxury, and that we are immune to coercion and intimidation. Why on earth should we observe the petty fidelity of ordinary women?"

> 那小姐對妹子道:「我兩人忍死在此, 只為祖父母與兄弟遠戍南北, 欲圖一見, 不期在此遭人輕薄, 不如一死, 以得清白。」小小姐道:「不遇盤根錯節, 何以別利器! 正要令人見我們不為繁華引誘, 不受威勢迫脅, 如何做匹婦小諒?」[34]

The impracticality of the elder sister echoes the impracticality that Fang Xiaoru was accused of in the final commentary. The idea of *pifu xiaoliang* 匹婦小諒 "petty fidelity of an ordinary woman" is worth considering. The younger Tie girl argues for the value of a heroic death (if death must be), versus a "wasted death," such as that of "ordinary women in some unknown gully." In so doing, she defends a more activist form of resistance. From this perspective, *rensi* 忍死 "holding on to life for the sake of a higher cause," or "forbearing from dying," is deemed a higher virtue than simply committing suicide without putting up a fight, or without finding an appropriately public venue to display it.

There is a measure of irony in the predicament of the Tie girls: it is precisely by being chaste that they attract legions of admirers, who after all are brothel patrons. It is interesting to compare the Tie girls with the daughter of Hu Run, one of the famous loyal ministers remembered in the prologue. Like the Tie girls, Hu Run's daughter is sent to the courtesan quarters by Yongle. There, she preserves her chastity by disfiguring her appearance, shaving her head, and neglecting her personal hygiene. Hu's daughter purposely destroys her beauty, and refuses to write poetry, claiming that she is not capable of it. For all we know, her beauty and her poetry might have been on a par with those of the Tie girls, but her deliberate silence and voluntary disfigurement stand out as a striking example of complete refusal to condescend to the world, a purely ascetic choice.[35] The Tie girls, on the other hand, simply do not wear makeup and don white mourning clothes, but in so doing their beauty is not only unmarred, but on the contrary rather enhanced. And unlike Hu's daughter, they are more than willing to write poetry on demand.

In the modern era, Lu Xun singled out the story of the Tie daughters as representative of the way in which the violence and brutality of traditional China was systematically rewritten and whitewashed.[36] He believed that this story was fabricated by later writers to create a satisfying "harmonious ending" (*quzhong zouya* 曲終奏雅) out of a harrowing account of mutilation.[37] In fact, the authenticity of this story, and even the very existence of the Tie daughters, was a matter of doubt well before Lu Xun's time. Qian Qianyi 錢謙益 (1582–1664) rejected the poems attributed to the Tie daughters as spurious and unbefitting,[38] and Chu Renhuo 褚人獲 (fl. 1675–1695) doubted the very existence of the Tie daughters.[39] According to Qian Qianyi, these spurious poems are representative of the texts and stories that were circulated about the Jianwen period, mostly fabricated by later "aficionados" (*haoshi zhe* 好事者). (Indeed, it seems that virtually all the major Jianwen martyrs had acquired at some point *two* virtuous daughters: Fang Xiaoru, Wang Shuying, Huang Guan, and Tie Xuan.)[40] And, as seen in the tail commentary quoted earlier, Lu Yunlong himself noted how nobody really believes that the ending should be so rosy, but that is "what people like to hear."

The narrator manages to transform Yongle from an arrogant and rebellious prince into a benevolent ruler in a seemingly unproblematic way. But many details remain troubling to the modern reader. The military confrontation between the Prince of Yan and Tie Xuan is depicted in strikingly similar terms to the battles between Nurhaci and the controversial Ming general Mao Wenlong, which Lu Renlong had narrated just a couple of years earlier in his novel *A Record of Fervent Loyalty* (1630). Like Mao, Tie Xuan attacks the army from the north with firearms.[41] Zhu Di even pronounces similar lines to Nurhaci's general, Tong Yangxing 佟養性, who fought against Mao Wenlong.[42] In other words, a parallel may be established between the Prince of Yan and the Manchu.

To his last breath, Tie Xuan abuses and curses Yongle. Yet by the end of the story, Yongle is hailed as a sage ruler by both narrator and commentator. As we have seen in the passage quoted above, Yongle is depicted as an enlightened ruler already in his exchange with Gao Xianning. However, what definitively consecrates Yongle as a virtuous ruler is his forgiveness of Tie Xuan's daughters. One day, Yongle asks Ji Gang, one of his courtiers, what happened to all the womenfolk of traitorous ministers (*jianchen zinü* 奸臣子女) who had been sent to serve in the brothel and in the palace laundry service.[43] Upon hearing that Tie Xuan's daughters managed to preserve their chastity, Yongle is moved to compassion. He declares them "worthy to be called the daughters of a loyal minister" (*bu kui zhongchen zhi nü* 不愧忠臣之女).[44] Stating that Tie's daughters are every bit as virtuous as the worthy daughters of a loyal minister is a highly ambivalent pronouncement. There is a paradox here: it is by pardoning the offspring of the minister who had so fiercely opposed him and whom he had brutally executed only a few years earlier that Yongle becomes a sage ruler (*shengzhu* 聖主), as opposed to a deviant hero (*jianxiong* 奸雄) à la Cao Cao. The chastity of the Tie daughters functions as the litmus paper that proves at once the worth of Tie's daughters *and* Yongle's stature as a sage ruler.[45]

It is interesting to compare "Tie Xuan and his Daughters" with another story that celebrates a loyal minister in Feng Menglong's *San Yan*, that is, "Shen Xiaoxia Encounters the Expedition Memorial" 沈小霞相會出師表 (*YSMY* 40). In this story, the loyalty of Shen Lian 沈煉 (1507–1557), who dares to openly oppose the notorious Grand Secretary Yan Song 嚴嵩 (1480–1562) and his son Yan Shifan 嚴世蕃, is celebrated but also subtly ridiculed.[46] In his exile, Shen is depicted as a literatus turned storyteller, à la Jia Fuxi 賈鳧西: "Every day, Shen Lian expounded stories to local residents about loyalty, filial piety, and the deeds of men of honor and justice in history" 沈煉每日間與地方人等, 講論忠孝大節, 及古來忠臣義士的故事.[47] Particularly amusing is the description of how Shen trains his followers to use effigies of the villains Yan Song, Li Linfu 李林甫, and Qin Kui 秦檜 made out of straw and cloth as targets for daily shooting exercises. This is a form of loyalty that borders on childish foolishness. The interlineal commentator wryly remarks: "Do not do something just for the sake of gratification" 快心之事莫做.[48]

Shen Lian's two sons, Shen Gun 沈袞 and Shen Bao 沈褒, conform to their father's idealistic notion of loyalty. Jia Shi 賈石 (whose role in the story may be compared to that of Gao Xianning) tries in vain to persuade them to flee instead of staying behind to await sure death. Jia Shi labels their behavior a "minor act of filial piety" (*xiao xiao* 小孝) that would compromise the more crucial duty of continuing the family line.

In both stories, the narrative opens with an account of the deeds of a famous loyalist hero. However, in both cases the heart of the narrative lies in recounting what happens to the survivors. In Feng Menglong's story the most memorable character is undoubtedly the ingenious concubine Wen-shi, who manages to ensure the survival of her husband, Shen Lian's elder son. She is no doubt a more colorful character than the Tie sisters. However, the story of Tie Xuan engages in an exploration of different modes of loyalty that is not to be found in Feng's story. Tie Xuan plays a significantly more active role than Shen Lian. The fact that the villain is turned into a legitimate ruler halfway through the story also brings in the issue of the necessity of compromise.

~

"Cheng Ji and the Jianwen Emperor" offers a version of the popular legend in which Jianwen survived a fire in the palace and wandered incognito throughout the empire for several decades disguised as a monk. This widespread legend appears in a number of historical writings as well as fictional accounts and dramatic adaptations.[49] The proximate source for Lu Renlong's story is most likely Li Zhi's biographies of Cheng Ji and Gao Xiang, which appear consecutively in his *Sequel to a Book to Hide*.[50]

In the story, Cheng Ji studies for the examinations together with his good friend Gao Xiang 高翔. The two young scholars have opposite temperaments but get along very well. One day a foreign monk stops at the Vimalakirti temple where Cheng and Gao are residing. While Gao Xiang looks down on the monk, Cheng treats him most warmly. The monk predicts that one of them will become a loyal subject (*zhongchen* 忠臣), and the other a wise advisor (*zhishi* 知士), and he gives Cheng Ji a divination book before bidding farewell. By observing the constellations Cheng Ji predicts the rebellion of the Prince of Yan, but no one believes him and he is thrown in jail. When his prophecy turns out to be true, Cheng Ji is released from prison and given a post, thanks to the intercession of Gao Xiang, who has in the meantime become a censor. When the capital falls to the northern army, Cheng Ji exhorts Jianwen to flee as a monk. While Gao Xiang is brutally executed by Yongle, Cheng Ji escorts the deposed emperor in his wanderings through the south and southwest of the country for forty years. In his old age, Jianwen finally manages to return to the capital. His task now accomplished, Cheng Ji disappears with the foreign monk.

The prologue of this story uncharacteristically dwells on a figure of remote antiquity, Jie Zhitui 介之推 (referred to as Jie Zitui 介子推 in the text), whose deeds constitute an obvious parallel with those of Cheng Ji. According to the legend, Jie faithfully assisted Chong'er 重耳, the future Duke Wen of Jin, during his eighteen years of exile in the seventh century BCE. At one time, Jie Zhitui even cut off a piece of his thigh to save his master from starvation. Yet Jie's legendary loyalty was met by an equally legendary forgetfulness on the part of his ruler. After failing to be rewarded, Jie Zhitui quietly withdrew to mount Mian, and was later accidentally burnt to death by Duke Wen's inept emissaries.

Jie Zhitui embodies an ideal of loyalty that is emphatically decoupled from the notion of reciprocity (*bao*). In contrast with those who urge him to request a reward from the ruler, Jie reasons:

> "When I sliced my thigh to feed my lord back then, I only did so with the intention of saving his life, and to fulfill my duty as a subject. I certainly did not have any reward in mind. If I were to do as they say and demand to be rewarded, it would be as if I had given out a loan and now I expect to get it back. How could this apply to the bond between ruler and subject?"

> 我當日割股, 也只要救全主上, 全我為臣的事, 並沒個希望封賞意思。若依着他們, 畢竟要報我, 恰是放債要還模樣, 豈是個君臣道理。[51]

In the monetized economy of the late Ming, the notion of reciprocity can become dangerously akin to a commercial transaction. Yet, in this story Jie Zhitui himself is not spared a note of sarcasm. He is depicted as a pedantic and almost ludicrous character:

> Jie thought to himself: "They really want to force me to come out. Back then, if I hadn't fled, I would have been accused of craving profit. But if I come out now, it would mean that I crave life. How can this world tolerate such a greedy person as myself? Much better to die and be done with!"

> 子推見了道:「這定是要逼我出去的緣故了。我當日不走是貪利, 今日出去是貪生。世上安可着我這貪夫? 不如死了罷。」[52]

The interlineal commentary gives him the coup de grâce: "In the end, he craved fame! (*tanming* 貪名)"[53] Here both narrator and commentator join hands in subtly ridiculing an excessively intransigent ideal of loyalty. They also suggest that the logic of *bao* may ultimately be inescapable. No such intimations of ridicule apply to the figure of Cheng Ji, however. He is thus presented as a modern exemplar of the loyal subject who not only updates but also outdoes the ancient model.

The Spectrum of Loyalty

There are some parallels between the characters of Cheng Ji and Gao Xianning in "Tie Xuan and His Daughters."⁵⁴ Both ensure the survival of their designated beneficiaries, the deposed Jianwen emperor and the offspring of the former mentor Tie Xuan, respectively. In both cases, fire is used as a ploy. While Gao is able to find a rural oasis for Tie Xuan's younger son, Cheng Ji finds a religious refuge for the deposed emperor. As in "Tie Xuan and His Daughters," this story too stages competing models of loyalty. These are mainly embodied in the two characters of Gao Xiang and Cheng Ji. Their opposing views on official duty, loyalty, and martyrdom are captured in the following conversation with the foreign monk at the beginning of the story:

> The Western monk said to Gao: "You too are a fit 'vessel for the state.' But just like Master Cheng here, your rank and reputation will be outstanding, but you will not succeed in the end. As for Cheng, at least he can look forward to dying a natural death." Gao Xiang laughed and replied: "Achieving rank and fame is part of our duty. I don't care if I don't succeed. As for 'dying a natural death,' a man of mettle who lives in this world should act candidly and honestly. As a son, he should die for the sake of filial piety, and as a subject, he should die out of loyalty. Simply slit the throat, sever the neck, and his name will be recorded in the historical annals. What's the point of [being content to] merely grow old and die by the window?" Cheng Ji just happened to hear these words as he was bringing in the tea, and he said: "Brother Gao, I say that Shi Rong's death was of no use to Wei. Much better to follow the example of Ning Wuzi who held on to life to serve his ruler!"

> 那西僧又對高仲舉道:「檀越亦是國器, 但與此間程檀越, 功名都顯而不達. 程檀越還可望令終。」仲舉笑道:「功名是我們分內事, 也不愁不顯達. 若說令終, 大丈夫生在世間, 也須磊磊犖犖, 為子死孝, 為臣死忠, 便刎頸決脰, 也得名標青史, 何必老死牖下。」此時程君楫正烹茶來, 聽了道:「高兄, 我道士榮殺身, 無濟于衛。倒不如甯武子, 忍死全君。」⁵⁵

To illustrate his position, Cheng Ji uses the case of Ning Wuzi 甯武子, a Wei minister who helped his ruler, Duke Cheng, when the latter was imprisoned by the leaders of Jin during a legal dispute against Yuan Xuan, a Wei noble accused of plotting against the duke. As recorded in the *Zuozhuan*, Ning Wuzi served as the Duke's assistant, while Shi Rong served as the Duke's representative in court (presumably in charge of speaking on behalf of the Duke during the trial). The Duke lost the case and as a result Shi Rong was executed, while Ning Wuzi was considered to have been loyal to the duke and was thus pardoned. Later, Ning Wuzi took care of the Duke by sending him food and clothes after the latter was imprisoned by Duke Wen of Jin.[56] Ning Wuzi and Shi Rong enact a similar dynamics of contrasting models to Cheng Ying and Gongsun Chujiu in "Tie Xuan and His Daughters." Cheng Ji argues that it is preferable to hold on to life to protect one's ruler, rather than to opt for a heroic but ultimately wasteful sacrifice of the kind envisioned by Gao Xiang. It is an extremely delicate balance between loyal devotion and sagacious self-preservation.

As the titular couplet of the story suggests, both Cheng and Gao end up realizing their aspirations. For his part, Gao fulfills the ideal of the loyalist martyr. As in "Tie Xuan and His Daughters," the narrator does not linger on the description of Gao Xiang's death. (According to some historical records, Gao was executed by "slow slicing," like Tie Xuan.) Yet Gao Xiang and the other loyal heroes in the story, such as Yan Zhenzhi and the eunuch Wu Liang, remain in the background. Once again, it is the realm of moral pragmatism and activism that is placed at the forefront, and the narrative interest lies in what happens to the survivors. As the title of the story suggests, one of the crucial attributes of Cheng Ji is his sagaciousness (*zhi* 智). *Zhi* is usually translated as "wisdom," but as Hanan has pointed out in his discussion of Feng Menglong's *Zhinang* 智囊 (Sack of Wisdom), *zhi* refers not to a contemplative kind of wisdom, but rather to something akin to "applied intelligence."[57] The story emphasizes the subject's shrewd sense of expediency and ability to cope with historical contingencies.[58]

The aura of Taoist wizardry that characterizes Cheng Ji in the biographical source, and other vernacular adaptations such as the one found in *West Lake Stories*, is somewhat downplayed in "Cheng Ji and the Jianwen Emperor." Instead, the narrator takes pain to establish Cheng on firmly Confucian grounds by emphasizing his filial devotion to his parents (who are made to conveniently die well before the Yongle usurpation occurs, so that Cheng can properly mourn them for the prescribed three years) and regret at abandoning his wife to assist the fleeing emperor (the wife promptly commits suicide to show *her* unwavering devotion, and to avoid troubling his conscience). By contrast, Gao Xiang's sacrifice is made to be enormously costly for his family and associates. His own death is accompanied by the execution of his relatives to the ninth degree (the original biography had it to the third degree only).[59]

Lu Yunlong's final commentary settles the relative merits of the two modes of loyalty in no uncertain terms. His judgment clearly echoes the one offered by Li Zhi in the original source:

> Those who died out of principle or went into hiding when Yongle "cleared away the disaster" were truly loyal subjects.[60] Yet, if an official hears that his ruler must wander about with no fixed abode, how can he not feel disheartened whenever he thinks about it? But Compiler Cheng [Ji], who endured many hardships to protect his lord, truly deserves to be considered as a supreme example of loyalty.
>
> 請 [靖] 難中一干死節行遁諸君子，真忠臣也。然業為君臣，聽其流離道路，每一念及，能無憮然乎? 則程編修之間關衛主，固一 忠之尤耳。[61]

In sum, both "Cheng Ji and the Jianwen Emperor" and "Tie Xuan and His Daughters" articulate contrasting views of loyalty. In both cases, the more activist and pragmatic version of loyalty is praised as the superior form—the form that was most urgently needed in the difficult times the Lu brothers lived in. But as we shall see in the following section, with the fall of the Ming the meaning and performance of loyalty seemed to take an absolutist turn.

Loyal Subjects Amid the Ruins

Bell in the Still Night includes two stories about loyal subjects set during the fall of the Ming. Both may be seen as examples of the genre of "fiction on current events" that was briefly in vogue during the seventeenth century.[62] The first story, titled "Chongzhen's Loyal Minister and His Wife" (full title: "The Faithful Minister Vehemently Kills Himself, His Heroic Wife Serenely Dies a Martyr's Death" 貞臣慷慨殺身, 烈婦從容就義, *QYZ* 1), is a fascinating, firsthand document about how the traumatic events of 1644 (and implicitly, the disheartening experience of the Southern Ming) might have reshaped Lu Yunlong's perception of loyalty and martyrdom. The story tells of Wang Wei 汪偉 (*js* 1628), an upright member of the Hanlin academy who is remembered among the piteously few officials who committed suicide after the Chongzhen emperor hanged himself on Coal Hill as the rebel armies overtook the capital in the spring of 1644.

This story offers a gripping account of the Ming fall. The prologue is exceptionally long (about 1,800 characters, taking up over one-third of the total length of the story) and rather anomalous. It does not resemble a typical argumentative prologue, nor does it provide anecdotes or "teasers" to prepare the reader for the main story. Rather, it offers a passionate defense of the Chongzhen emperor and his policies, dense with details and filled with bitter accusations of inept officials who could have saved the day. Even after Wang Wei is introduced in the story proper as a character who stands in stark contrast to the political factions and trends of his time, the narrative energy is clearly expended on the scathing criticism of the high-talking but ineffectual officials, along with Donglin party sympathizers:

> In truth, [Wang Wei] never put on airs, or put up a front, very much unlike those people nowadays who talk about the Donglin party, deliver Confucian lectures, and value "spiritual affinity." These people swarm toward profit but hide away when there is danger. Day in and day out, they fish for fame and recognition, while in secret they are constantly after money and forming cliques. Day in and day out, they talk of loyalty and principle, but when facing an actual emergency they invariably betray the country and forget the ruler.
>
> People praise them as so many Jizis and Bi Gans,[63]
> Their reputation is higher than Xu You and Bo Yi.[64]
> When you meet them face to face it's all "Yes! Yes!"
> But in their heart they have already reneged.
>
> 實不是扯架子、裝門面，似近來說東林，講道學，重聲氣的，見利便趨，見害便躲。平日釣譽沽名，暗裡一味抓錢結黨，平日談忠道義，臨機一味背國忘君。
>
> 人稱箕比，譽重由夷
>
> 謀面只是，徵心已違。[65]

Before the fall, around 1628, Lu Yunlong had composed a eulogy to celebrate Chongzhen's ousting of Wei Zhongxian and his clique, titled

"Eulogy for Overcoming and Exterminating the Great Iniquity" (*Ke qing da dui song* 克清大憝頌). In the preface he criticizes a certain category of "loyal" ministers for their excessive self-righteousness and ineffectuality:

> In the Tianqi reign [1620–27] there were two or three [high-minded] gentlemen who, though not necessarily motivated by personal gain, were nonetheless paranoid about "checking evil at the outset," and fiercely "abhorred evils [as deadly foes]." If now and then there were those who advocated more moderate views, these gentlemen were not pleased with them. Hence, not only did they look askance at the slanderers and corrupt, but they even refused to mix with those who were fair-minded. In their keenness to keep their sleeves clean, they completely failed to take into account actual emergencies.

熹廟時二三君子不必有自功心, 然防微過甚, 嫉惡過猛。間有進持平之說者, 勿悅也。故不惟為讒邪睊目, 中正者亦弗與。乃猶銳于袪清, 不解審緩急之勢。66

In this passage, Lu Yunlong expresses his frustration with the intransigence and lack of strategic skills of the so-called virtuous officials of the Tianqi era, deeming them largely responsible for the disastrous outcome. His criticism echoes his harsh appraisal of some of the famous martyrs of the Jianwen era voiced in the final commentary to the story "Tie Xuan and His Daughters" discussed earlier. The target of his criticism is likely to be those members of the Donglin party who bluntly opposed Wei Zhongxian but ultimately only brought calamity on themselves.

Lu Yunlong gives discrepant portraits of celebrated martyr figures in his fictional and nonfictional writings. A case in point is his treatment of Yang Lian 楊漣 (1571–1625), the censor who in 1624 submitted a memorial enumerating twenty-four crimes committed by Wei Zhongxian and subsequently died an atrocious death at Wei's hands.[67] In *The Story of Wei Zhongxian: A Book of Indictment*, Lu Yunlong conforms to a more celebratory image of the loyalist hero, while he articulates his criticism in his essays and interlineal commentaries. A Chinese scholar has suggested that this difference in attitude may be due to a difference in audience.[68] In fact, the distinction is not so clear-cut. For one thing, the audience consuming the novel was after all also likely to read the interlineal commentaries that came with it. More to the point, however, the portrait of the loyalist hero in the novel itself is subject to the "deflation of heroism" that Andrew Plaks has seen as one of the defining features of Ming *xiaoshuo*.[69] For example, Yang Lian's arrest and journey to the capital are recounted in great detail. Yang Lian lectures the crowds who have come to his rescue and even threatens to commit suicide then and there if they don't let him go. Along the route, Yang Lian is depicted as a public spectacle, surrounded and almost harassed by crowds of fans.[70]

In "Chongzhen's Loyal Minister and His Wife," however, there seems to be no space for modulations in the performance of loyalty. In the 1628 eulogy Lu Yunlong had expressed criticism of certain self-righteous officials for their ineffectuality, but he would still consider them fundamentally virtuous and well intentioned. However, by the time the Ming had fallen, those same officials are indicted as downright nefarious and hypocritical. The spectrum of choices seems to have become narrowed dramatically.

Wang Wei and his wife stand in striking contrast to the surrounding narrative, as if they were stylized figures pasted onto a realistic and densely descriptive painting. This contrast epitomizes the tension between the exemplary impulse and the chaos of historical reality. The loyal subject appears to be the embodiment of an ahistorical ideal that is disjointed from the chaotic ambiguity of history in the making. Unlike more conventional narratives of loyal subjects that have a clear (and often colorfully characterized) villain, here no single entity, but rather the entire society—save for the handful of loyalists listed at the end of the prologue—functions as a villain.

In the midst of the rampant corruption and malfeasance in the examination system—where everything from an official position to a simple administrative document could be purchased—Wang Wei's ascent to one of the top government positions is nothing short of a miracle. Yet for all his integrity, Wang is confined to a Cassandra-like role, whereby he continuously decries the gravity of the situation, while his suggestions and predictions are systematically ignored. In his last, futile attempt to muster forces to resist the bandits who have already entered the capitals, all he sees in the streets of Beijing are hordes of officers and common people in festive clothes, ready to welcome the rebels.[71]

Wang Wei and the Chongzhen emperor mirror each other in their moral temper as well as their utter isolation. Significantly, both commit suicide. Here there is no longer space for moral pragmatism and strategies of survival—moral heroism, in its most extreme form as suicide, seems to be the only viable option. While the Chongzhen emperor is said to have forced Empress Zhou to commit suicide and to have personally killed several of his concubines before taking his own life, Wang Wei's wife acts in complete, almost mechanical, accord with her husband. Her intention to commit suicide along with Wang is not probed but simply assumed.[72] In short, Lady Geng's heroic quality (*lie* 烈) is highly formulaic. Her most memorable gesture is to remind her husband, as he is about to hang himself, that he ought to choose the east (left) beam for the purpose, not the one to the west.[73] Moral heroism is here almost reduced to ceremonial fastidiousness. The subjunctive "as if" world of ritual order has become the only symbolic corrective, the only refuge from the chaotic "as is" world of the crumbling Ming dynasty.[74] Significantly, the couple's determination and composure as they prepare to die is described as "impassioned" or "vehement" (*kangkai* 慷慨) and "serene" (*congrong* 從容), respectively. While these two attributes are used in opposition to one another in a popular proverb, with the implication that the latter represents a more arduous ideal, here we see an attempt to reconcile the previous opposition. Both can be equally laudable attributes of true martyrdom.[75]

The narrator's concluding remarks, introduced in a strikingly personal fashion: "I say . . ." (*wo dao* 我道), cast a somber light on the actual efficacy of such model of moral heroism:

"I casually write about these exemplars, so as to inspire a sense of shame [in the readers]. I only fear to meet with obtuse mouths and recalcitrant ears, for that would surely be a hopeless situation." 聊書榜樣以發愧心, 只恐口頑耳頑, 這便是箇無如之何了.[76]

What a difference from the optimistic faith in the power of vernacular stories to elicit shame and fear in the reader as expressed in the *San Yan* prefaces!

Another story in *Bell* is set during the Chongzhen era (Chongzhen is here given as "the current emperor" *jinshang* 今上, which suggests an earlier date of composition than the story "Loyal Minister Wang Wei and His Wife"). This story, titled "The Divine Instructor Warned Him Three Times, The Director of Grain Transport Did Not Escape Death" 神師三致提撕, 總漕一死不免 (QYZ 14), tells of the life and death of the virtuous minister Yang Yipeng 楊一鵬.[77] The story reads very much like a hagiography, complete with supernatural elements. Yang's downfall occurs in 1635, when the city of Fengyang, the ancestral village of the Ming founder, is ravaged by bandits, who also desecrate the imperial tombs. Yang Yipeng and another official are deemed responsible and thrown into jail. The other official is eventually pardoned, while Yang is executed.

The moral message of this story is particularly ambiguous. There is a discrepancy between the hagiographical tone of the narrative (which stresses Yang's integrity) and his merciless execution at the end. The supernatural elements that constitute a parallel thread of the story—Yang is periodically visited by spirits in the guise of nuns and holy monks urging him to withdraw from officialdom lest calamity strike—seem to suggest that one should abstain from government service, a point quite at odds with the main narrative. A similar opposition between service and withdrawal is presented in the brief anecdote narrated in the prologue. This tells how Zhuo Jing 卓敬, a Jianwen loyalist, while still a young boy chanced on an immortal who predicted that he would rise to prominence in later years, but that he would also meet a violent death. He therefore urged him, in vain, to withdraw.[78] Perhaps, having supernatural figures who point to the fundamentally ahistorical (or counterhistorical) option of abstention from government service is the only solution to the dilemma in which the narrator seems to find himself at the end of this story: a loyal and earnest official in his sixties is executed, for no real fault of his own, by the Chongzhen emperor, who is deemed to be a just and virtuous ruler.

∽

The loyalty stories discussed in this chapter reveal the tension between moral illustration and historical narrative. Lying just beneath the seemingly simple surface is a layering of dissonant discourses on loyalty, martyrdom, and survival in the wake of intra- and interdynastic transitions. The stories seem to deliberately exorcise scenarios in which political duty is at odds with filial obligation, focusing instead on representing loyalty as being in harmony with filiality even in times of trouble. While martyrdom for one's ruler is celebrated in the *Exemplary Words* stories, it is also framed as an extreme outcome rather than an indispensable or defining attribute of a loyal official. The compiler and commentator prefer more pragmatic examples, as demonstrated by the narrative gusto with which they depict ingenious survival strategies. Gao Xianning in "Tie Xuan and His Daughters," in particular, may be seen as emblematic of the second generation that survives the trauma of the intradynastic transition—in an eerie prefiguration of the impending Manchu conquest. However, such a pragmatic stance seems no longer to be a compelling or viable option in the *Bell in the Still Night* stories, written on the eve of the Ming collapse and its immediate aftermath.

Chapter 4

Female Exemplarity and the Violence of Virtue

Chastity (usually understood as the defense of one's virginity for maidens, and conjugal fidelity for married and widowed women) is traditionally considered the bedrock of female virtue, though its relative importance in the constellation of qualities that went into the construction of female exemplarity did not remain unchanged throughout the long course of Chinese history. Scholars have long noted that early records of female paragons such as the foundational *Exemplary Women* (*Lienü zhuan* 列女傳) by Liu Xiang valorized a wider range of virtues and traits than simply chastity. These virtues were mostly centered on kinship-based norms, but some room was left for qualities that went beyond the domestic sphere, such as wit, stylistic mastery, and political sagacity—what Lisa Raphals has called the "intellectual virtues."[1] Even within the kinship-based norms, the image of the exemplary wife often encompassed the notion of gentle remonstrance, which on the one hand subtly problematized the classic dictum that "the husband should be righteous, and the wife should be compliant" (*fu yi fu ting* 夫義婦聽), while on the other hand it reinforced the analogy with the ruler-subject and father-son relationships, which also prized the role of gentle remonstrance in certain circumstances.[2]

By contrast, in late imperial collections about exemplary women, chastity almost entirely overshadowed other exemplary traits. Further, chastity was construed in increasingly narrow terms as an act of heroism or martyrdom by which the wife (or fiancée) resists violent sexual assault or family pressure to get remarried. This shift is encapsulated in the semantic narrowing of the terms used to designate virtuous behavior.

While the terms themselves remained largely the same, their meaning changed, sometimes dramatically. *Jie* 節, originally a gender-neutral attribute indicating integrity or the quality of being principled, has been used since at least the Song dynasty onward to indicate almost exclusively the virtue of wifely fidelity or chastity when applied to women.³ *Zhen* 貞 (often used in tandem or interchangeably with *jie*) underwent a similar shift, from the idea of integrity and steadfast loyalty to sexual purity, chastity, and virginity.⁴ Other terms, such as *yi* 義, *lie* 烈, and *xian* 賢, underwent analogous semantic shifts.⁵

Scholars have long traced the rise of a "cult of female chastity" as a distinctly Ming and Qing cultural phenomenon. Two aspects related to the chastity cult that are especially relevant to the four stories discussed in this chapter are the contentious practice of female suicide⁶ and the ambiguous role played by the male literati biographers who wrote profusely on chaste women. Three of the four stories end with the heroine's suicide, and suicide itself is framed as a problematic, if admirable, choice in one story (*XSY* 10). All the stories, moreover, close with an explicit mention of the literatus, or literati, who recorded the heroine's deeds. If female chastity became a cult, the male literati who wrote account after account of virtuous women could be seen as its theologians and officiants. Their stance toward their subjects may seem uniformly eulogistic, but it is rarely devoid of other, implicit agendas. The celebration of female exemplars was almost always accompanied by an invitation to reflect on the analogy between male loyalty and female fidelity. According to this analogy, chaste wives are the domestic counterpart of loyal subjects who refuse to serve a second ruler, as expressed in the adage "a faithful minister does not serve two rulers, a heroic woman does not marry a second husband" 忠臣不事二君, 烈女不更二夫. Faithful maidens (*zhennü* 貞女) in particular became powerful tropes for the literati who remain unflinchingly loyal to a ruler they would never be given the chance to serve (typically because of their failure to pass the civil service examinations).⁷ But many late Ming writings were marked by what Martin Huang has termed the "collapse of th[e] analogical relationship" between male loyalty and female fidelity.⁸ Growing numbers of literati lamented that chaste women were not simply equal, but actually far superior to men, and that it was much easier to find heroic women than loyal ministers in actual life.⁹ In other words, the praise and glorification of chaste women was often used as a polemic denunciation of male deficiency.

The stories discussed in this chapter deal with the kind of exemplary women who in many ways fit the expectations of the late Ming audience for *lienü zhuan* (exemplary women) literature. This should come as no surprise since three of the four stories deal with presumably historical characters and incidents and have a corresponding classical language source, explicitly mentioned at the end, while the fourth story clearly follows the blueprint of the exemplary biography even though the historicity of the figures and events narrated is most tenuous. "Injustice to Tang Guimei" (*XSY* 6) tells of a young widow who commits suicide to avoid compromising the reputation of her corrupt mother-in-law, who had tried to coerce her into marrying her own ex-lover. Its plot is paralleled in "The Beauties and the Bumpkins" (*QYZ* 2), which features not one but two such virtuous women who are the victims of a lascivious mother-in-law. "The Heroic Woman and Her Mother" (*XSY* 10) recounts the drama of a young widow who commits suicide against the advice of all those around her and with the acquiescence of her own mother. Lastly, "The Faithful Widows of the Xiao Family" (*XSY* 16) narrates the life of a chaste wife and equally chaste concubines who refuse to remarry after their husband's death in order to raise the orphans. These stories are exceptional not so much in that they feature exemplary "chaste widows" (*jiefu* 節婦) and "martyred or heroic widows" (*liefu* 烈婦)—these figures are found ubiquitously in vernacular fiction—but in that the virtuous women are the central heroines of these stories.[10] Never before had vernacular stories been so closely, and explicitly, imitating exemplary biographies in classical language.

For this reason, these stories offer an ideal vantage point to illuminate the rhetorical and ideological differences between classical language biographies and vernacular *huaben*. The vernacular stories, as one would expect, typically flesh out the characters' background and motives for action, often adding subplots and incidents to the terse biographical account. Most significantly, the vernacular stories feature what I have called "discursive frame." Typically, the plots are built around a moral conflict of sorts, which, however, is not presented as an interiorized dilemma, in that there is no depiction of hesitation or inner torment over the proper course of action. Rather, the dilemma is externalized, so that the significance of the heroine's act, the alternative courses of action, and the claims of competing values are discussed by a more or less colorful crowd of relatives, servants, friends, and neighbors. What was portrayed as an individual, private drama in the original biography becomes an issue whose social ramifications are explored in the vernacular story.[11] Such a discursive frame thus opens a textual space in which a debate over the moral choice can be articulated. It also fulfills other functions, occasionally serving as comic relief and foil for the seriousness of the heroine. It furthermore reflects a historical reality, since relatives and neighbors were called to testify as witnesses in the process of verification necessary to confer honorific titles on the family of women of exceptional conduct.¹²

As narrative texts, these stories may at first glance appear to follow the basic ordeal motif in which a virtuous heroine must overcome one or more ordeals to prove her resolution.¹³ But we see opposite tendencies in the variations around this basic motif. On the one hand, there is a magnification of the ordeal facing the heroine, and a magnification of a singular kind at that. Rather than roving bandits, floods, or tigers, the villain is found within the domestic walls. The villain here is the monstrous mother-in-law, and to a much lesser extent, the vile husband. On the other hand, we also see stories in which the ordeal is minimized, if not altogether erased. The heroine must overcome not a real antagonist, but the audience's (both diegetic and actual) incredulity that such acts *can* be accomplished. The heroines' world of supererogatory commitment is pitted against everyday common sense, practical calculations, and even the natural feelings that bind mother and daughter.

Tang Guimei, or the Drama of Filiality and Chastity

The titular character in "Injustice to Tang Guimei" (full title: "To Preserve Her Virtue, the Daughter-in-Law Holds Steadfastly to a Pure Heart; Covering Up Her Mother-In-Law's Faults, Her Pure Verse Echoes for All Centuries" 完令節冰心獨抱, 全姑醜冷韻千秋, *XSY* 6) is a young woman sent as a live-in daughter-in-law into the family of widow Zhu 朱, who runs a business as an innkeeper. Originally a demure and proper woman, widow Zhu has gradually become depraved after the death of her husband. She starts an affair with one of her tenants, Wang Hanyu 汪涵宇, a rich merchant from out of town. When her son Zhu Yan 朱顏 finds out about his mother's promiscuous behavior, he falls ill and dies of shame. On his deathbed, Tang Guimei swears to remain faithful to him. Wang Hanyu bribes the widow to talk Guimei into marrying him, but the girl adamantly refuses. One day, as she is rejecting Wang's advances, she accidentally hits the widow, who drags her to court with the charge of unfilial behavior. Guimei declines to defend herself to protect her mother-in-law's reputation. As a result, she is tortured and thrown into jail by the district magistrate Mao, who has also been bribed by Wang Hanyu. After a few days, Hanyu ransoms her, again with the intention of forcing her to marry him. Seeing that there is no honorable way out—she cannot betray her husband, nor can she publicly denounce her mother-in-law's lascivious conduct—Guimei hangs herself from an old plum tree in the garden. A quatrain proclaiming her innocence is found on her body. Wang Hanyu tries to escape with the money and gifts he had previously given widow Zhu, but he is seized by the enraged neighbors. Magistrate Mao is later dismissed for corruption, while the widow is sentenced to pay for Tang Guimei's funeral and falls into poverty.

The plot of "Injustice to Tang Guimei" is strongly reminiscent of the celebrated Yuan play *Injustice to Dou E* (*Dou E yuan* 竇娥冤) by Guan Hanqing 關漢卿 (ca. 1241–1320), which the late Ming reading public could access in several more or less heavily edited editions, including the most influential *Selection of Yuan Plays* (*Yuanqu xuan* 元曲選, 1615–1616) by Zang Maoxun 臧懋循 (1550–1620).[14] Lu Renlong, however, was not simply spinning a literary motif. He based his story on a historical incident that had a vast resonance at the time (although the historicity of the incident has been disputed by modern scholars).[15] Tang Guimei's biography was first written down by the famous literatus Yang Shen 楊慎 (1488–1559), although the proximate source used by Lu Renlong was most likely the version included with an added commentary by Li Zhi's in his *A Book to Burn* (*Fenshu* 焚書, c. 1590).[16] Here is the text of Yang's biography:

> The heroic woman was surnamed Tang, her given name was Guimei. She hailed from Guichi county in Chizhou prefecture [mod. Anhui]. When she came of age she married a man surnamed Zhu. Her husband was poor and spineless, while her mother-in-law was cruel and lascivious. In her youth the mother-in-law had an affair with a wealthy merchant from Huizhou. During the Hongzhi reign [1487–1505], the wealthy merchant returned to Chizhou. When he caught sight of Guimei, he immediately fancied her. He stroked his chest, saying to himself, "I'm not deranged, why should I stick with the old crone for no reason?" Therefore he secretly bribed the mother-in-law with gold and silk. Seeing that there was a profit to be made, the mother-in-law tried every possible trick to convince Guimei to sleep with the merchant, but Guimei did not pay her heed. She was forced, caned, prodded with a hot poker until there was not a piece of skin left intact on her body—but still she could not be prevailed upon. Then she was sued on the charge of unfiliality and brought to court. The assistant prefect (*tongpan*) Mao Yu of Cixi had also received bribes from the merchant, and he redoubled the punishment. She came close to dying several times. The merchant, who still lusted

after her, hoped that she would change her resolve and so he had the mother-in-law bail her out. All the relatives and neighbors urged Guimei to speak the truth, but she said, "If I do, I will clear my name but I would defile my mother-in-law's. This goes against filial piety." That evening she changed into her formal attire and she hanged herself under the old plum tree in the back courtyard. The following morning, the mother-in-law, not knowing what had happened, set out to go into her room to beat her, brandishing a mulberry cane in her hand, and cursing as she walked, "Evil slave, if you had followed my request early on, you would have had gold and silk, and enjoyed much merrymaking to boot. What was the purpose of bringing such suffering upon yourself?" She went into her room and not seeing her there, she searched for her until she came to the plum tree, and that is how she learned of her death. The mother-in-law wailed out loud most piteously. Relatives and neighbors made a loud din, screaming, "When she was alive you accused her of unfiliality. You should only be pleased now that she's dead. What's up with this display of grief?" The mother-in-law replied, "If she were alive, I would still have some hope. Now that she is dead, the merchant will surely retract his bribes. I am crying over the loss of gold and silk, not for the sake of this evil slave!"

The corpse hung from the tree for three days, yet her face looked as if alive. All the woodcutters and young shepherds shed tears for her. Every year, around the end of the fourth month (plum month), her figure could be seen faintly until it gradually faded away. Because the officials in charge encountered obstruction from the prefectural authorities, her case was never brought up (for official reward).

烈婦姓唐氏, 名貴梅, 池州貴池人也。笄年適朱姓, 夫貧且弱。有老姑悍且淫, 少與徽州一富商有私。弘治中, 富商復至池, 一見婦悅之, 自捫心曰:「吾無頭風, 何以老嫗虛拘哉。」乃密以金帛賂其姑。姑利其有, 誨婦淫者以百端, 弗聽。迫之, 弗聽。加以箠楚, 弗聽。繼以炮烙, 體無完膚, 終不聽。乃以不孝訟于官。通判慈谿毛玉亦受商之賂, 倍加官刑。幾死者數。商猶慕其色, 冀其改節, 復令姑保出之。親黨咸勸其吐實。婦曰:「若然, 全吾名而污吾姑, 非孝也。」乃夕易袿襡, 雉經于後園古梅樹下。及旦, 姑不知之也, 將入其室挺之, 手持桑杖, 且罵且行, 曰:「惡奴早從我言, 又得金帛, 且享懽樂, 今定何如而自苦乎?」入室無見, 尋之至樹下, 乃知其死。姑大慟哭之。親黨咻之曰:「生既以不孝訟之, 死乃

Female Exemplarity and the Violence of Virtue 111

稱嫗心, 何哭之慟?」姑曰:「婦在, 吾猶有望。婦死, 商人必倒贓。吾哭金帛, 不哭此惡奴也。」尸懸於樹三日, 顏如生, 樵夫牧兒咸為墮淚。每歲梅月之下, 隱隱見其形, 冉冉而沒。有司以礙於府官之故, 終不舉。[17]

The comparison between the classical biography by Yang Shen, Li Zhi's commentary, Lu Renlong's vernacular retelling, and Lu Yunlong's commentary illustrates the shifts in the moral characterization across genres and historical moments. As expected, the vernacular narrator fleshes out the background of the main characters. Contrary to the original biography, the narrator portrays Guimei as the daughter of a village schoolteacher, who proudly boasts his membership in a Confucian family (*rujia* 儒家, *siwen zhi jia* 斯文之家) and raises his daughter on a diet of canonical texts such as the *Classic of Filial Piety* and *Exemplary Women*.[18] Thus, Guimei's moral integrity is presented as shaped by the Confucian written canon, or better, by what percolates from that canon into the humble household of a village schoolmaster in a Jiangnan locality at the turn of the sixteenth century. This detail runs counter to the original biography, where there was nothing to suggest that Guimei came from an educated if impoverished family, but even more significantly, it turns Lu Yunlong's main argument into a moot point. In the preface, Lu Yunlong had argued for the moral superiority of "ignorant women" (*yufu* 愚婦) over so-called erudite scholars, a point that echoes Li Zhi's own trenchant commentary to Yang Shen's biography.[19] This curious discrepancy between story and commentary suggests that, at least in this case, the author of the commentary was familiar with the original source but somehow failed to read the vernacular retelling in close detail—or that the story was composed separately from the preface. Whichever the case, the tension between literacy and moral integrity is not an item on the narrator's polemic agenda. Rather, Lu Renlong's choice to rewrite the heroine as literate may be construed as an attempt to give Tang Guimei a voice, to shift the characterization from one of victimhood to one of agency—although the gesture itself is not devoid of ambiguity. The quatrain found on Tang Guimei's body echoes the countless songs and poems invariably attributed to women who encountered a tragic (but presumably silent) death in successive retellings of their stories by zealous literati of later ages.[20]

The vernacular story also develops the character of the father and the husband. Mr. Tang is said to be concerned with the issue of "outward respectability" (*timian* 體面), yet he spectacularly fails to check the background of the Zhu family. In a subtle gender reversal (which prefigures the later development, when Guimei becomes a heroic figure while her husband remains a weak figure in the background), the prospective husband's delicate and refined *looks* are all that it takes to convince old Tang to marry his daughter to him.[21] Here Lu Renlong is probably taking inspiration from the characterization of the heroine's father in *Injustice to Dou E*.

As for Zhu Yan, Guimei's husband, he is depicted as a delicate and bookish young man, in striking contrast with his mother. When he starts to suspect that his mother is having an affair, he vainly tries to persuade her to hand over the innkeeping business. Once his suspicions are confirmed, he falls sick and dies. In contrast, the original biography has the husband still alive, although "poor and weak," when the tragedy unfolds. Like Guimei's father, Zhu Yan is worried that his family's reputation as a "family of scholars" (*dushu renjia* 讀書人家) might be blemished—a detail that sits at odds with the rest of the narrative.[22] True, the boundaries between merchant class and officialdom had became considerably blurred by this time. We might surmise, for example, that Zhu Yan's father had gone into the innkeeping business after failing the examinations, and that his son is devoted to continuing the "scholarly" tradition of the family. What is notable is that the morally positive characters in this story are stereotypically coded as literate. This is at odds with Lu Yunlong's preface and Li Zhi's commentary, as we have noted above in the case of Tang Guimei's characterization. Moreover, like Guimei, Zhu Yan can be said to be a victim of filial piety. His inability to mend his mother's ways is his curse. Yet no mention is made of him thereafter.

The most conspicuous difference between Yang's biography and Lu's vernacular version is the more sympathetic characterization of widow Zhu. The graphic description of the mother-in-law's physical abuse of Guimei in the original biography is considerably toned down in the vernacular story (no hot pokers!). The woman's reaction upon discovering Guimei's body is curtly described as one of utmost fright, while the theatrical exchange with the neighbors to explain that she is crying for her loss of money is altogether absent. The "monstrous" mother-in-law of the original biography (to use Katherine Carlitz's term) is thus somewhat humanized in the story.[23] There is an additional episode in the vernacular story, a lengthy flashback recounting how the widow became a woman of easy virtue, which takes a good third of the total story length. This episode reads like a romantic/erotic tale grafted onto the body of the exemplary biography. It might be tempting to read the story as a titillating tale of adultery uneasily masquerading as an exemplary tale. On the contrary, I argue that Lu Renlong is paying homage to the conventions of the *huaben* genre that had accustomed its readers to saucy details and bedroom scenes. In doing so, however, he also adds complexity to the moral characterization. While the description of Mrs. Zhu's sexual adventures may simply be read as a foil to Guimei's virtuous behavior, the choice to show her as an originally demure and proper woman who gradually became corrupted (in the original biography, she was already promiscuous in her youth) is worth analyzing.

The lonely young widow's propensity to sexual arousal is a stock situation in fictional narratives from this period, as Keith McMahon has noted.[24] The narrator even inserts a *fu* poem that portrays widow Zhu's predicament sympathetically. We are far from the lapidary characterization in Yang Shen's biography: "The mother-in-law was cruel and lascivious" (*gu han er yin* 姑悍而淫).[25] The interlineal commentaries, ascribed to a "Hero among women from Qinhuai" 秦淮女中丈夫, remark on the verisimilitude of the depiction ("a true depiction!" *shiqing* 實情, "so true!" *zhen* 真), and later, in the seduction scene, on the craft of the narration ("nicely filled out with vivid details!" *dianzhui yi jia* 點綴亦佳, "describes him as a novice [at the beginning of their affair]" *xushi chu shi wei shengshou* 敘事處是為生手) or on the typicality of the narrative situation ("a marvelous encounter" *qiyuan* 奇緣, "no pain no gain" *haoshi duomo* 好事多磨).[26] There is virtually no moralizing comment in this section. Later, as the narration switches back to the present, the commentator switches gears as well, by focusing on the moral appraisal of the characters ("what a filial son!" *xiaozi xiaozi* 孝子孝子, "The Huizhou [merchant] is what can be called a motherfucker" *Huiren suowei runiangzei* 徽人所謂入娘賊, "she's as firm as metal tempered a hundred times" *bailian jin* 百煉金".[27] So, is the insertion of the "merry adventures" of widow Zhu simply an added embellishment, serving no ideological purpose? While this episode undeniably represents an excursion into a different subgenre (the romantic/erotic), within the larger framework of the moral/heroic tale—a subgenre that seems to be governed by its own rhetoric and stock situations at both textual and paratextual levels, as we have seen—the depiction of the process through which a young widow is seduced also reveals the narrator's interest in analyzing motives.

As expected, the vernacular story also ties up some of the ends left loose in the biography: the corrupt magistrate is dismissed for corruption, the wealthy merchant is caught by the neighbors, the cruel mother-in-law is reduced to poverty (the marginal commentary notes with satisfaction that "there is retribution!" *you baoying* 有報應).[28] What remains unchanged, though, is the fate of the heroine: her shadow is still seen lingering on by the old plum tree even after the villains have been punished. It is only through Yang Shen's biography, as Li Zhi remarks in the commentary, that Tang Guimei finds posthumous (and extradiegetic) vindication.

The story of Tang Guimei illustrates not just chastity, but also filial piety—that particular brand of gender-specific filial piety that is directed toward one's mother-in-law. Indeed, it is *because of* filial piety that Guimei ends up a martyred widow (*liefu* 烈婦) instead of remaining a chaste widow (*jiefu* 節婦). This point is raised in Li Zhi's commentary, a portion of which is incorporated as a tail commentary to the vernacular story:

> The two words "filial piety and heroism" are the distinctive stylistic touch of the great historian Yang [Shen]. Guimei's death is heroic indeed! But what does filial piety have to do with it? This is because the reason why Guimei preferred to die rather than clear herself was her mother-in-law. Otherwise, why would she not express her burning anger and hatred toward the merchant who had tried to win her over by means of bribes, and instead chose to endure death in order to conceal the truth?
>
> 孝烈二字, 楊太史特筆也。夫貴梅之死, 烈矣。于孝何與? 蓋貴梅所以寧死而不自白者, 以姑之故也。不然, 豈其不切齒痛恨于賄囑之商, 而顧忍死為諱哉?[29]

In Yang Shen's biography, Tang Guimei's unconditional adherence to the principle of chastity is never questioned; rather, it is the tacit assumption on the basis of which the tragedy unfolds. There is thus an implicit hierarchy between chastity and filial piety. While the first admits no doubt, the second is implicitly questioned. Guimei faces the *hypothetical* choice to either adhere to the principle of filial piety unconditionally, or not (I call the choice *hypothetical* in that she is shown to have no hesitation in acting the way she does). Her predicament is that she can either be filial de jure or de facto, but not both. Were she to speak the truth, the *legal* charge of unfiliality could have been cleared, but in so doing, her mother-in-law's reputation would be sullied, and thus Guimei would *in fact* be acting unfilially. This paradoxical situation may in itself constitute a critique of the perversion of the legal system that made it possible in the first place. But it also questions the validity of unconditional adherence to a social bond regardless of the worth of its object. It is precisely this state of affairs that is ruthlessly manipulated by the mother-in-law.[30]

In the vernacular story, the conflict is more squarely between chastity and filial piety, as articulated in Lu Yunlong's preface. Significantly, Guimei's course of action is not presented as self-explanatory. The biography already featured Guimei's relatives and neighbors (qindang 親黨) as a dramatized, if minimal, audience that gives Guimei the chance to explain her reasons, but the vernacular story greatly elaborates their role and significance. Guimei's kin and neighbors are constantly observing, judging and misjudging, criticizing and commending. It is precisely in this discursive frame constituted by kin and neighbors that the validity of values is tested. The standpoint of the neighbors is that of "common sense" and even common justice as opposed to the absolute ethical imperatives in the mental world of the heroine. A neighbor named Li Zhi (Li the Straight) reproves Guimei, saying, "*She* [your mother in-law] may be inhumane, but *you* are acting against justice. Not only has that old slut been keeping a lover for herself, but now she has also framed you on trumped-up charges. The scoundrel Wang has been scheming to take other men's wives, and has instigated this lawsuit. Tomorrow let's all go to the circuit intendant to plead for a redress!" 她不仁, 妳不義。這樣老淫婦, 自已養漢, 又要圈局媳婦, 誑告。汪蠻謀占人家婦女, 教唆詞訟, 我們明日到道爺處替她伸冤。[31]

The vernacular story also introduces the character of the maid, Xiaomei 小妹, who plays a small but significant role within the discursive frame. Xiaomei voices the argument of expediency when she tries to persuade Guimei to give in to her mother-in-law by arguing that since she lives in such a dubious household, no one will believe that she is chaste anyway. As the interlineal commentator remarks, such reasoning (the logic of "might as well") has ruined countless people.[32] It is to Xiaomei, and not the chorus of neighbors as in the original biography, that Guimei reveals her reasons and articulates her dilemma:

"When my husband was about to pass away I swore that I would continue my duties to the family and keep chaste to him—how could I forget my former promise out of fear for the present suffering? But now, the neighbors down the street are determined to fight mother on my behalf. They would clear me from the charge of unfiliality, but by doing so, they would attach a bad reputation onto mother as an unchaste woman, and how could that do? I am unable to serve and support her as instructed by my husband, how could I bear to defame her on top of that?"

「丈夫臨終, 我應承守他, 斷不失節。怎怕今日苦楚, 忘了? 只是街坊上鄰舍, 為我要攻擊婆婆, 是為我洗得個不孝的名, 卻添婆婆一個失節的名, 怎好? 我不能如丈夫分付奉養她, 怎又污衊她?」[33]

Ironically, the well-meaning neighbors contribute to precipitating the heroine's choice to commit suicide. Yet on a different level, kin and neighbors, in their capacity as witnesses, constitute also the necessary link between the often voiceless martyr and the literatus, whose unfailing presence characterizes these accounts. Li Zhi's commentary quoted at the end of the story (partially quoted earlier) captures the complex link between female heroism and male writing most powerfully. Li draws attention to the written biography as a form of *cultural capital* for both the narrated subject and her family, and the author of the biography. Particularly in the case of women from obscure families, having a biography written by a national celebrity such as Yang Shen would play a tremendous role in propelling their case toward official recognition, or, beyond official court reward, literary public fame.[34] The writer also invariably dons the garb of the sympathetic and morally enlightened individual. These carefully crafted biographies would often be included in the collected writings of that author, or find their ways into various anthologies and compilations, thus further cementing the fame of their author. Tang Guimei's chastity and filial piety are not simply celebrated as such, but rather used as a pretext to criticize the shortcomings of corrupt officials, such as the muddle-headed magistrate Mao. Her exemplarity is also used as a foil to indict the crowds of phony, fame-seeking officials who would pay a fortune to have their biography written by such celebrities as Yang Shen—yet failed to obtain one.[35]

Lu Yunlong's own brief final commentary highlights the cleverness (*qiao* 巧) by which Guimei was able to preserve her chastity without compromising her mother-in-law. This is not dissimilar to the praise bestowed on other virtuous exemplars who combine integrity with sagacious deliberation. And yet the adjective, *qiao*, sounds very much like a merely cerebral appreciation. The death of Guimei, seen in this light, sounds like little more than an ingenious solution to a puzzle in moral casuistry, quietly discussed by a circle of literati friends on a placid afternoon.[36]

∾

The plot of "Injustice to Tang Guimei" is paralleled and amplified in the second story from *Bell in the Still Night*, "The Beauties and the

Bumpkins" (full title: "The Country Boors Profligately Enjoy the Twin Beauties, The Limpid Stream Engulfs Two Precious Jades" 村犢浪占雙嬌, 潔流竟沉二璧, QYZ 2). In fact, the story of Tang Guimei is explicitly mentioned in the final commentary.[37] Here we have not just one, but two virtuous daughters-in-law, Niu Sannuo 鈕三娜 and Gu Xiaoda 顧小大. Chen-shi, the lascivious mother-in-law, has several lovers who seem to conveniently come in pairs, and whose moral fiber is progressively more debased. Unlike Tang Guimei, Niu and Gu are not widowed, but their vile husbands, significantly named Hu Youren 胡有仁 and Hu Youyi 胡有義 (which could pun with "Has no humaneness" and "Has no sense of duty"), turn out to be just an added curse. The husbands are often away from home, and when they are present they side with their mother. They are the particular targets of the author's criticism.

Niu and Gu's drama of moral choice is thus rendered more exacerbated and absurd than Tang Guimei's. Their dilemma is between the conflicting demands of fidelity to their boorish husbands, and filial piety toward their depraved mother-in-law. Both virtues are thus absolutized and decoupled from their object. Ritual duty is severed from any hint of contamination with notions of reciprocation (*bao*) and affection (*qing*). Guimei's husband was also portrayed as a rather spineless figure, but their brief conjugal life was depicted as blissful and harmonious, and even sexually satisfying for both parties (so much so that widow Zhu's lust was roused when she overheard the sound of their lovemaking).[38] On the other hand, widow Zhu is depicted in a more sympathetic light than in the biography, as we have seen. But in "The Beauties and the Bumpkins" no such redeeming elements are found.

The social milieu is lower than "Injustice to Tang Guimei." The men in the Hu family are stonemasons. Niu Sannuo's father is a poor peasant, while Gu Xiaoda's is a tofu peddler. None of the characters in this story can read or write. In this sense, the unfailing presence of the sympathetic literatus (in this particular story, Zhu Ziqiang 朱子強) becomes all the more necessary.[39]

There is no court trial, no torture or imprisonment, but the domestic inferno skillfully portrayed in this story feels all the more perverse in its quotidian horror. The affection and sorority that develops between the girls is the only redeeming element. It is this sense of communion and like-minded spirit (*tongxin* 同心) that is praised by the commentator in the end as the most extraordinary facet in this story.

Death thus becomes the only possible outcome, and the two sisters-in-law's shared decision, preparation, and execution are movingly described. Yet, one wonders, to what extent can such extreme choice be seen as the heroic enactment of moral norms externally imposed? And to what extent can it be read as a self-affirming gesture and vigorous denunciation of the debased reality that surrounds them? One of the most disturbing details is that Niu is six or seven months pregnant when she decides to commit suicide. It is this element that problematizes her action—and by extension, her like-minded sister-in-law's action as well. Their suicide thus reads like a final gesture to affirm their loyalty not so much toward their husband or mother-in-law, but to themselves and their own sense of personal integrity.

The Suicide Widow and Her Mother

The plot of "The Heroic Woman and Her Mother" (full title: "A Heroic Woman Endures Death and Commits Suicide to Follow Her Husband, A Wise Lady Sets Aside Her Feelings to Let Her Daughter Fulfill Her Intent" 烈婦忍死殉夫, 賢媼割愛成女, XSY 10)[40] is very slim. The heroine, Chen Zhi'er 陳雉兒, is a dutiful wife and daughter-in-law whose husband dies after only two years of marriage. Zhi'er is determined to commit suicide to honor her husband, against the counsel of everyone around her, including her in-laws and natal family. She finally succeeds after several failed attempts. Just as in the story of Tang Guimei, this story is based on a classical language biography explicitly mentioned in the conclusion. This is the "Biography of Heroic Woman Gui" 歸烈婦傳, by Gui Zimu 歸子慕, the younger son of the famous literatus Gui Youguang 歸有光 (1507–1571).[41] It is purportedly a firsthand account of events that occurred during the late Wanli era (the heroine was the wife of the author's nephew).

Save for an episode about a temple pilgrimage inserted at the beginning, the vernacular story follows the classical language source very closely. Throughout the text, Zhi'er is simply referred to as the "heroic wife/martyr widow" (*liefu* 烈婦) instead of by her personal name—a usage reminiscent of the exemplary biographical genre. The narrator even adds the conventional hagiographical motif (absent from the source text) of the birth of the heroine marked by an unusual dream of her mother.[42] More significantly, the discursive frame, here constituted by the mother, the parents-in-law, and other relatives and servants who witness the event, was already present in the source text, though it is further elaborated and dramatized in the vernacular story.

Chen Zhi'er's first suicide attempt is narrated in an arresting scene. As her husband is lying dead on the bed, Zhi'er wails loudly, then catches sight of a sword lying by the pillow and grabs it to slash her throat. Because the blade is dull, she only manages to inflict a superficial cut before she is stopped by her mother, while the mother-in-law hurries to snatch the sword. This fast-paced sequence of actions is immediately followed by a formal speech in which Zhi'er enumerates her reasons for committing suicide lucidly and dispassionately, as if she were speaking in front of a judge.

> "There are four reasons why I ought to die. First, I have no children who need my care, and who may be a source of attachment for me. Second, mother and father-in-law are well on in years, so later on I will have no means of support. Third, I am only twenty-two years old, and the days ahead are far too many. Fourth, mother and father-in-law have their own children who will take care of them, so there is no need for my service."

> 我有四件該死: 無子女要我撫育, 牽我腸肚, 這該死; 公姑年老, 後日無有倚靠, 二該死; 我年方二十二, 後邊日子長, 三該死; 公姑自有子奉養, 不消我, 四該死。[43]

The contrast between the fast, messy actions and loud cries on one hand and the composed and eloquent speech on the other is jarring. Zhi'er's poise seems to preempt the kind of condescending dismissal of female suicide as irrational, irresponsible, and selfish found in eighteenth-century literature and legislation about such acts, as eloquently analyzed by Janet Theiss.[44] The possibility that the widow's suicide could be construed as a case of "treating life lightly" was ever present. In the Qing dynasty, a Kangxi edict of 1688 deplored wives who took their lives after their husband's death and in the absence of other extenuating circumstances. Another edict by Yongzheng in 1728 argued similarly for the superiority of chaste widows over those who chose suicide.[45] But anxiety about the definition of proper and improper suicide and different gradations of virtue was already widespread in the Ming. Zhi'er's reasons echo with the instructions that the famous loyal minister Yang Jisheng 楊繼盛 (1516–1555) left behind for his wife on the eve of his execution. As Yang wrote, only those women who had no children could be entitled to end their own lives to follow their husbands. If a widow were to commit suicide even though she had young children to raise, she would be dying a useless death (Yang uses the metaphor of the swan's down, borrowed from the celebrated "Letter to Ren An" by Sima Qian). She would be considered a "woman who does not understand the higher principle!" 不知道理的婦人.⁴⁶

Another vernacular story included in *Rocks Nod Their Heads* entertains the argument that a lifetime of chaste widowhood is in fact more arduous, and thus more exemplary, than an impetuously committed suicide. In the story "Lu Mengxian Looks for His Wife on the Yangzi River" 盧夢仙江上尋婦 (*SDT* 2), Li Miaohui 李妙惠 is forced to remarry by her parents-in-law after her husband is mistakenly thought to be dead.⁴⁷ Seeing that Miaohui is determined to commit suicide rather than go along with the remarriage plan, her in-laws seek help from Miaohui's aunt, widow Fang. The glib-tongued Aunt Fang persuades her niece to desist by reminding her of her duties toward her late husband, arguing that to commit suicide would deprive her in-laws of the financial income they would obtain from her new husband, and also expose them to public infamy (they would be accused of having driven their daughter-in-law to suicide). Moreover, Aunt Fang argues, it is far more difficult to be a chaste widow than a heroic one, since the former requires a lifetime of effort and sacrifice, while the latter is done quickly and on the spur of the moment.⁴⁸ However, the discourse of virtue is ambiguously used in this story as a rhetorical tool to serve a morally questionable cause (the in-laws are characterized as greedy and unenlightened)—unlike what we see in Chen Zhi'er's story.

After Zhi'er has enumerated her reasons, her mother Zhou-shi reminds her that her husband's own parting words had encouraged her to return to her natal home and look after her mother, who had no other offspring. Zhi'er retorts that those deathbed words are not to be taken seriously. Rather, she argues, what counts are the words that her husband had once said to her, on a night when they overheard the pitiable laments of a neighboring woman, a childless young widow. On that occasion, her husband had said that it would have been much easier for her to commit suicide and be done with it, instead of enduring a lifetime of misery and temptation.

Lastly, it is Zhi'er's parents-in-law's turn to try to dissuade her from committing suicide. They appeal to the argument of reputation and official recognition. In particular, the father-in-law mentions the living example of her great-aunt, Mao-shi, who had successfully endured a lifetime of chaste widowhood, and was now being awarded an official recognition. But Zhi'er refuses to yield to such argument, protesting that "Everyone has their own allotted share of fortune and misfortune. Mother and Father, you are both advanced in years, while I am still young. With such a long stretch of months and years ahead, it is impossible to foresee the turn of events. How could I dare to look up to great-aunt [as a model to emulate]? Better to die and be done with!" 「人各有幸有不幸, 今公姑都老, 媳婦年少, 歲月迢遙, 事變難料。媳婦何敢望祖姑, 一死決矣。」[49]

These lines, as in Zhi'er's other speeches throughout the story, are lifted almost verbatim from the original source.[50] As a result, the heroine is speaking in (almost) classical Chinese, a rhetorical strategy that could signify the level of detachment of a heroine who no longer partakes of the (vernacular) world of the living.[51] It could also be read as a symbolic gesture to signify that the kind of exemplarity embodied by the heroine is, or remains, otherworldly—it cannot be fully integrated, assimilated, and translated into the vernacular world inhabited by the other characters, and, by extension, the readers. The efficacy of state rewards to promote or validate virtuous behavior is also questioned in other stories, as we have already seen. Lu Renlong is generally suspicious of the official reward system, on two main accounts. First, honors are all too often unjustly distributed, privileging rich and powerful families who were well connected with the official channels of power.[52] Second, official rewards would seem to encourage a pettily utilitarian mentality. Lu Renlong's stance comes close to that of the rigorous moralist, according to whom people should be rewarded because they do good, and not do good so that they may be rewarded. The irony in Chen Zhi'er's story is that in the end she still gets rewarded by the state for her chaste martyrdom.[53]

In the final analysis, though, feelings are the hardest to suppress. What makes this story remarkable is its exploration of the relationship between mother and daughter. As in the story of Tang Guimei, this story stages a conflict between chastity and filial piety. However, the angle of the narration and human emotions described are entirely different. From a ritual point of view, the bond between biological mother and daughter is seen as much diminished after the daughter's marriage, even though historical records about actual practice suggest a different picture. The bond between mother and daughter is here described as purely emotional and affective, which makes the tragedy all the more gripping. As it turns out, it is not the mother who wins over her daughter's suicidal determination, but rather the daughter who manages to turn the mother from an antagonist to a helper. It is very hard to forget the climactic scene in which the mother hears the unmistakable sound[54] made by her daughter, who has just hanged herself:

> At this moment, the flow of air in Zhi'er throat was obstructed, and as the knot around her throat tightened she made a loud, gasping sound. Her mother had heard everything, and

thought: "This girl really does not want to live anymore!" So she pretended not have heard, and she fiercely gagged her mouth with the blanket.

此時咽喉間氣不達，擁起來吼吼作聲。他母親已是聽得他，想道：「這人是不肯生了。」却推做不聽得，把被來狠狠的嚼。[55]

Zhi'er's mother-in-law, however, also overhears the sound and immediately comes to rescue Zhi'er. The other family members are bewildered and reproach Zhou-shi for failing to hear her daughter even while sleeping in the same room. They misunderstand her (in)action, in the same way that they temporarily misunderstand (and even malign) Zhi'er's actions.

The heroine's eloquent speeches and calculated determination, her ability to counter each of the arguments made to persuade her not to take her life—ranging from filial duties toward her in-laws and natal family, to the lure of official rewards and the concrete example of a chaste widow within her own clan, and even her husband's deathbed instructions—are a powerful evidence to support modern scholars' claim that it was individual women who concretely defined the content of the chastity code, often in defiance of parental or state instructions and expectations.[56]

The most significant, if somewhat indirect, critique of the figure of the heroic widow comes from the narrator, not the commentator. In both the prologue and the conclusion of the story, Lu Renlong argues for a fundamental equivalence between the heroic (*liefu* 烈婦) and the chaste widow (*jiefu* 節婦). He writes:

> Nowadays everyone says that "it is easy to sacrifice one's life fervently, but it is harder to do so serenely."[57] They don't know that those women who have the mettle of a chaste widow would surely be capable to act as a heroic one, and likewise, those who have the spirit of a heroic widow, would surely be able to steadfastly maintain their purity like a chaste widow.

如今人都道慷慨易，從容難，不知有節婦的肝腸，自做得烈婦的事業；有烈婦的意氣，畢竟做得節婦的堅貞。[58]

In denying that there is any fundamental difference between a heroic and a chaste widow, the narrator questions the inevitability of suicide. Just as in the loyalty stories discussed in chapter 3, the argu-

Female Exemplarity and the Violence of Virtue 123

ment suggested here is that chastity does not necessarily entail suicide.

In the preface to the story, Lu Yunlong seems to be as interested in celebrating the story and the story's author as he is in celebrating its heroine. He writes, "a formal eulogy in parallel prose, or an official plaque to commemorate chastity and martyrdom cannot measure up to Lu Renlong's so many words [i.e. his vernacular adaptation], which can disseminate the story of the heroic woman to places far and wide, and consign her to eternal glory." 然而一篇四六呈, 一個貞烈匾, 又不如君翼數語, 能播烈婦于遐荒, 垂烈婦于不朽矣.[59] The celebration of the heroine is indissolubly tied to the celebration of the male writers (and here in particular, the vernacular writer) who have spun the woman's life into an extended narrative.

The Faithful Widows of the Xiao Family

The sixteenth story in *Exemplary Words*, "The Faithful Widows of the Xiao Family" (full title: "Three Chaste Widows from Neijiang Stay Loyal, Two Orphans from Chengdu Succeed in the Exams" 內江縣三節婦守貞, 成都郡兩孤兒連捷, *XSY* 16), is a tale of chaste widows and exemplary mothers. Different from the previous stories, this story draws two of its virtuous heroines from the usually forgotten ranks of concubines. This is the only story among those discussed in this chapter that ends happily for the women involved. Yet as a narrative text it is the least successful of the three, which is due in large measure to the absence of villains or conflict.

In the story, Xiao Teng 蕭騰 and Xiao Lu 蕭露, two brothers from a gentry family, have a wife, a concubine, and a son each, named Shijian 世建 and Shiyan 世延. The two brothers die in close succession, but not before urging their respective concubines to remarry. But the concubines, Chen-shi and Li-shi, refuse to leave the Xiao family despite the initial pressure from the principal wives, their own parents, and the crowd of matchmakers. Before long, Yin-shi, the principal wife of the elder brother, also dies. The three remaining widows join forces in raising the two orphans and overseeing their education. In due time, the orphans pass the examinations with distinction. They get married and have successful careers.

The classical source is once again a biography by Yang Shen titled "The Two Virtuous Women of the Xiao Family from Neijiang County" (*Neijiang xian Xiao-shi shuangjie ji* 內江縣蕭氏雙節記).[60] In his vernacular adaptation, Lu Renlong departs from the biography in one major respect: he does not focus on the concubines only, but he turns Wu-shi, the principal wife of the younger brother, into a female exemplar on a par with Chen-shi and Li-shi.

As noted, there is no villain and no conflict in the source text. In the vernacular retelling it is the discursive frame, here consisting of a handful of bad advisors, that comes closest in function to a villain—if a rather ineffective one. The bad advisors include Wu-shi's younger sister, the concubines' natal family members, and the meddlesome matchmakers. Wu-shi's sister repeatedly tries to dissuade her from encouraging her husband to take a concubine, and, later, from treating the concubine too well, lest she becomes arrogant and unruly. But Wu-shi does not pay heed, and proceeds to sell her jewelry to procure the concubine, Li-shi, and to welcome her into the house. For her unperturbed determination and ability to turn off the "background noise," the commentator praises her in hyperbolic terms: "For letting all the chatting and nagging go by her ears unheeded, Wu-shi can truly be considered a holy sage among virtuous wives!" 家庭之變多起于旁人唆聳, 而吳氏任耳邊瑣瑣而不聽, 真賢良之神聖矣！[61] While Wu-shi's sister and her colorful tirades are clearly meant to have a comic function, the grim scenarios of domestic disharmony she paints to dissuade her sister are all too real—down to the case of a neighbor's wife who was driven to commit suicide after her husband became infatuated with a concubine.

The parents of the concubines, too, try to persuade their daughters to remarry, insisting that they are still young—and moreover one of them, Chen-shi, is still childless, while the other, Li-shi, though she bore a son, would still not have any entitlement in the Xiao family.

The matchmakers, together with the other professional category they are frequently paired with in these stories (doctors), are the target of the authors' satire. Matchmakers are collectively depicted as meddlesome, untrustworthy, and glib-tongued. Moreover, they loudly compete against each other, just like the charlatan doctors who hasten the poor brothers to their death. These matchmakers belong to an altogether different universe, as remote from that of the main heroines as a gentleman (*junzi*) is from a petty man (*xiaoren*), as one interlineal comment points out.[62] One of the elements of the exemplary nature of these three women is their unflinching resolution, and their imperviousness to gossip and evil advice, as Lu Yunlong notes in the first of two tail commentaries.[63]

In spinning out this exemplary tale, Lu Renlong is not free of bitter undertones. This is a story of spectacular success: all parties involved are duly praised and officially rewarded, the widows with official honors, the sons with successful careers. Yet Lu Renlong seems to bitterly remark that the final success is contingent on the perfect functioning of a just system. He makes a comparison between the now and then, that is, the Chongzhen reign and the Jiajing reign. While in the Jiajing reign examination officers were relatively just and honest, the present times are dominated by all kinds of cheating and abuse.[64] Lu Renlong suggests that even sons raised by mothers as exemplary as those of Mencius or Ouyang Xiu would fail to become successful officials under the present corruption.

In the tail commentary, which is uncommon for its openly autobiographical quality, Lu Yunlong praises his own mothers (he is the son of a concubine who has raised five children together with the main wife). His mothers, he laments, are as virtuous as the widows of the Xiao family, but no biographer has conferred immortality on them.

∼

The stories discussed in this chapter have been criticized by modern Chinese scholars for their depiction of what are perceived as suffocating female exemplars. In striking contrast with the sympathetic portrayal of "fallen" heroines in *San Yan* stories or other late Ming collections such as *Antagonists in Love* (*Huanxi yuanjia* 歡喜冤家), in *Exemplary Words* "women are made into sacrificial victims at the altar of feudal morality," as one Chinese scholar has put it. Yet, and contrasting somewhat paradoxically with this kind of reading, the same stories have also been praised as *realistic* depictions of the predicament of women under the tremendous social and psychological pressures of the time.[65] While it is obviously erroneous to judge these texts on the basis of modern notions of ideological "progress" or "regression," or according to feminist criteria, the second kind of fallacy—the tendency to read and mine fictional texts as if they were accurate accounts of historical or sociological reality—is perhaps more insidious. These are, after all, literary texts—texts that articulate visions of female exemplarity, which are determined and shaped as much by historical reality as by rhetorical conventions. At the same time, these stories *can* give us a depiction of evolving mentalities and discourses around values and normative behaviors.

These stories paint a conservative image of female exemplarity, which is in line with the biographical texts from which these stories are derived. Still, by populating the stories with noisy neighbors and onlookers, the author breaks the silence and diffuses the pathos around the solitary heroines of the biographical texts. Their moral choices are made at once more arduous and more transparent: more arduous because of the contrast between the logic of common sense and expediency voiced in the discursive frame and the intransigent observance of ethical imperative embraced by the heroines, and more transparent because the reasons and motives behind the heroines' choices are made more explicit in the process. At the same time, the author also explores the domestic repercussions of extreme moral choices, such as in the story of Chen Zhi'er where the mother-daughter relationship is brought to the forefront. Unlike the case of the loyalty stories, Lu Yunlong prefaces and tail commentaries do not seem to be as concerned with investigating the nature and implications of fidelity, be it heroic or chaste. Rather, the commentator is more interested in celebrating the *stories*, and those stories' authors, that celebrate female exemplarity. Prose accounts of the lives of these women are deemed to be superior even to the official honors and plaques conferred by the emperor, about which both narrator and commentator express ambivalence and skepticism. This self-celebratory gesture is a familiar component of the discourse on female chastity in the late Ming.

Chapter 5

Interchangeable Brothers

It is perhaps not a coincidence that two "derivative" anthologies published at the eve of the Ming fall placed a story of exemplary brothers as their first piece. The popular *Extraordinary Spectacles Old and New* (*Jingu qiguan* 今古奇觀, ca. 1640), which comprises a selection of stories from *San Yan* and *Er Pai*, opens with the story of the three virtuous Xu brothers (originally XSHY 2).[1] *Illusion*, the anthology that appropriated stories from *Exemplary Words* and whose preface was discussed in the introduction, opens with the story of the selfless Yao brothers (originally XSY 13). The fragility and inherent ambiguity of the brotherly bond makes it an ideal starting point in these fictional projects that aim to reaffirm traditional relationships and role-specific duties.[2] Typically listed as the fourth, or sometimes third, of the Five Cardinal Relationships, the bond between brothers stands in a somewhat curious middle ground. There are two distinct connotations in the traditional notion of *ti* 悌 or "brotherliness." In the first connotation, *ti* can be translated as the "brotherly deference" the younger brother should ideally have toward his elder brother(s). As stated in the *Mencius*, the relationship between juniors and seniors should be based on the principle of precedence (*xu* 序).[3] With this meaning, *ti* 悌 is treated as an ancillary virtue of filial piety, with which it is often discussed in one breath as *xiaoti* 孝悌 (filiality and brotherliness). If in the parallel conception of society the bond between father and son is naturally extended to the relationship between ruler and subject, brotherly deference is seen as the basis for deference toward elders outside the family—the foundation for an orderly and harmonious society.[4] Another important connotation of *ti*, however, cuts across this strictly hierarchical conception, and it emphasizes instead an idea of harmonious and mutual relationship between brothers. In this second meaning *ti* may be translated as "brotherly affection" or "brotherly love," and it is sometimes grouped together with the paradigmatically egalitarian and voluntary bond of friendship, as *youti* 友悌.[5] This more egalitarian notion of brotherly bond is reflected in property inheritance laws, which generally provided that all brothers had an equal claim to the family assets in spite of the inequality of status.[6] This principle was reaffirmed by the Ming founder Zhu Yuanzhang.[7] Rather than this legally based equality of claims, however, the notion of brotherly love is best embodied in the ideal of the *frérèche* family, with married brothers living together *without* division of family assets.

The notion of fraternity as egalitarian is confirmed in Alfonso Vagnone's *Illustrations of the Grand Dao* (*Dadao jiyan* 達道紀言, 1636), a collection of moral sayings organized by the Five Cardinal Relationships. This work devotes an unusually large space to the fraternal relationship, which is placed third, after the ruler-minister and father-son bonds. Actually, a great majority of the entries in this section are devoted not to relationships between blood brothers, but rather to those between younger and older.[8] The former entries stress the idea of harmony, balance, mutual help, and mutual yielding[9]—all qualities that are central to the stories of exemplary brothers discussed below.

The blurring of boundaries between brotherly bond and friendship is usually understood as a movement *from* the friendship bond (an egalitarian, horizontal, hence potentially dangerous relationship) *to* the brotherly bond. That is to say, friends can become "brothers," as illustrated in the widespread practice of sworn brotherhood. However, one is left to wonder about the extent to which it may have operated the other way around, namely that the ideal brotherly bond could be modeled on exemplary friendship, which was greatly valorized in the mid and late Ming (see chapter 6).[10]

In one conception, the bond between brothers is thus perceived as strictly hierarchical and it is often collapsed with the father-son relationship; in the other, it is configured as a horizontal relationship characterized by amity and reciprocal support—something that presupposes interdependence and, from a narrative point of view, *interchangeability* of the characters. The reason for the relative paucity of exemplary brothers in fictional stories—notwithstanding the prominent position given to two such tales in *Illusion* and *Extraordinary Spectacles*—may thus be both ethic and aesthetic. There are stories of exemplary brothers in which the younger brothers are represented as de facto filial sons of the elder brother who, in turn, has symbolically replaced the dead or missing father. Such is the case with the story of Xu Wu and his brothers (to which I will return below), and with some of the tales in the literary language collection *Samsara Tales to Awaken the World* (*Lunhui xingshi* 輪迴醒世, early seventeenth century).[11] Other stories conversely represent brothers who take turns yielding property or positions to one another, or who gladly replace each other in jail, as in the story of the Yao brothers, which was placed first in *Illusion* (originally *XSY* 13).[12]

Stories of estranged brothers are more numerous. In early southern drama, plots of estrangement and reconciliation typically featuring an evil older brother opposing a virtuous younger brother seem to have been quite popular (for example in plays such as *Killing a Dog to Admonish the Husband* or *Shagou quanfu* 殺狗勸夫 and *Little Butcher Sun* or *Xiao Sun tu* 小孫屠). In contrast, such reconciliation is not often granted in vernacular stories from this period—in fact some stories even depict fratricide.[13] These tales of brotherly estrangement are a clear inversion of the stories of exemplary brothers. The cause of falling out among brothers is typically greed and disagreement over the inheritance—the reverse of the ideal amicable relationship depicted in the exemplary stories. Many of these stories dwell on protracted and unsavory legal battles and fall into the "court case" or *gong'an* category. And whereas in exemplary stories the brothers are often cast as "friends," in tales of estranged brothers, friends and brothers are seen as competing figures, and the friends usually turn out to be no friends after all.

Exemplary Brothers

Among the rare stories of exemplary brothers is "The Yao Brothers" (full title: "To Repay His Teacher's Kindness, a Student Clashes with the Local Bully; A Younger Brother Takes the Older Brother's Place in Jail" 擊豪強徒報師恩, 代成獄弟脫兄難, *XSY* 13). The story tells of two brothers, Yao Juren 姚居仁 and Yao Liren 姚利仁, who are equally upright and chivalrous. They take classes with the local teacher Fang Fangcheng 方方城. Their classmates are the studious but poor Hu Xinggu 胡行古, and two good-for-nothings, the rich Fu Ergu 富爾縠 and Xia Xue 夏學, his hanger-on. When teacher Fang dies his pupils pay their respect at his house, and it is during that occasion that Fu Ergu catches sight of the teacher's beautiful daughter, Huiniang 慧娘, whereupon his lustful appetites are immediately whetted. The scene is described with grotesque humor: at the sight of the girl "his eyes popped straight out like a crab's, while his entire body went as soft as a slug" 雙隻眼直射似螃蟹,

一個身子酥軟似蜓蝣.¹⁴ Xia Xue promptly concocts a plan to make the girl Fu's concubine: he convinces the widow to accept money and gifts from Fu Ergu as a loan, only to claim later on that it was in fact a betrothal gift. The widow refuses to acquiesce since Huiniang had already been promised to Hu Xinggu, and she returns all the money to Xia Xue, minus five taels that had already been spent for the funeral expenses. The Yao brothers immediately take sides with the teacher's family, and Yao Juren volunteers to pay back the five taels within five days.

But Fu Ergu and Xia Xue come up with another trick: they send Fu's servant to the Yaos' to collect the money the very next day, with the result that Juren gets infuriated and shouts at the servant. Meanwhile, Fu and Xia kill another servant who had been gravely ill and accuse Juren of the murder. With the help of the devious Zhang Luo 張羅, who flaunts some legal expertise, Juren is thrown in jail and forced to confess under torture. Liren, however, convinces his brother to let him take his place, so that he can go back home to his newly wed wife and continue the family line. The two brothers look perfectly alike, so that nobody is aware of the exchange. After a few years and after a son is born, Juren's wife convinces him to replace Liren in jail, so that he in turn can get married to the girl he had long been engaged to, and continue his branch of the family line. Meanwhile Zhang Luo has continued to extort money from Fu Ergu since he is in possession of evidence for the murder (he has told the victim's father to hide away the ruler that was used to kill him, and also part of the money that was paid to bribe the coroner). As a result, Fu is gradually ruined. One day Zhang inadvertently spills out the truth to Hu Xinggu, who has by now become a magistrate. Fu Ergu, Xia Xue, and Zhang Luo are duly punished and Yao Liren is released and reunited with his family.

The prologue of "The Yao Brothers" is significant for the way it frames the story as an exemplary tale. It opens with the customary poem, which laments the "ways of the world" where brother turns against brother, and invites the reader to consider instead the example of virtuous brothers from the past. The prose section that follows is an elaboration of both motifs present in the poem. There is first a short argumentative section that deplores the all-too-common enmity among blood siblings, and enumerates the common causes: the parents' partiality for one son over another, the influence of petty wives who do not get along with their sisters-in-law, the influence of bad friends or meddling maids and servants. The argumentative section concludes with a pantheon of brotherly paragons (only partially overlapping with the figures mentioned in the poem): Sima Guang 司馬光, who showed unwavering deference to his older brother even after he had become a top official;[15] Zhao Li 趙禮, who offered to be eaten by the starving bandits in lieu of his elder brother, arguing that he was plumper;[16] the three Tian 田 brothers, who decided not to divide the family property when the redbud tree in their courtyard suddenly withered; Niu Hong 牛弘, who was not bothered when his younger brother shot his ox; Sun Chong'er 孫蟲兒, who forbore his elder brother's abuse with a happy face; Wang Lan 王覽, who protected his older stepbrother Wang Xiang's 王祥 from his mother's attempt to murder him.[17] In this impressive list of brotherly exemplars, famous historical people such as Sima Guang are cited side by side with semilegendary figures such as Wang Lan or the Tian brothers, and with entirely fictional characters such as Sun Chong'er, who is featured in the play *Killing a Dog to Admonish the Husband*. The list ends with a reference to Zheng Lian 鄭濂, an early Ming historical figure who was officially honored for his filial and brotherly behavior. There is general praise of the Ming as a dynasty that most highly honors these twin values (here referred to as *xiaoyou* 孝友). The story of the Yao brothers is then introduced as a natural supplement to these illustrious precedents, only closer in time to the author and his audience.

After reading the story, however, one may wonder about the relevance of the argumentative section of the prologue. As it turns out, none of the common pitfalls in the path of virtuous behavior listed here plays a role in the story. Virtually no mention is made of the parents, except that they die early on. Liu-shi 劉氏 and Ru Huan 茹環 are both flawlessly virtuous wives and sisters-in-law: Ru Huan refuses to be married to somebody else after her fiancé Liren is sent to prison, while Liu-shi takes her into the family and urges her husband to replace his brother in jail. As for the influence of bad friends, one may say that the brothers are too self-righteous to have any. So what was the point of mentioning all these? While it is a rather common narrative device in short stories to present in the prologue an instance (or several instances) that are opposite to the case narrated in the main story, here no *case* is given. The argumentative section is purely so, no historical or fictional anecdote is invoked. What the narrator is pointing his finger at here is thus unmistakably the actual world of the reader, his lived or witnessed experience. This section ends with an apostrophe to the reader—a rhetorical strategy relatively rare in *Exemplary Words*: "Let me ask you: aren't brothers born from the same womb? Aren't they made of the same flesh and blood from their parents? How is it possible that [the relationship among them] could become distorted so?" 試問人, 這弟兄難道不是同胞? 難道不同是父母遺下的骨血? 為何顛倒若此?[18] This point is also echoed in the preface, where Lu Yunlong expresses the wish that the callous ones would break into a cold sweat once they read this story.[19]

The past exemplars are thus explicitly introduced as a *repertoire* of models of conduct, rather than as a single uniform mold to which the reader ought to conform: in times of peace you should be like A, in times of turmoil you should be like B, younger brothers should be like X, older brothers should follow the footsteps of Y, and so on. The narrator does not unconditionally praise all the famous exemplars: he has for example a caustic judgment of the Tian brothers who, in his view, "do not really amount to real men. How can they fail to make up their own mind, instead of waiting for a plant in order to be stirred?" 他不是漢子, 人怎不能自做主張, 直待草木來感動?[20] There is no further attempt on the part of the narrator to bridge the gap between the reality of the audience's life and the flawless behavior of the brothers in the story—this may in part account for the relative lack of appeal of this story. The two brothers ultimately remain rather indistinct and wooden figures.

Feng Menglong's story "Three Devoted Brothers Win Honor by Yielding Family Property to One Another" 三孝廉讓產立高名 (*XSHY* 2) also presents a portrait of exemplary brothers. This story tells of Xu Wu 許武 and his two little brothers. Having lost his parents, Xu Wu finds himself in charge of managing the family property and raising his brothers. He accomplishes both tasks admirably by supervising the work in the fields during the daytime and painstakingly instructing his brothers at night. He thus gains a reputation as a virtuous brother, which leads to his appointment at court. After a few years of meritorious service, Xu Wu resigns to return home and arrange for his brothers' marriages, as well as his own. He then proceeds to divide the family property. To everyone's surprise he does so most inequitably, by appropriating the best house, lands, and servants for himself. His younger brothers, however, accept his terms without a word of complaint. Because of this, the reputation of the younger brothers is now spread far and wide, and they are soon appointed by the emperor. It is only after the two brothers have had in turn their chance to make a career that Xu Wu reveals that he had intentionally divided the property unequally. He then gathers the neighbors and village elders to redo the division, this time in an equitable manner.

The story is set in the Han dynasty. Indeed, one of the running themes is the comparison between the golden age of the Han and the lamentably corrupted times of the narrator and his readers. As the narrator eagerly explains in the numerous asides, the Han had a wonderfully fair system to recruit officials, in which recommendations based on reputation of personal integrity played a crucial role. Ironically, the story of Xu Wu deals precisely with the skillful manipulation (if for a virtuous end) of that allegedly most sound system. Public opinion is a protean entity. When the village elders are called to redo the tripartition of family property and see that all three brothers keep demurring and trying to yield the best share to one another, they start to suspect that they are only "hypocrites fishing for fame" 便是矯情沽譽.[21] The story can thus be read as a subtle commentary on the debate on the notions of "fake" and "genuine" (*zhen* 真/*jia* 假) and the ambiguous nature of fame (*ming* 名) that preoccupied the minds of many late Ming literati.

In terms of characterization, the Xu brothers may be said to encompass both aspects of ideal brotherly bond delineated earlier, that is, "brotherly deference" and "brotherly affection," but there is never a blurring of identity between the figure of the elder brother Xu Wu and the two younger brothers. Their relationship is highly asymmetrical. Xu Wu remains the singular and uncontested hero throughout the story, unlike the Yao brothers, who are by any measure mutually interchangeable figures.

Estranged Brothers

Evil brothers fighting over property or being led astray by bad friends or greedy wives are more common stock in vernacular stories.[22] Let us first take a brief look at two sample stories of bad brothers from *San Yan* and *Er Pai*, before discussing a remarkable story of brotherly estrangement from *Bell in the Still Night*.

Both Feng Menglong's "Magistrate Teng Solves the Case of Disputed Inheritance with Ghostly Cleverness" 滕大尹鬼斷家私 (*YSMY* 8) and Ling Mengchu's "The Deceitful Accomplice" (*EK* 16)[23] feature greedy brothers who try to cheat their younger brother(s) out of their rightful share of inheritance, only to end up being outsmarted. In "The Deceitful Accomplice" the protagonist Chen Qi 陳祈 is loath to share the rich family property with his three little brothers, and he is persuaded by his rich and devious friend Mao Lie 毛烈 to mortgage the best lands to him. The plan is to redeem the lands from Mao Lie once the division has been done, so that Chen Qi can enjoy them alone. But Mao Lie in turns cheats Chen Qi, and the dispute is only solved in the underworld court. In the story, Chen Qi's younger brothers have no voice at all. Chen Qi is only allowed a partial redemption after he pays his dues. Ironically, his close association with Mao Lie is depicted at the beginning as being "closer than blood siblings" 勝似同胞一般.[24]

If Chen Qi is allowed to regain at least some measure of the reader's sympathy after he becomes in turn a victim of deceit, Ni Shanji 倪善繼, the elder brother in "Magistrate Teng," is depicted as a ruthless and unfeeling man throughout the story. Shanji is not outsmarted by an evil friend but by his own father, who had set up a plan to ensure that a generous share of the family inheritance would go to his younger son, whom he bore in his old age. In the prologue of the story, the narrator deplores the brothers who fall out with each other over family property, by arguing that it is foolish and unfilial. In the commercialized world of the narrator and his audience, family bonds are seen as being in direct competition with material possession, and are appraised in terms of gain and loss. The narrator argues for the much higher value of a harmonious brotherly bond compared to land property. The well-worn metaphor of brothers as one's hands and feet (*shouzu* 手足) is here reactivated: "Fertile lands and wealth, if lost, can be won back some day, but loss of a brother is no less than loss of a hand or a foot that would leave you maimed for the rest of your life." 譬如良田美產, 今日棄了, 明日又可掙得來的; 若失了個弟兄, 分明割了一手, 折了一足, 乃終身缺陷.[25] Ultimately, greed over family property almost always leads to a third party taking advantage of the situation. Here the third party (the proverbial fisherman who takes advantage of the clam and the snipe fighting with each other) is Magistrate Teng, who deftly pockets a much more substantial "commission fee" than the one Prefect Ni had promised in his secret testament.

~

The mood of the eighth story in *Bell in the Still Night*, "Fratricide in the Rear Garden" (full title: "Insensate Words Lead to Murder, Steadfast Endurance in the End Redresses the Injustice" 狂言竟至殺身, 堅忍終伸大怨, *QYZ* 8), is vastly different from the light and at times flippant tone of Feng Menglong's story. The story is framed as an exemplary tale of a virtuous widow who manages to avenge her husband's murder; indeed the second half of the story focuses on the figure of Qian-shi 錢氏, the youngest brother's widow, and her sons. Of particular interest, however, is the first half of the story, which offers one of the most memorable depictions of brotherly estrangement. There is a fratricide, and there are Cains—but there is no Abel. Even though the youngest brother is brutally murdered, he is no innocent victim. In fact, the narrator sharply condemns him as an arrogant fool who has brought disaster on himself.

The characterization of the brothers is very different from those in Feng Menglong's or Ling Mengchu's stories. Ling in particular plays with literary types; Chen Qi's younger brothers have no voice at all. By contrast, when reading "Fratricide in the Rear Garden" one has the distinct impression that the author is working with actual characters and events, however filtered through a literary lens. Unlike the stories discussed above, the cause of brotherly estrangement is not simply money. Rather, the influence of wives and friends, deplored in the prologue of "The Yao Brothers," is here given full dramatization. But other factors, not mentioned in other stories, are analyzed as well, such as differences in temperament and a rise in the family fortune. The author is interested in providing us with a sociological portrait, and the story could be read as a bitter commentary on the dark side of upward mobility within one generation.

The story tells of three brothers of the Shui 水 family, Bojin 伯繙, Zhongwei 仲帷, and Shumian 叔冕. This is how the gradual process of mutual estrangement is depicted:

> When they were young and they played together, even if the elder brother was at times bossy, and if the younger brothers were a bit disobedient, they would not make too much of it. Once the fight was over, they would make peace again, and nobody would bear a grudge. By the time they reached fifteen or sixteen years of age, when the elder brother lectured the younger ones, they would sometimes be bothered by his haughty condescension; and when the younger brother started to display some signs of talent, the older brothers would on occasion resent his insolence. But this too did not matter much. It was only when they got married that their three "strands of entrails" became six (i.e. spirit of division set in). Now, among the sisters-in-law, there are those who give themselves airs on account of family background, others who flaunt their good looks, others still who boast their fat dowry, and there are also those who are overly proud of their talent and skills. Add to this parents-in-law who indulge in foolish favoritism, and servants and maids who are adept at sowing discord, and calamity is sure to follow.

在小時節，弟兄頑耍，大的或者僭些強，小的或者有些不遜，都無成心，爭過便好，不致嫌隙。到了十五、六歲，為兄的教訓些語言，為弟或者嫌他做大；為弟的略露些圭角，為兄或者嫌他凌上，這也還不碍。一到到了做親，前番三條肚腸，如今六條肚腸了。妯娌之間，有把家世自矜的，有挾人品自是的，有擁粧貲自尊的，有恃才技自滿的，又加起公姑妄有重輕，奴婢好為搬鬭，這翻却不好了。[26]

As the narrator tells us, the three wives of the Shui family come from different backgrounds, as they joined the family at different moments in the father's career. Gao-shi, the eldest brother's wife, married into the family before the father earned his *juren* degree. She is from a poor Confucian family and has a petty and money-loving nature. Wang-shi, the second brother's wife, is from a rich landowning family. Qian-shi, wife of the youngest, entered the family at the apex of the father's career, and she is thus from an old and prominent family (*shijia* 世家).

The brothers' temperament and education are likewise variously molded by the different stages of their father's career. The eldest brother Bojin, who has grown up during the humble days of his father's career, is not interested in studying. He is socially inept and only good at guarding the family treasure. Zhongwei, the second brother, is only slightly more talented and has established a reputation for himself mainly through family connection and money. Shumian, the most talented of the three, has had the advantage of an early education. As a result:

> Bojin accused his younger brothers of not knowing the hardship of farming labor, and not having a clue on how to manage a household. Zhongwei derided his big brother for his miserliness and Shumian for his frivolity. For his part, Shumian looked down upon his elder brother's vileness and his unwillingness to enjoy his good fortune, and scorned his second brother for being a humbug without real talent.
>
> 伯縉說這兩弟不知稼穡艱難, 不曉做家。仲帷笑大兄的纖嗇, 叔冕的輕佻, 叔冕又鄙薄大兄的齷齪, 肚中不亨; 二兄盜名, 沒真實本事。[27]

The wives too have each their own firm share of power within the family. To aggravate the situation, each brother befriends unworthy men, parasites and drinking mates, who help fan the flames of discord. Gradually Bojin and Zhongwei strike an alliance at the expense of the youngest brother. The latter has become more and more unruly. He is often drunk and acts recklessly: he beats up his brothers' servants, chases away the nuns who were visiting Wang-shi, and lectures Gao-shi for whipping a servant who had broken a bowl. Shumian seems completely unaware of his brothers' growing discontent. Even as his wife Qian-shi warns him to be more guarded with his words and actions, Shumian replies nonchalantly, "This is just my nature, ever since I was born! Among siblings, if there are things to say of course they should be said openly. I refuse to play the idiot and the deaf and dumb!" 直是我性生來的, 嫡親弟兄, 有話便說, 我做不得這樣如痴、如聾啞巴的.²⁸

In the end, Bojin and Zhongwei decide to murder Shumian. They lure him into the rear garden and beat him to death, with the help of some family servants. They confront their father with the *fait accompli*, so that he has no choice but to cover for his sons' crime, lest he lose them too. Qian-shi, bringing her three small boys, comes to the garden and is told that her husband was killed by the father on account of his refractory nature. She guesses the truth, but does not utter a word of complaint in order to protect her orphans. She conceals the club with which the husband was murdered, and the blood-stained clothes.

The second half of the story charts Qian-shi's patient plan of revenge. Only after her sons are grown up and married does she reveal to them, on her deathbed, the truth about their father's death. The case is brought to court, Shumian's corpse is reexamined (the attitude toward autopsy is vastly different from Wang Shiming's story discussed in chapter 2), and the brothers, as well as their accomplices, are apprehended. Quite remarkably, the story has an open ending: Bojin is the only one to be put to death, while Zhongwei and the two servants manage to get away. But Fazu, the eldest son of Shumian, is going to file again with the magistrate, and the narrator expresses his certainty that the culprits will be duly punished sooner or later. This unusual ending strongly suggests that the story may be based on an actual court case that was still ongoing at the time of the composition.²⁹

The harmonious relationship among Shumian's three sons may be read as a corrective to the negation of brotherly values embodied by Bojin, Zhongwei, and Shumian himself. The narrator tells us that the boys' early years of education under their mother's strict guidance are nurtured through stories of filial sons and loyal ministers: "Whenever they would come across figures of loyal ministers and filial sons, she would never tire of explaining it in detail, her single-minded devotion poured into the task of raising them to be principled, filial and upright men. Her sons understood this completely." 到那忠臣孝子, 不厭祥細, 一意指引他們要做個有氣節、能孝義的人, 這班兒子也都領會得。³⁰

Ultimately, the golden virtue praised by the narrator is forbearance (*ren* 忍). This is the secret to a harmonious family, as taught by the example of Zhang Gongyi 張公藝 of the Tang, who wrote out 100 *ren* characters when asked to explain by the ruling emperor how his multigenerational family could peacefully live under one roof.³¹ Forbearance is seen not only as the foundation of ethical conduct (倫理所賴) but as the recipe for survival (實亦性命攸關).³² It would be hard to find more compelling reasons to abide by moral norms than those offered in this story, published around 1645.

∽

As we have seen, the brotherly bond is potentially the most vulnerable among the Five Cardinal Relationships, being subject to a curious kind of "double pull." On one hand, brotherly affection is conceptualized as a corollary of filiality in its emphasis on the hierarchical distinction between older and younger. On the other, it fades into a kind of friendship between equals. Stories of exemplary brothers were relatively rare, but stories of brotherly strife were much more common. The last story discussed in this chapter, "Fratricide in the Rear Garden," may be read as a powerful dramatization of the tension between the hierarchical and horizontal conceptions of the fraternal bond—what Adrian Davis has called the "contested nature of fraternity" in late imperial China.³³ The older brothers commit murder by invoking the safeguarding of the family reputation, which is threatened by the younger brother's reckless behavior. But they also justify their murder by brandishing the formidable accusation of unfiliality. In this perspective, the story is a travesty of the classical exhortations to brotherly harmony, and it becomes a tragic caricature of all that can go wrong in such relations. Stories of exemplary brothers conspicuously display what I have called the trope of "interchangeability," emphasizing the idea of equality rather than precedence. But even the story of fratricide, with its complex characterization of the three brothers and its unsympathetic portrait of the victim, stresses their fundamentally equal share of responsibility in the ensuing tragedy.

Chapter 6

Friends in Need and Friends in Deed

As the editors of a recent anthology of writings by the controversial figure Li Zhi have put it, friendship (*you* 友) "was a favorite topic" among late Ming intellectuals.[1] Vernacular stories that feature tales of idealized male friendship are best read against the backdrop of the vibrant debate on the significance of friendship among literati circles in the late Ming. This chapter tackles the following questions: What do the heroes of these stories concretely *do* for each other? How is their friendship constructed as "exemplary"? Is there a perceived tension between friendship and the fulfillment of other normative bonds, such as filial duty, and how is such tension reconciled in the narrative? How do these representations reflect, complicate, or transcend the intellectual debate on friendship that took place in the late Ming? While writers such as He Xinyin and Li Zhi advocated a radical reevaluation of friendship, and attributed cosmic power to it, the vernacular stories discussed in this chapter emphasize the reharmonization or reincorporation of friendship within the structure of kinship and family.

Friendship was traditionally ranked as the last—hence comparatively least important—among the Five Cardinal Relationships. Occupying the somewhat uncharted territory between family (the province of the father-son, husband-wife, and older brother–younger brother relationships) and the state (regulated by the ruler-subject bond), friendship had been treated with suspicion for its potentially subversive implications, while also being exalted for its liberating and nonhierarchical nature. On the one hand, friendship dangerously approached "cliquism" and factionalism (*peng dang* 朋黨). A number of early medieval texts that are often regarded as the earliest "theoretical" pieces on friendship are in fact so many denunciations of its degeneration into cronyism. For example, Zhu Mu's 朱穆 (100–163) *Discourse on Severing Friendship* (*Juejiao lun* 絕交論), Cai Yong's 蔡邕 (133–192) *On the Rectification of Relationships* (*Zhengjiao lun* 正交論), Ji Kang's 嵇康 (223–263) *Letter on Breaking Off Friendship with Shan Tao* (*Yu Shan Juyuan juejiao shu* 與山巨源絕交書), and Liu Xiaobiao's 劉孝標 (462–521) *Expanded Discourse on Severing Friendship* (*Guang juejiao lun* 廣絕交論) find faults with the corruption and degeneration of friendship, and conclude with the speaker advocating withdrawal from such private intercourse altogether.[2] Here, "friendship" (*you*) and "establishing relationships" (*jiao*) refer to "private associations," the nature of which was however very much public in that it could clearly be manipulated, used and abused for political advancement. These texts could be read as emblematic of a period of political division and short-lived dynasties, when volatile political alliances could have fatal repercussions on the lives of famous literati such as Ji Kang. These texts ultimately speak about the choice between service and reclusion faced by literati officials more than they provide philosophical ruminations on the nature of friendship. It is noteworthy that these texts talk about the *severability* of the friendship bond. Unlike filial piety, or chastity, or loyalty, friendship does not admit of an unworthy object and it can and *should* be severed when the friend turns out to be not worthy of this designation.

On the other hand, friendship had also been exalted for its nonhierarchical and reciprocal nature, for its element of agency and deliberation. The ideal friend was perceived as "a critic, a teacher, and a fellow traveler on the Way."[3] Ideal friendship was forged on the basis of commonality of spirit and intent (*tongxin* 同心, *tongzhi* 同志), cutting across social status, age, or provenance (though, in fact, common geographical provenance was one of the most powerful tools of networking).[4] Even so, the subversive potential of a freely entered association was always lurking beneath the surface. According to common rhetoric, man-made bonds (*renhe* 人合) were recast as "heavenly" (*tiansheng* 天生, "bonds one is born into"). For example, marriage was customarily depicted as "predestined affinity" (*yinyuan* 姻緣, *yuanfen* 緣分). As for the ruler-subject relationship, though there was an ongoing debate on its voluntary or involuntary nature, it was generally agreed that a devoted son "owed it to his parents and to the state to serve."[5] Friendship too, in spite of being hailed as the quintessentially egalitarian and voluntarily embraced bond, was not immune to such rhetoric, as shown by the common practice of sworn brotherhood. Through the act of swearing brotherhood, a bond that was originally egalitarian is recast as a hierarchical one, since one always needs to distinguish between an older and a younger brother, based on a predetermined characteristic such as age. This could be seen as an indication of the anxiety generated by a bond that is neither familial nor political. At the same time, however, as we have seen in the previous chapter, the relationship between brothers is itself charged with ambivalence, as it encompasses both a hierarchical conception (seniority) and a more egalitarian one (an equal right to family inheritance), which is dramatized in the trope of interchangeability. Indeed, the fraternal bond is the only one that admits of such permeability with the friendship bond—which would be unthinkable if applied to the parent-child or ruler-minister relationship.[6]

The Late Ming Discourse of Friendship

Some of the traditional views of friendship were subject to scrutiny and debate during the sixteenth and seventeenth centuries. This period witnessed an unprecedented surge of positive re-evaluation of friendship—a surge that some scholars have termed the "cult of friendship."[7] Perhaps this is not surprising: after all the late Ming is the great age of poetry clubs, literary societies, assemblies for the discussion of learning (*jiangxue* 講學), benevolent societies, societies for moral edification (*xingguo hui* 省過會), and so on.[8] Lu Miaw-fen and Martin Huang have both highlighted the crucial role played by the assemblies for the "discussion of learning" (*jianghui* 講會 or *jiangxue* 講學) in the discourse and the practice of male friendship.[9] Such assemblies became vastly popular, especially among Wang Yangming's followers in the mid and late sixteenth century. They were typically held at private academies (*shuyuan* 書院) or monasteries, which were often located in scenic areas away from the hubbub of the mundane world. The popularity and influence of literati assemblies were in turn fostered by the dramatically increased mobility of literati during the latter half of the dynasty. The advancement of the commercial transportation system provided the infrastructure that made it possible to realize the ancient ideal of "seeking friends from the four corners of the world" (求友四方), or "befriending virtuous scholars from all over the empire" (友天下之善士).[10]

The valorization of friendship is a crucial part of a broader argument that sought the reconfiguration of the Five Cardinal Bonds, as discussed in the introduction. In the writings of He Xinyin 何心隱 (1517–1579), a scholar associated with the "left-wing" Taizhou school, friendship is hailed as the highest form of human interaction. In one essay he writes:

"When heaven and earth are in communion, there is great peace. And communion is fully realized in friendship." 天地交曰泰, 交盡於友也.[11] In another piece, "Letter to Ai Lengxi" (Yu Ai Lengxi shu 與艾冷溪書), He singles out the two social bonds of ruler-minister and friends (as opposed to family bonds) as most crucial for the harmonious unification of the world. He writes: "Although father and son, brothers, husband and wife are also relationships that lead to the way succeeding under heaven, it is difficult to employ them to unify all men. Only when the relationship between ruler and minister is in place can the heroes of the world be gathered.[. . .] Only through friendship can the brilliant talents of the empire be gathered." 夫父子昆弟夫婦, 固天下之達道也, 而難統乎天下。惟君臣而後可以聚天下之豪傑.[. . .] 惟友朋可以聚天下之英才.[12] According to He, the paramount embodiments of the two bonds are Yao and Shun, and Confucius respectively. Li Zhi famously summed up He Xinyin's attitude toward friendship as follows: "[Of] the five human relations he discarded all but one, devoting himself entirely to the cultivation of the relation between teacher and friend, and sage and worthies." 人倫有五, 公舍其四, 而獨置身于師友賢聖之間.[13] As Theodore de Bary suggests, here Li Zhi is speaking as much about He as he is speaking about himself.[14] Li Zhi himself devoted a great part of his *First Collection by the Pond* (*Chutan ji*, 1588) to the friendship bond, which he conflates with the teacher-disciple bond.[15] Other prominent thinkers of the late Ming, such as Gu Dashao, valorized friendship along similar lines, sometimes endowing friendship with a quasireligious value.[16]

A crucial implication of the elevation of friendship above the other four bonds is the characterization of the family as a less-than-ideal place for the individual to spiritually thrive. The relatively conservative thinker Lü Kun 呂坤 (1536–1618) developed the argument in this direction. Lü judges friendship as the fundamental bond on which all the other four rest. He writes:

> Friendship is a bond of utmost importance, therefore it is listed side by side with the other bonds such as that between ruler [and minister] and that between father [and son], to constitute the Five Cardinal Relationships. Without friends it is not possible to achieve success in life. A ruler rules by way of laws, and in so doing he is the one who governs us. The father acts through kindness, and "goodness should not be demanded" [between father and son].[17] Brothers are content with getting along, and do not wish to hurt their feelings of mutual affection by engaging in criticism [the way friends would do].[18] Women

are in charge of the domestic affairs, and cannot follow men's pursuits [outside the house]. When there is a fault that needs to be corrected, the son, however much he dares to argue for it, will finally be deterred by suspicions that have to be avoided. When facing a stern teacher, one usually is cautious and restrained, so that it is hard to detect any faults. When at home, one is on intimate and affectionate terms [with his family members], so that serious matters cannot enter the picture. It is only with friends that one can spend a lot of time together, from morning till evening, unlike in the case of the teacher, which whom one only spends limited time. [It is only around friends that] one is not hampered by either affection or moral principles, unlike in the case of family relations, with whom many subjects are taboo. As soon as there is a shortcoming in one's moral conduct, or a slackening in the pursuit of one's goals, the friend will reproach one for it. If one is doing well, the friend praises and urges one [to continue on the right path]. If on the other hand one is in dire straights, the friend comes to the rescue.[. . .] This is why friendship is the basis upon which all the other four bonds rely.

友道極關係, 故與君父並列而為五。人生德業成就, 少朋友不得。君以法行, 治我者也。父以恩行, 不責善者也。兄弟怡怡, 不欲以切偲傷愛。婦人主內事, 不得相追隨。規過, 子雖敢爭, 終有可避之嫌。至於對嚴師, 則矜持收斂而過無可見。在家庭則狎昵親習而正言不入。惟夫朋友者, 朝夕相與, 既不若師之進見有時, 情理無嫌, 又不若父子兄弟之言語有忌。一德虧則友責之, 一業廢則友責之。美則相與獎勸, 非則相與匡救。[. . .] 是朋友者, 四倫之所賴也。[19]

Friendship is presented here as a liberating alternative space in contrast with political duty and with the family, where the individual is inevitably constrained by all kinds of rules. Both feelings of affection and ritual duty are seen as impediments to a frank conversation among family relations. Open and honest conversation is only possible among friends. However, the purpose of such heart-to-heart conversation is strictly conceived in terms of personal moral improvement. It is incumbent on the friend to dispense praise and censure whenever appropriate, in an honest and dispassionate way that is precluded to both kin and teacher. The leisure, freedom, and absence of taboos one can enjoy in the company of friends are here conceived only in morally positive terms. There is no mention of the fact that the same leisure and absence of constraints could be misused and lead instead to mutual degeneration.

While he may not have been aware of the vibrant debate on friendship at the time,[20] Matteo Ricci's (1552–1610) first work in Chinese, *On Friendship* (*Jiaoyou lun* 交友論, 1595), certainly contributed to this debate, and there is ample evidence that the work was widely circulated and read, both as a manuscript and in its printed form.[21] Ricci's choice of subject is also indicative of the contemporaneous interest on friendship in Europe, as testified by the deluge of essays on the topic published in the sixteenth century.[22] Ricci's treatise on friendship is actually not much of a treatise at all. It may be more adequately described as a digest of sayings, or collection of *chreia*, culled from classical authors such as Aristotle and Cicero.[23] The collection of moral sayings *Illustrations of the Grand Dao* (*Dadao jiyan*), compiled about four decades later by another Italian Jesuit named Alfonso Vagnone, also gives prominent space to the friendship bond.[24] While several of the maxims included in Ricci's and Vagnone's compilations resonated with the radical valorization of friendship promoted by literati such as He Xinyin and Li Zhi, the disparate and aphoristic nature of their books also lends itself to resonances with the more conservative stance embraced by the stories in *Exemplary Words*. In the following discussion of the friendship stories in *Exemplary Words*, I will refer to Ricci's treatise, as well as to the pronouncements of late Ming literati on the topic of friendship, in an attempt to put these different texts in conversation.

The discourse on friendship is not confined to prose essays and letters exchanged among elite literati, or treatises compiled by foreign missionaries, but rather spans several genres including poetry, drama, fiction—and short fiction. For example, Kimberly Besio has analyzed the plays and stories on the legendary friendship of Fan Juqing 范巨卿 and Zhang Yuanbo 張元伯 to show how fiction and drama provided an arena "in which an idealized masculine literati identity could be constructed and contemplated."[25] However, if the glorification of friendship in drama and fiction can be considered part and parcel of the "cult of friendship," it reflects a different perspective from the theoretical writings. If literati such as He Xinyin, Li Zhi, and Lü Kun, in spite of individual differences, unanimously emphasized the importance of friendship above and beyond the other four human relations, they did so having in mind a kind of idealized intellectual communion among "fellow travelers on the Way." Vernacular stories, on the other hand, depict a quite different heroics of friendship. The world of these stories is the world of spectacular acts of generosity and selflessness done on behalf of a friend, something that is often found in literature on the *youxia* 游俠 (wandering knights). If anything, it is in the biographies and anecdotes about the followers of Wang Yangming that traces of this heroics of friendship can be found, rather than in their own writings. For example, both Yan Jun 顏鈞 (1504–1596) and He Xinyin were known for their exceptional devotion to their friends. Yan Jun reportedly accompanied an official friend who had been exiled to a distant post (very much like Shi Keli in "Qin Zhu the New Liuxia Hui"). He also went on a "filial quest" to search for and bring back the remains of his teacher-friend Xu Yue after the latter was killed on the battlefield (not dissimilar to Guo Zhongxiang in "Wu Bao'an Abandons His Family to Ransom His Friend").[26]

No discussion of friendship in vernacular stories can ignore the most famous and celebrated friendship stories from Feng Menglong's collections. There are three such stories in *Illustrious Words to Instruct the World*: "Yang Jiao'ai Lays Down His Life for the Sake of Friendship" (羊角哀捨命全交, *YSMY* 7), "Wu Bao'an Abandons His Family to Ransom His Friend" (吳保安棄家贖友, *YSMY* 8), and perhaps the most famous of them all, "The Chicken-and-Millet Dinner for Fan Juqing, Friend in Life and Death" (范巨卿雞黍死生交, *YSMY* 16), on the Fan-Zhang "matter" mentioned above. Several modern scholars have seen these three friendship stories as evidence of Feng Menglong's fascination with the theme of friendship between literati.[27] Yet it is important to distinguish between the Fan-Zhang and Yang-Zuo stories on one hand and the Wu Bao'an story on the other. The first two stories appear in Hong Pian's 洪楩 (fl. mid sixteenth century) collection *Stories from the Qingping Mountain Studio* (*Qingping shantang huaben* 清平山堂話本) of the 1550s, from whence Feng Menglong lifted them to include in his collection of 1620, without making any substantial changes. In contrast, the story of Wu Bao'an was most likely adapted from a Tang classical tale by Niu Su 牛肅 (fl. 804), included in the *Extensive Records of the Taiping Reign* (*Taiping guangji* 太平廣記, 981).[28] It is therefore this story that we should consider more carefully to get a sharper sense of Feng's notion of friendship. At the same time, this story is the only one in this group that deals with the potential conflict between family and friendship ties. I will return to this story in the section devoted to the analysis of "Wang Mian the Exemplary Friend."

Another friendship story in *Common Words to Warn the World*, titled "Yu Boya Smashes His Zither in Gratitude to an Appreciative Friend" (俞伯牙摔琴謝知音, *JSTY* 1), is about the legendary friendship between the Jin official and exquisite zither player Yu Boya and the humble woodcutter Zhong Ziqi 鍾子期, who became the proverbial friend "who appreciates his tune" (*zhiyin* 知音). While this legend is mentioned in a number of ancient texts, the proximate source for the *San Yan* story is probably a vernacular story from the Wanli period, titled "Friendship between the Rich and the Poor" ("Guijian jiaoqing" 貴賤交情), substantially revised by the author.²⁹ The *San Yan* story, like its Wanli source, emphasizes how the friendship between Yu and Zhong reaches across the social divide. However, it should also be noted that the kind of ideal friendship based on the appreciation of music described in the story is no less elitist than the ordinary friendship based on social status. The villagers of the orotundly named Hamlet of Gathered Worthies 集賢村 are ridiculed in one sweep as a bunch of ignorant rustics, and even Zhong Ziqi's father has to admit his lack of "ear."

Most friendship stories in *San Yan* are about relationships that span the chasm between life and death. "Yang Jiao'ai Lays Down His Life" and "The Chicken-and-Millet Dinner" in particular feature supernatural elements to show how the friends' mutual devotion continues after death—indeed can only find its true fulfillment after death.³⁰ By contrast, stories in *Exemplary Words* focus on worldly friendships, on how exemplary friendship can in fact be achieved in this lifetime. Moreover, *San Yan* stories are about legendary characters from the distant past. They often end by narrating how the local populace has built tombs or shrines devoted to the exemplary friends, which are the object of uninterrupted and fervent worship to the present day. In so doing the *public* aspect of these friendships is emphasized. Far from being private affairs, these friendships are publicly celebrated and upheld as models for the populace. In *Exemplary Words*, on the other hand, the Ming is celebrated for producing its own outstanding crop of exemplary friends that update and surpass the models of the past. However, the narrator or commentator still deplore the present times and present people for neglecting the virtue of friendship.

With one notable exception (the story of Wu Bao'an), *San Yan* tales celebrate friendship without calling into question the possible tension between kinship and friendship ties. Yang Jiao'ai and Zuo Botao are conveniently devoid of any family ties whatsoever. Fan Juqing and Zhang Yuanbo have compliant wives (though perhaps Zhang's mother could be seen as an element of dissonance, as she voices the "common sense" opinion that the friend will not show up). In contrast, stories in *Exemplary Words* show how friendship ties not only avoid conflict with family and/or state, but are in perfect harmony with both.³¹

Two important motifs that have been explored in modern scholarship, namely, sworn brotherhood and its links with "gang morality," and friendship as homosexual bonding, will not be addressed here.³² Rather, the focus of the following discussion is the way in which friendship is represented in the stories from *Exemplary Words* as a core value, officially sanctioned. The discussion will focus on two issues: the material dimension of idealized friendship, that is to say, the idea of friendship as performed and embodied through material help, and the position of friendship within the Five Cardinal Relationships system.

Wang Mian and the Domestication of Exemplary Friendship

The focus of this section is "Wang Mian the Exemplary Friend" (full title: "The Friendship Oath Lasts Forever, Two Jade-like Beauties Are Brought Back from a Distant Land" 千秋盟友誼, 雙璧返他鄉, *XSY* 14). When read side by side with "Wu Bao'an Abandons His Family," the story of Wang Mian depicts a model of friendship that, far from being in conflict with the demands of family bonds, is seamlessly integrated with it. Wang Mian 王冕 (1287–1359) is a well-known historical figure from the end of the Yuan dynasty.[33] Most readers are probably familiar with the portrayal of Wang Mian in the first chapter of the eighteenth-century novel *The Scholars*, in which he is depicted as an eccentric recluse, exquisite plum blossom painter, and a most devoted filial son. Lu Renlong, however, ignores these traits to cast Wang Mian as a paragon of loyalty toward his friends. He is described as a man of exceptional talent and erudition, who prefers not to embark on the official career. In Hangzhou, he strikes up a friendship with Lu Tai 盧太 and Liu Ji 劉基 (also a well-known historical figures from the Yuan-Ming transition).[34] Wang proves to be an exceptionally trustworthy friend in two main episodes.

In the first episode, Wang Mian comes to the rescue of Liu Ji, who, having run afoul of a corrupt official, is impeached and sentenced to death. Braving the ire of the Mongol Chancellor Toghto 脫脫, Wang submits an eloquent memorial in defense of his friend. As a result, Toghto not only releases Liu, but even offers a position to Wang Mian. But Wang refuses, predicting that calamity will soon strike. In the second episode, Wang comes to the rescue of his other friend Lu Tai, who is serving in Luanzhou, a remote city in the north. Lu Tai has fallen ill, and shortly before dying he sends a letter to Wang imploring him to look after his two daughters. Wang promptly sells his possessions and hurries to Luanzhou. Once there, he finds that Lu Tai's older daughter has sold herself into the family of a local Mongol magnate to pay for her father's funeral expenses, while the younger daughter and a servant are reduced to begging. Wang manages to ransom the elder daughter for a dear price; he then brings his friend's remains and the two girls back to their hometown Hangzhou. He later ensures that the girls are both married to respectable scholars.

This story does not provide much insight into the nature of the friendly bond between Wang Mian, Lu Tai, and Liu Ji. We are not even told how their friendship begins, and we are given only a glimpse of what they do together—there is one passage in the story where the friends are described as roaming around the scenic spots of Hangzhou, and enjoying themselves in a wine-and-poetry gathering by the West Lake. Rather, the story emphasizes that friendship is to be gauged by the extent to which the hero is willing to help his friends in distress.

This point is made most explicitly in the story preface by Lu Yunlong: "If friendship is not shown in times of distress, where else can it be shown? Could it be that [you can discern friendship] only while sharing wine cups or when hanging on to those who are in power? That is why in discussing friendship one should really use this model." 然友不在淪落中見, 于何處見? 祇在酒杯趨附中歟? 故論友者當以此為法。[35]

A similar down-to-earth approach to friendship is captured in a maxim in Matteo Ricci's *On Friendship*. The fifth entry reads: "When life is peaceful and without trouble, it is difficult to distinguish the true from the false friend. Only when difficulties arise do the true feelings of a friend reveal themselves." 時當平居無事, 難指友之真偽。臨難之頃, 則友之情顯焉。[36]

This entry is a reworking of Cicero's proverbial passage in his treatise on friendship, *Laelius De Amicitia*: "Amicus certus in re incerta cernitur," (lit. The true friend is discerned during uncertain times), usually rendered by the English proverb "A friend in need is a friend indeed" (which nicely captures the alliteration of the Latin original).[37]

The point that friendship can only be tested in times of trouble may in itself sound vapid and clichéd, just as any proverb can be seen at once as a distillation of ancient wisdom and a banalization of it through countless, often cursory, repetitions. However, if we read this passage against the backdrop of the literati debates mentioned earlier in this chapter, we can begin to see it in a different light. This passage can be read as a reaction against the excessive intellectualism and abstraction of the various "essays on friendship." One may well praise the cosmic power of friendship, but in the end it is only at times of sore need that genuine friendship can be told from false, that is, from a relation based merely on profit and interest. Moreover, like the now less common variant of the English proverb, "A friend in need is a friend *in deed*," this is not merely a restating of ancient wisdom but an active reinterpretation.[38] By underlining the necessity of testing friendship through material help and concrete action in times of hardship, Lu Yunlong suggests that what matters to the author is not so much providing a philosophical answer to the question "what constitutes true friendship," but rather to show what friendship *does*, and by extension, what it *should do*. Most notably, the rhetoric of disinterestedness pervasive in literati debates is here reconciled with a notion of friendship as commensurate with—indeed, almost quantifiable by—the extent to which one is willing to sacrifice for a friend in times of difficulty. This is expressed in terms of specific amounts of money or a measurable material sacrifice (such as a long and arduous journey).

Here we see a departure from the more famous stories of exemplary friendship in the *San Yan* collection. *San Yan* stories are typically about friendship in life and death (*shengsi jiao* 生死交). In the story of Fan Juqing and Zhang Yuanbo, Zhang kills himself just so he can make the appointment with his friend who lives far away (the assumption being that ghosts can travel much faster than humans). By contrast, "Wang Mian the Exemplary Friend" depicts a this-world friendship in a more realistic setting, with real-life situations. Further, this story explicitly addresses the relation of friendship to other cardinal relations, notably political duty and family ties. In spite of his traditional aura as a recluse, at the end of this story Wang Mian is depicted as a supporter of the Ming founding. Thus Wang's reclusion is portrayed as a matter of political loyalty (even if it is a proleptic one, thanks to Wang Mian's gifts as prognosticator) rather than an absolute choice.[39]

The idea that friendship ties can span the service vs. reclusion divide contrasts with the spirit of the medieval letters on "breaking off relations" mentioned earlier. There does not seem to be any apparent conflict between friendship and loyalty here. Both Lu Tai and Liu Ji serve as officials under the moribund Yuan, while Wang Mian refuses to serve—and yet the friendship between them is not in the least compromised.[40] Such a coexistence of different political choices among close friends may perhaps be read as a reaction against the excesses of political factionalism witnessed during the Wei Zhongxian era and its aftermath—that is, the time when these stories were published.

There is one moment in the story, however, where Wang Mian seems to entertain the possibility of serving even the Yuan. On his way to rescue Lu Tai in Luanzhou, Wang Mian runs into the Yuan army sent to crack down on the bandits.[41] He is once again offered a position as military advisor by the Mongol Chancellor Toghto. Wang refuses on the account that he has to help his friend. In declining the offer, however, there is one moment of hesitation. When Gong Bosui asks him to become Toghto's advisor and thus help them defeat Zhang Shicheng, Wang Mian replies:

> "Sir, with an overbearing minister at court, how can a general, however mighty, accomplish anything at the frontier? Now, if he succeeds in the campaign, he will be suspected of 'having enough power to threaten the ruler'; if on the other hand he fails, this will immediately cause malicious tongues to wag. This is just the dilemma of Chancellor Toghto lacking the basis to either go forward or retreat. But even so, since I enjoyed the undeserved honor of a brief acquaintance with the Chancellor, it would only be fitting that I should put my efforts to serve him. However, my friend has passed away in Luanzhou, leaving behind two daughters, whom he has entrusted me to escort back to Hangzhou. Chancellor Toghto here still has you, sirs, to assist him. Those two girls in Luanzhou, however, have no one else to rely on."

> 「先生，焉有權臣在內，大將能立功於外？今日功成則有震主之威，不成適起讒譖之口，方為脫公進退無據。雖是這般說，小生辱脫公有一日之知，當為效力。但是 我友人歿在灤州，遺有二女，托我攜歸杭。脫公此處尚有公等，二女灤州之托，更無依倚。」[42]

Wang Mian's verbal jugglery reminds one of Gao Xianning's equally astute way of disengaging himself from Yongle's request to take office, while at the same time fending off his accusation of wanting to bury the remains of an executed traitor, in the story "Tie Xuan and His Daughters" discussed in chapter 3. More importantly, however, here the famous recluse seems to be considering for a moment the possibility of serving the Yuan, not out of a sense of political loyalty but due to a bond of *personal* acquaintanceship with the Chancellor Toghto, to whom Wang owes the favor of rescuing his friend Liu Ji.

The second and main episode of the story, in which Wang Mian rescues Lu Tai's daughters, turns to the relation between friendship and family ties. This is also dramatized in an anecdote included in the prologue to the story. The anecdote relates how Du Huan 杜環, also a historical figure from the early Ming dynasty,[43] welcomes in his home the mother of his late father's friend. The lady had found herself with nowhere to go after her son's (Du Huan's father's friend) death. Although she did have another son, he had completely abandoned her to her own fate.

Du Huan gladly takes the old lady in and treats her with unswerving devotion for no less than twenty years. After she dies, he buries her with all the proper rites due by a filial son toward his deceased parent. In both this anecdote and Wang Mian's rescuing of Lu Tai's daughters in the main story, the emphasis is not on helping the friend himself but rather the friend's family, either upward in the family's hierarchical scale, as in the case of Du Huan, or downward as in the case of Wang Mian. Friendship ties seem to provide here a convenient surrogate for the exercise of filial duty for both Du Huan and Lu Tai's daughters.

In a fascinating detail, the narrator tells us how Du Huan, and his equally virtuous wife, even have to put up with the old lady's pettiness and irascibility, once the woman had grown too comfortable in her position as "mother" and "mother-in-law." "As time went by, Zhang-shi began to forget that she was just a guest, and she even put up her old airs of grand lady of the house, quick-tempered and exceedingly demanding. Yet Du Huan and his wife did not mind it in the least." 那張氏習久了, 卻忘記自己流寓人家, 還放出舊日太奶奶躁急求全生性來, 他夫妻全不介意。[44]

The old lady's overbearing attitude toward Du Huan and his wife does not result in a rift or termination of their relationship (as one would normally expect of a friendship tie). Rather it is met with the perfect subservience of a filial couple. In this anecdote, we have the transformation of a bond originally based on a twice-removed friendship tie (Zhang-shi being the mother of Du Huan's father's friend) into—for all practical purposes—an actual kinship tie.

What the Du Huan anecdote does not entertain as a fictional possibility (a possibility in the moral imagination) is: What would happen if Du's mother were still alive and around the house? Or if her other son were virtuous and filial? Such a narrative possibility is explored in Feng Menglong's story "Wu Bao'an Abandons His Family," to which I shall now turn. The story tells of two men, Wu Bao'an and Guo Zhongxiang. Although they never met, Guo Zhongxiang helps Wu Bao'an to get a post in the army where he is serving. Before Wu is able to take up his post, however, the army is badly defeated, and Guo is taken prisoner. There is no one to pay the exorbitant ransom the barbarians require for his release. For ten years, Wu Bao'an works indefatigably to save enough money to ransom Guo, all the while abandoning his own wife and son. Several years later, after he is released, it is Guo Zhongxiang's turn to help his friend. Wu Bao'an had died while serving in a distant town. Guo brings back his friend's remains to the latter's hometown for proper burial, and he takes care of his friend's son, finding him a job and a wife and dividing his estate with him.

As the synopses suggest, the two stories seem to stand on opposite ground when it comes to the relation between friendship and family obligations. The story of Wu Bao'an seems to pit the two directly against each other. Yet I argue that this story does so in a more ambivalent way than its title announces. To start with, Wu Bao'an abandons his wife and son, *not* his parents. In the traditional logic of male bonding and "gallant fellow" (*haohan* 好漢) culture, one's own wife and children are often seen as readily expendable for the sake of a friend, as epitomized in the proverb "brothers are like hand and feet, wife and children are like clothes" 兄弟如手足, 妻子如衣服, where "brothers" more often than not refers to sworn rather than actual brothers.[45] Guo Zhongxiang also goes in search of his friend only after he has completed his duties as a son, that is, after his father has died—in fact, there is a hiatus of several years between Guo's release and his sudden impulse to go in search of his friend.

It is rather in the latter half of the story that the contraposition between friendship and kinship ties becomes trickier. Here we have a recounting of Guo Zhongxiang's strenuous pilgrimage to bring back his friend's remains. This part reads like a straight narrative of filial journey: the care with which Guo marks the friend's and his wife's bones and carefully wraps them in silken bags, the extent to which he goes to mourn them after the burial, living in a shed by the grave mound, are all paradigmatic behaviors of a filial son. The problem is, Wu Bao'an *does* have a son, and a very virtuous one at that, unlike the callous son in the Du Huan anecdote. When Guo and Bao'an's son travel back home, a rather comical struggle ensues between the two (in spite of the pathos of the situation)—a struggle over who gets to carry the basket containing the bones.[46] It is this part of the story that contains the most subtle subversion of the relative ranking of family and friendship, whereby friendship is not only in competition with the filial bond but actually usurps it, in that Bao'an's son is practically robbed of the possibility of showing *his* filial piety.

By contrast, in the Du Huan anecdote and in Wang Mian's story, friendship and family ties are seamlessly and unproblematically intertwined. To go back to the Du Huan anecdote, we have seen how Du Huan is the only one willing to provide a shelter for the old lady. Du Huan's sense of duty (*yi* 義) toward his late father's friend's mother stands in for the filial piety that should be there but is missing, just as an artificial limb (also *yi*, as in *yizhi* 義肢) stands in for the natural limb that is missing. Seen from a different angle, Zhang-shi also "fills in" for the missing mother figure, thus completing Du Huan's family. Likewise,

Wang Mian, who had become virtually disentangled from family connections early on in the story (his wife dies, and no mention is made of his parents or offspring), by the end of the story is mourned as a beloved father by his friend's daughters. Friendship becomes here a way to reconstruct a dismembered family. It is shown as complementary to, and seamlessly integrated with, the paradigmatic father-son relationship.

The idea that friendship can be seen on a continuum with filiality is actually found in Matteo Ricci's "On Friendship." "A devoted son will keep the friends that his father has made just as he inherits his father's possessions and property." 孝子繼父之所交友, 如承受父之產業矣。[47] The use of the term *xiaozi* here must be considered an instance of cultural accommodation, as it does not appear in the version included in the late-sixteenth-century collection of sayings consulted by Ricci.[48] It is notable that the Italian Jesuit included this maxim at a rather prominent place, as the fourth entry, after several sayings that illustrate the classical Aristotelian definition of the friend as a "second self" (*di er wo* 第二我) and "half of oneself" (*wo zhi ban* 我之半). However, another maxim that pertains to the relationship between friendship and family ties falls short of similarities with the moral framework embodied in the story of Wang Mian. This entry reads: "Friends surpass family members in one point only: it is possible for family members not to love one another. But it is not so with friends. If one member of a family does not love another, the relationship of kinship still remains. But unless there is love between friends, does the essential principle of friendship exist?" 友於親惟此長焉, 親能無相愛親。友者否。蓋親無愛親, 親倫猶在。除愛乎友, 其友理焉存乎。[49]

While to the Chinese ear this maxim may resonate with the ancient Mencian dicta that "father and son should not demand goodness of each other" and that "it is for friends to demand goodness from each other,"[50] the story of Du Huan represents an illustration of how the boundaries between real kinship ties and surrogate kinship ties based on friendship can become very slippery indeed.

In "Wang Mian the Exemplary Friend," Wang Mian's selfless dedication toward his friends does not find explicit reciprocation, unlike in the *San Yan* stories. This detail suggests a subtle shift toward a valorization of friendship as an intrinsic value. The end of the story is remarkably anticlimactic. We do not see Wang Mian being specifically rewarded for his good deeds. The only reward one can speak of is an extradiegetic one: Wang Mian is celebrated and upheld as an exemplary friend by the narrator and the commentator of this story (who also takes this opportunity to chastise the current moral decay). Moreover, friendship relations are represented as networks of friends, which naturally and harmoniously extend to the friends' family members. Rather than celebrating friendship as an exclusive and idealized relationship that binds two soul mates together across life and death as in "Wu Bao'an" and the other *San Yan* stories, Lu Renlong portrays friendship relations in their larger social context.

Exemplary Friendship and Male Chastity

Another story found in *Exemplary Words*, titled "Qin Zhu the New Liuxia Hui" (full title: "He Retained His Composure Even with a Girl Sitting on His Lap in Order to Fulfill His Friend's Entreaty; He Vigorously Upheld Rightness and Correctness While Opposing a corrupt Minister" (不亂坐懷終友託, 力培正直抗權奸, *XSY* 20), brings to the forefront the theme of resistance to sexual temptation as a test of true friendship. Like "Wang Mian the Exemplary Friend," this story also focuses on networks of friends, and on the idea of helping the friend's friend. The story tells of Qin Zhu 秦燾, a student in the imperial college. On his way back to the capital after mourning his parents, he visits his friend Shi Keli 石可礪 in Yangzhou. Shi asks him to deliver a beautiful "skinny mare" that he has selected as a concubine for his friend, Secretary Dou 竇主事 in Linqing 臨清. Everything is set up for trouble: Qin Zhu is young and unmarried, the girl is ravishing, and the two are traveling by themselves on a small boat. As if that were not enough, their journey takes them through Lake Gaoyou 高郵湖, notorious for its huge and ravenous mosquitoes "as big as geese" 蚊子大如鵝. The girl has to share the bed with Qin since she does not have a separate mosquito net for her bed. Yet despite all these, Qin remains impervious to temptation. When they reach their destination in Linqing, Secretary Dou is understandably unwilling to believe that the girl is still a virgin. However, after he has seen evidence to the contrary, he praises Qin as a new Liuxia Hui, the proverbial paragon of male virtue. Once in the capital, Qin Zhu passes the exams and obtains a *jinshi* degree, not without the help of Dou, who has in the meantime been promoted to a post in the capital. However, because in a memorial he has criticized the policy of the Grand Secretariat, he is demoted to serve in the remote Rong county in Guangxi. On his way to the post, Qin stops once again by Yangzhou. Shi Keli insists on accompanying him on this dangerous journey. When they reach Lake Dongting, they are attacked by pirates. Shi Keli is about to decapitate the pirate leader, but Qin Zhu stops him. The pirate leader then stops his men from slaughtering and pillaging the boat: Qin's good deed immediately pays back!

In Rongxian, the scenery is of utter desolation: the *yamen* is dilapidated, and the staff is composed by a motley crew of scruffy clerks. Shi Keli takes leave of his friend. The local administrator is a country fellow of the minister that Qin had offended, and he immediately becomes Qin's nemesis. He first purposely sends him on a dangerous mission to collect taxes from the recalcitrant Miao tribes. However, it turns out that the Miao village chief is none other than the pirate whom Qin had once saved. With his help, Qin is able to collect plenty of tributes to bring back. The local official then accuses Qin of having received bribes by the Miao tribes. However, his attempts to ruin Qin all come to a naught when Dou arrives in the area, to take up his new post as prefect. Later, Qin receives a series of promotions. In the end, Qin, Shi, and Dou all end up serving in the Yangzhou area.

In the prologue, the narrator launches into praise of true friendship, which is unshaken by the ups and downs of fortune. True friendship stands at the polar opposite of the shallow form based solely on interest, the one decried in the famed "Expanded Discourse on Severing Friendship" by Liu Xiaobiao. The narrator then proceeds to quote a number of famous or infamous examples of friends past and present. Among the former we find Fan Juqing and Zhang Yuanbo, the legendary couple of trustworthy friends who did not forget their "chicken and millet" appointment, and Pang Tong and Sima Hui, who freely went to each other's houses without bothering to distinguish between host and guest. Among the Ming examples, the narrator mentions Wang Shizhen 王世真 (1526–1590) and Yang Jisheng: Wang bravely stood by Yang's side when the latter got in trouble, agreeing to take care of his wife and son after his execution.[51] There was also the case of Ma Shiquan 馬士權 and Xu Youzhen 徐有貞 (1407–1472): when Xu Youzhen was imprisoned, Ma Shiquan, his protégé, protected him. Xu promised his daughter to him, but after being released from jail, he went back on his word. Yet Ma did not resent it at all. The narrator mentions even more recent cases: when Wei Zhongxian was in power, among those who attacked the Donglin members Yang Lian 楊漣 and Zuo Guangdou 左光門 were people who had befriended them; and likewise, when Cui Chengxiu 崔呈秀 and Wei Zhongxian were impeached, among the impeachers were men who had called themselves bosom friends of Wei and Cui. It is noteworthy that here, for the sake of argument, the narrator treats villains and martyrs equally: both were victims of people who had dubbed themselves friends.

This story, partially based on preexisting sources (the episode of the escorted concubine is probably derived from an entry in Tao Zongyi's

陶宗儀 fourteenth-century miscellany *Record of a Break from Plowing*, or *Chuogeng lu* 輟耕錄), foregrounds a theme that was not present in *San Yan* stories, namely the resistance to sexual temptation as a test of friendship.[52] In the preface, Lu Yunlong praises the protagonist for outdoing even the famous paragon of male chastity, Liuxia Hui, arguing that the latter endured the temptation of sleeping with a beautiful girl for one night only, while Qin Zhu endured it through a journey of several weeks. Moreover Qin is deemed superior to the young man from Lu (Luguo nanzi 魯國男子), who refused to give shelter to a widow whose house had been burned down, claiming that he was not as imperturbable as Liuxia Hui.[53] Lu Yunlong's praise of Liuxia Hui and censure of the man from Lu also illustrates the different attitude toward these moral exemplars when compared to the author of *Rocks Nod Their Heads*. In "The Reckless Scholar" (莽書生強圖鴛侶 *SDT* 5), the man from Lu is considered the only plausible model of male chastity, along with Dou Yi 竇儀 (a Song dynasty erudite), while the legend of Liuxia Hui's imperturbability simply "cannot be vouched for."[54] What is seen as an unattainable model of dubious historicity by one writer is considered barely adequate by the other.

Male chastity is a staple attribute of manly heroes, as typified for instance in the figure of Guan Yu from the *Romance of the Three Kingdoms*. In "Qin Zhu the New Liuxia Hui," however, Guan Yu is not even mentioned. Rather, male chastity is tied with success in the examination, a common motif in late Ming vernacular stories that is often linked, sometimes explicitly, with the business of morality books and ledgers of merit and demerit.[55] This story pattern is typically strongly governed by the logic of *bao*. Indeed, for an aspiring official, resisting sexual temptation is tantamount to winning the lottery of moral credit, as no other act of "hidden merit" (*yinzhi*) is considered more arduous to accomplish; likewise, failure to observe restraint inevitably leads to disaster. As we have seen in the other chapters, *Exemplary Words* stories tend to valorize virtue (be it filial piety, or loyalty, or chastity) as an intrinsic value, while maintaining an ambivalent attitude toward the notion of *bao*. This story, then, seems to be an exception. However, unlike most stories of male chastity rewarded with phenomenal success in the exams, *bao* here does not manifest itself as supernatural intervention, but rather as human help. By weaving together the theme of friendship with the pattern of the "chaste scholar rewarded," Lu Renlong humanizes the workings of *bao* while turning friendship into its own reward. That is, by delivering the concubine "in pristine condition" to his friend's friend, Qin Zhu acquires yet another trusted friend, who then helps him pass the exams. Even so, the extent of Dou's help toward Qin is actually quite trivial: Dou simply instructs him to use a cuttlefish bone to erase wrong characters on the exam paper, and to include the phrase "huangdi bixia" 皇帝陛下 (Your August Majesty) in the essay. Moreover, the narrative of the protagonist's success in the exams is interspersed with lively passages of trenchant satire against the corruption in the examination system and the bogus scholars who curry favor left and right to achieve fame and status. Even after his unexpected triumph at the exams, Qin is immediately banished to a dangerous locality for his outspokenness. In other words, the true reward of Qin's moral rectitude is in the friendship ties he has acquired, or reconfirmed, along the way, rather than in a successful career itself.

It is interesting to compare the construction of male chastity vis-à-vis female chastity in this story. The female counterpart of Qin Zhu (and Liuxia Hui) as paragon of chastity is the martyr girl commemorated as "Lady Bare-Sinews" (*loujin niangzi* 露筋娘子).[56] According to the legend, a woman was traveling with her sister-in-law by lake Gaoyou, and they both took shelter for the night in a merchant's boat. While the sister-in-law went to sleep in the merchant's bed to escape from mosquitoes, the woman refused to do so, with the result that she died the same night on the boat, eaten alive by mosquitoes. While male chastity is here represented as sexual restraint in a situation of being in close quarters with a beautiful girl, female chastity simply does not contemplate any hint of physical proximity. Thus the moral temper of the Yangzhou "skinny mare" is highly questionable. The hero's exemplarity inevitably comes at the expense of the girl's probity.

∽

When read against the backdrop of the late Ming literati debate, friendship stories discussed in this chapter reveal a measure of anxiety toward the radical reconfiguration of values proposed in certain theoretical essays. These stories furthermore tend to cast the bond of friendship in quite different terms from the ethereal communion of souls between "fellow travelers of the Way" that is described in the philosophical writings. The figure of the *shi you* 師友 (teacher and friend or teacher-friend) is not altogether absent in stories of exemplary friendship, but it remains relatively rare. Rather than telling of friends helping each other in the arduous process of moral self-cultivation, these narratives favor chivalric exploits of generosity: exemplary friends are those who would find a job for the other, who would risk their lives to save the other from political trouble, who would take care of the deceased friend's children as if they were their own, and so on. In all these tales, the insistence on the physical and material sacrifice and quantified (if only symbolically, rather than literally) monetary disbursement the friends undergo for one another tends to cast the friendship bond in very material terms.

Late Ming writers of tales about exemplary figures needed to silence, even repress, a great deal to construct a serene and ideal model for action. The story "Wang Mian the Exemplary Friend" celebrates friendship while showing how friendship ties do not conflict with political duty or with family obligations—in fact, the aloof recluse may even be coopted into service out of friendship, and friendship ties can function as surrogates for family ties when those are missing or dysfunctional. The moral framework of vernacular stories is often dismissed as simple didacticism (good deeds are always rewarded, bad deeds infallibly punished) in a mechanical application of the principle of *bao*. But the stories discussed here seem to suggest that virtue is its own reward—indeed the only reward for moral action one could hope for—both in these stories and in the troubled historical reality of the end of the Ming.

Concluding Note

The rubric of "conventional morality" hardly captures the spectrum of moral choices and the discourse around these choices articulated in vernacular stories from *Exemplary Words*, *Bell in the Still Night*, and other story collections from the tail end of the Ming dynasty, in the 1630s and 1640s. When read in light of the larger historical and intellectual context, these stories reveal a deep engagement with contemporary debates and an earnest effort to update the classic models of virtuous behavior beneath the apparently naive narrative surface. By examining how the Five Cardinal Relationships and attending virtues are depicted in the stories, I have sought to uncover the specificities to each, as well as the tensions beneath the underlying ideal of the "five relationships completed and perfected" (*wulun quan bei* 五倫全備)—which is also the title of one of the most vituperated moralistic plays from the fifteenth century.

Friendship stories, for example, reveal an anxiety toward the radical reconfiguration of values proposed by sixteenth- and seventeenth-century literati seeking to elevate the friendship bond above the other four bonds, but they also emphasize the material dimension of friendship bonds about which most theoretical essays remain silent. Tales of brotherly devotion seek to give substance to a bond that is always on the brink of disappearing into either filiality or friendship, while exposing the tension between hierarchical and horizontal conceptions of brotherhood. Stories of chaste wives bring the often tragic heroines that late imperial readers had become accustomed to find in biographies and gazetteers onto the center stage of vernacular stories. By staging a crowd of noisy onlookers, these stories cast the heroines' actions and choices as at once more arduous and more transparent than in the source texts. Stories about loyal subjects reveal an intriguing fascination with specific moments of intra- or interdynastic transition, and with narratives of loyalty as a family-wide, rather than individual, virtue, thus avoiding scenarios in which the demands of filiality and political duty clash with one another.

If stories written on the eve of the Ming collapse articulate strategies for compromise and survival, stories published in the aftermath of the Manchu conquest suggest that the spectrum of loyal behaviors has narrowed dramatically. Lastly, tales of filial prowess contain a surprising range of concrete embodiments of this most preeminent virtue within the Confucian ethical system. Some stories betray an anxiety about the breakdown of family units or absence of authority figures by focusing on sons engaged in filial quests to retrieve a missing parent. Other stories portray characters facing impossible choices, such as that between a mother and a father, or between a mother and a wife. And they conspicuously display the body as a surface on which virtue is inscribed, particularly in the case of female virtue stories. Overall the testimony offered by these stories problematizes the still widespread perception of the late Ming as a libertarian, individualistic, and morally decadent era.

Unlike the seventeenth-century didactic novels such as *The Bonds of Matrimony: A Cautionary Tale* (*Xingshi yinyuan zhuan* 醒世姻緣傳) and Ding Yaokang's 丁耀亢 (1599–1669) *A Sequel to Jin Ping Mei* (*Xu Jin Ping Mei* 續金瓶梅, 1662), which show an intense and sustained preoccupation with the workings of retribution throughout their complex plots, vernacular stories about the Five Cardinal Relationships stand in a more ambiguous relationship with the principle of *bao*. The stories seem to be caught between a Mencian vision of virtue as its own reward and the logic of *bao* as *the* preeminent ethic and structural principle of vernacular stories. The authors show skepticism toward the system of official rewards, and do not shy away from stories in which the virtuous hero or heroine ends up succumbing to tragic circumstances. Nonetheless, virtuous behavior is often depicted as readily, even disturbingly, quantifiable in terms of money or physical objects—including body parts—being exchanged, as shown, for example, in "Mother Comes First," "A Slice of Liver for Grandma," and "Wang Mian the Exemplary Friend." Virtue in these stories seems inescapably material.

Arguably, one of the challenges in dealing with short stories is their inherently centrifugal nature, in spite of the authors' effort (itself admittedly unsystematic) to construct macrotextual coherence. Stories, even when curated in a collection, are not necessarily ideologically consistent with each other, nor is the text necessarily consistent with its paratext. In *Exemplary Words* there is often a slight tension between the argumentative sections (which offer explicit evaluative statements) in the text on one hand and the claims of the paratext on the other, over the "correct" interpretation. A case in point is the disjunction between the celebration of the illiterate commoners' moral achievement in the preface and the actual characterization in the story proper as in the story of Tang Guimei, which suggests that the commentator had the original biographical version in mind rather than its vernacular adaptation.

Lu Renlong and Lu Yunlong's stories of moral exemplarity offer a deep insight into what Confucian moral norms might mean to a late Ming reader. Despite the vivid details about examination corruption, village leader malfeasance, judicial malpractice, and general moral decay, they show a firm faith in the power of *exemplarity*, and a strong sense of mission as writers. Ironically, silences too may be telling. The kind of moral scenarios that are skirted, the issues that are passed over, may be representative of all that needs to be silenced and suppressed for the sake of this particular version of *poetic justice*. For example, the conflict between loyalty and filiality is carefully skirted in favor of the family tale motif, while the tension between chastity and filial piety (complicated by the double ties the woman owes to both the natal and the husband's family) is usually solved in favor of chastity. Silence and suppression may also be read as an implicit argument that the dichotomy posited in the proverb "loyalty and filial piety cannot both be fulfilled" is a *false* dichotomy, so long as one is sincere and committed.

A couple of decades later, in the 1660s, Aina jushi's story collection *Idle Talk under the Bean Arbor* offered one of the most trenchant critiques of the very idea of *exemplarity*, not just by debunking revered legendary figures that had become emblematic of particular virtues, but by resisting offering any serious alternative, to revel instead in the "luxury of ambiguity," as Hanan puts it.[1] The virtuous beggar Wu Ding'er in the fifth story, "The Little Beggar Who Was Truly Filial" (Xiao qi'er zhenxin xiaoyi 小乞兒真心孝義), may be seen as an attempt on the part of the author to build a new, post-Conquest filial exemplar. The prologue sets up a familiar contrast between the clever literati who use their knowledge only to become more adept at cheating and abuse, and the illiterate village rustics who have never heard of Confucius or the Duke of Zhou, yet have a firm moral compass and have not lost touch with their "child-like mind and heart." The reader is primed to expect that the impecunious protagonist is going to be just such an embodiment of pure ethical values. But in the climactic dialogue between the filial beggar and the local notable (a high point in the story, as remarked in the final commentary), this expectation is overturned. The notable man had happened to observe the curious ceremony put on by the beggar for his blind mother's birthday, and as he scoffs at the miserly offerings, Ding'er launches in an impromptu lecture on the true meaning of filiality, expounding on the passage from the *Mencius* about Zeng Xi, Zeng Shen (Zengzi), and his son Zeng Yuan.² As Ding'er reminds him, there are two kinds of filiality; the first (the genuine one) is the "nourishing of the will" (*yang zhi* 養志), the second (the lesser one) is the mere "nourishing of the body" (*yang ti* 養體). The supposedly unschooled and socially inferior character does not simply outshine the local notable in terms of virtue, but also in terms of scholarship—he is clearly an allegorical character who revels in the very kind of moralizing the story is supposed to debunk, and who hardly offers an appealing alternative to the Confucian pedants. When the notable, awed by Ding'er "utmost sincerity and purest filiality" (*zhicheng chunxiao* 至誠純孝), hurriedly offers him employment, Ding'er adamantly refuses, arguing for the incompatibility between officialdom and actual filial service, and denouncing the old idea of taking office as a means to bring luster to the family (conventionally considered a superior form of filial piety, vide *Classic of Filial Piety*) as hypocritical. This decoupling of office holding and filial piety (in contrast with *Exemplary Stories*, where the identity or equation between *zhong* and *xiao* had been one of the most cherished tenets) may be seen as an obvious echo of the times, or even as an indirect self-apology of a Ming remnant subject.³

The loyal paragon, too, is sardonically deconstructed in the seventh story, titled "Shu Qi Switches Allegiance at Mount Shouyang" (Shouyang shan Shu Qi bianjie 首陽山叔齊變節). This is a bitter satire of the revered princely brothers Bo Yi and Shu Qi, who refused to serve the rising Zhou and starved to death on Mount Shouyang. Shu Qi is transformed from revered paragon of integrity into an emblem of opportunism. But the story offers an even more troubling satire of reclusion and loyalism, not only in the characters of the phony "mountain people" (*shanren* 山人) who gather at Mount Shouyang following the lead of the famous brothers, but also through the character of Bo Yi. He is portrayed as a rather unappealing emblem of absolute integrity, as someone who is entirely disconnected from the world that surrounds him. From the very beginning, he is described as a man "aloof by nature" (*shengxing gupi* 生性孤僻) and "uncongenial" (*bujin renqing* 不近人情). For these reasons he is deemed unfit to be a ruler by his father, who bequeaths the throne to his younger brother Shu Qi instead.⁴ If Shu Qi's self-justification for seeking service under the new ruler sounds contemptible, Bo Yi's narrow-mindedness is no less risible. While Bo Yi sees the throngs who have gathered up the mountain and who are depleting its supply of ferns as "people who abide by principles" (*shangyi zhi ren* 尚義之人) and even as a good opportunity for the Shang cause to regain its momentum, his brother cynically sees them as people who are "looking for an excuse to indulge their pride" (*jieming yang'ao* 借名養傲) and "pretending to be recluses when they are in fact seeking service" (*tuoyin qiuzheng* 托隱求徵).⁵ In the end, Bo Yi, the paragon of political integrity, is reduced to a pile of desiccated bones in Shu Qi's chilling final remark: "Let me first secure fame in service. There will still be time enough later to collect my brother's bones at the Western Mounts!" 待有功名到手, 再往西山收拾家兄枯骨, 未為晚也.⁶

In recent years, China observers have noted how the traditional Confucian values that were attacked and rejected at several junctures during the violent upheavals of the twentieth century have made what appears to be a spectacular comeback. The impulse to reformulate supposedly perennial moral precepts and revisit supposedly timeless paragons of virtue is certainly very much alive and well in contemporary China. In 2013, the Party-state issued a revised set of the original *Twenty-Four Filial Exemplars*, which exhorts the twenty-first century's aspiring filial children to buy health insurance for their parents, teach them how to navigate the Internet, cook a meal for their elders, and take them on holiday trips—in lieu of tasting the parents' feces, defending them from a tiger's assault, or slicing a piece of flesh to cure them.⁷ It is noteworthy that, much like Hongwu's *Sacred Edict* with which this book began, these newest state-issued moral exhortations are presented as *abstract rules and norms*—they do not tell a story, nor do they offer exemplary heroes or heroines who embody these ideal precepts. But norms and rules remain elusively bland and distant—how many would disagree with either the old injunction of abstaining from "doing evil" or the modern exhortation to cook a meal for one's parents? In contrast, stories can be told and retold, heroes can be admired and vilified, enshrined and trashed. Stories and their heroes take roots in the popular imagination as they continuously change contours and acquire and shed details, simultaneously reflecting and interpreting their times.

Appendix

Exemplary Words and *Bell in the Still Night*

Texts, Editions, Authorship

In 1987, the French sinologist Chan Hing-ho fortuitously rediscovered a woodblock edition of *Exemplary Words for the World* (*Xingshi yan* 型世言) while doing research at the Kyujanggak changsŏ 奎章閣藏書 National University Library in Korea. This edition appears to be missing the first fascicule (*ce* 冊), which probably included one or more general prefaces, perhaps a statement of editorial principles, and full-page illustrations. The full title of the collection as it appears at the beginning of the first *juan* is *Zhengxiaoguan pingding tongsu yanyi Xingshi yan* 崢霄館評定通俗演義型世言, or *Exemplary Words for the World, Vernacular Retellings with a Commentary by Zhengxiaoguan* (the generic designation *tongsu yanyi*, which is usually found in the title of long novels, points to the vernacularization and popular fictionalization of historical texts originally written in classical Chinese). The collection was compiled by Lu Renlong 陸人龍, and edited, commentated, and published by his brother Lu Yunlong 陸雲龍. Chan has persuasively dated the publication of this collection to 1632. While modern histories of Chinese literature tend to lump *Exemplary Words* together with the "later" *huaben* collections (i.e., published during the Ming-Qing transition),[1] the dating of 1632 situates this collection squarely in the heyday of the *huaben* genre. Feng Menglong's immensely influential *San Yan* 三言 (Three Words)—the collective designation of the three story collections *Illustrious Words to Instruct the World* (*Yushi mingyan* 喻世明言, aka *Gujin xiaoshuo* 古今小說, 1620), *Common Words to Warn the World* (*Jingshi tongyan* 警世通言, 1624), and *Constant Words to Awaken the World* (*Xingshi hengyan* 醒世恆言, 1627)—had just been published in the previous decade. The second installment of Ling Mengchu's equally famous *Er Pai* 二拍 (Two Slaps)—the collective designation of *Slapping* the Table in Amazement (*Pai'an jingqi* 拍案驚奇) and *Slapping the Table in Amazement, Second Collection* (*Erke Pai'an jingqi* 二刻拍案驚奇)—came out in precisely 1632.

One striking feature of the Kyujanggak edition of *Exemplary Words* is the presence of individual prefaces for each story, and individualized commentators for each story. The prefaces are clearly set apart from the text of the story proper and written in a variety of calligraphic scripts. The commentators' pseudonyms bear relation to the content of the story. In the aftermath of the rediscovery of the Kyujanggak edition, some scholars took the forty different commentators' pseudonyms as proof of an exceptionally wide readership, encompassing men and women, officeholders and recluses.[2] Other scholars such as Chan Hing-ho, however, have argued that Lu Yunlong was in fact responsible for all the commentaries.[3]

With its forty stories, *Exemplary Words* is the only surviving collection of this size besides *San Yan* and *Er Pai*. Although *Exemplary Words* itself sank into oblivion in China by the early Qing, a great bulk of the stories found its way into other anthologies: the two virtually identical late Ming anthologies *Illusion* (*Huanying* 幻影) and *Slapping the Table in Amazement, Third Collection* (*Sanke Pai'an jingqi* 三刻拍案驚奇),[4] and the early Qing *Alternative Edition of Slapping the Table in Amazement, Second Collection*, known in Chinese as the "Bieben erke" 別本二刻 (or "Bieke" 別刻) edition of *Slapping the Table in Amazement, Second Collection* (*Erke Pai'an jingqi* 二刻拍案驚奇).[5] It was a fate not entirely dissimilar to that of the *San Yan* and *Er Pai*, which were in turn overshadowed by the anthology *Remarkable Spectacles Past and Present* (*Jingu qiguan* 今古奇觀) compiled almost certainly without Feng or Ling's consent. It was only after Chan Hing-ho's accidental rediscovery of *Exemplary Words* that the provenance of all the stories in *Illusion* and *Slapping the Table in Amazement, Third Collection*, as well as twenty-four stories in the "Bieke" edition became clear.[6]

The distinctive paratextual and typographic features in the original Kyujanggak edition of *Exemplary Words* were not preserved in the "Bieke" edition and in *Illusion/Slapping the Table in Amazement, Third Collection*. Both editions reshuffle the order of the stories, often providing new titular couplets, and both get rid of story prefaces and eyebrow commentaries entirely. If "Bieke" still preserves most tail commentaries and occasionally even the name of the commentator at the beginning of the story (but not the redactor), the *Illusion/Slapping the Table in Amazement, Third Collection* anthology does away with both, replacing instead the original commentator and redactor with a duo of compilers (*ji* 輯), Mengjue daoren 夢覺道人 and Xihu langzi 西湖浪子, uniformly throughout the anthology.[7]

Bell in the Still Night (*Qingye zhong* 清夜鐘, c. 1645) is a collection of sixteen stories, only ten of which are preserved in a couple of known editions.[8] Its authorship has been attributed, albeit not unanimously, to Lu Yunlong.[9] Some scholars have even suggested that *Bell in the Still Night* is the second installment of *Exemplary Words*.[10] Based on internal evidence, the work was published around 1645, during the Longwu reign of the short-lived Southern Ming. The surviving stories in this collection are all set in the Ming, and several stories touch on momentous historical events at the end of the Ming: the desecration of the imperial tombs in 1635 (*QYZ* 14), the bizarre episode of the contender to the throne Wang Zhiming after the Ming fall (*QYZ* 4), and the fall of Beijing and the suicide of Chongzhen in 1644 (*QYZ* 1).[11] Some of the stories narrate recent historical events, thus bringing the collection close to the subgenre of *shishi xiaoshuo* 時事小說 (fiction on current events) briefly in vogue during the seventeenth century.

Like *Exemplary Words*, *Bell in the Still Night* appears to be a thematically organic collection of stories. However, in contrast with *Exemplary Words*, the stories do not have an individual preface, nor do they have the abundance of interlineal commentaries and pseudonymous attributions that characterize *Exemplary Words*. Rather, there is a brief tail commentary, generally limited to a line or two. Some scholars have suggested that the author of the final commentaries is none other than Lu Renlong. If the suggestion is true, the two collections would represent a neat reversal of roles among the brothers—a tantalizing instance of the trope of brotherly interchangeability discussed in chapter 5.[12]

As mentioned in the introduction, the Lu brothers were active in the world of commercial publishing in Qiantang (Hangzhou) during the last two decades of the Ming. We have more information on the activity and social network of the elder brother, Lu Yunlong, who ran the fairly successful publishing house Zhengxiaoguan 崢霄館 in Qiantang. His collaborators include scholars from the Hangzhou area—Ding Yunhe 丁允和 (*juren* 1627) and He Weiran 何偉然 (*juren* 1651)—as well as family members, including Yunlong's son Lu Minshu 陸敏樹 (1616–1675).[13] Lu Yunlong's name is also associated with the famed Ming loyalist Li Qing 李清 (1602–1683).[14] Li Qing obtained his *jinshi* degree in 1631 and served in various posts until the collapse of the Ming. He refused to resume service under the Qing. Lu Yunlong published a collection of Li's writings titled *Remnant Records by Master Li Yingbi* (*Li Yingbi gong yulu* 李映碧公餘錄, 1637). In his preface, Lu addresses Li as his teacher, which has led Chan Hing-ho and others to conclude that Lu Yunlong was Li's disciple. Lu Yunlong's son, Lu Minshu, is also associated with Li Qing in the capacity of disciple: Minshu penned a preface to Li Qing's *A Female Tales of the World* (*Nü Shishuo* 女世說).[15] Li Qing's name is associated in another way with Lu Yunlong. Li is the putative author of the novel *An Idle Commentary on Monsters* (*Taowu xianping* 檮杌閑評, 1629),[16] which treats the same subject matter as Lu Yunlong's *The Story of Wei Zhongxian: A Book of Indictment*.

On the other hand, information on Lu Renlong, the younger brother, is very scarce. Like his elder brother, he authored a novel on current events, titled *A Record of Fervent Loyalty in the Liaodong Peninsula* (*Liaohai danzhong lu* 遼海丹忠錄, 1630), which was published by Zhengxiaoguan in 1630. Besides the story collection *Exemplary Words*, he also wrote a preface to the volume devoted to the aphorisms (*geyan* 格言) in the series *Must-Carry-Along Readings, Selected and with Commentary by Cuiyuge* (*Cuiyuge pingxuan xingji bixie* 翠娛閣評選行笈必攜, ca. 1631). He also collated other anthologies published by Zhengxiaoguan, such as *Homecoming to Ming Prose* (*Ming wengui* 明文歸, 1635). However, there is a complete documentary silence on Lu Renlong's activity following the latter publication.

A noteworthy aspect of Zhengxiaoguan's publishing activity is the practice of "calls for submission" (*zhengwen* 徵文, *zhengshu* 徵書). *Exemplary Words* itself might have been compiled by taking advantage of this method, as a scholar has suggested.[17] A volume from the series *Must-Carry-Along Readings*, which appeared around 1631, carries a notice asking readers to submit records of "unusual events," although the title of the intended publication is not specified.[18] A similarly phrased notice appears again in the 1633 edition of the bestselling anthology *Informal Essays by Sixteen Eminent Authors of the August Ming* (*Huang Ming shiliu mingjia xiaopin* 皇明十六名家小品), this time soliciting readers to contribute items for a planned second installment of *Exemplary Words*.[19] The practice of including a call for submission among the prefatory materials seems to have become increasingly common in the seventeenth century, particularly in the case of letter and poetry anthologies and examination essays collections.[20] However, one ought to distinguish between a call for "manuscripts" and a call for "stories" or "news items" as in the case of the notice printed in the *Informal Essays* anthology. In the latter case, readers were conceivably encouraged to submit news items or notation book entries (presumably in classical Chinese), which would then be rendered and expanded (*yanyi* 演義) into full-length vernacular stories by the compiler(s). It remains unclear, however, to which extent stories in *Exemplary Words* or *Bell in the Still Night* did in fact originate from this method, considering that most of the sources for the stories have been identified as literary texts by well-known authors or included in widely circulated compilations.

Notes

Introduction

1. I have used Victor Mair's translation, in "Language and Ideology in the Written Popularizations of the *Sacred Edict*," 327. A fascinating visual and textual document of the spread and popularization of the *Six Maxims* at the local level in the late Ming is Zhong Huamin's 鍾化民 *Illustrated Explanation of the Sacred Edict* (*Shengyu tujie* 聖諭圖解) of 1587, briefly discussed by Mair and fully translated into French by Édouard Chavannes as early as 1903; see Chavannes, "Les saintes instructions de l'empereur Hong-Wou (1368–1398), publiées en 1587 et illustrées par Tchong Houa-min." A photographic reproduction of a rubbing from the stele in the Xi'an museum can be found in Murray, "Didactic Picturebooks for Late Ming Emperors and Princes," 263. Johanna Handlin Smith discusses another example of use of the *Six Maxims* by the eminent member of the literati elite Gao Panlong 高攀龍 (1562–1626) in the context of lectures to community compacts (*xiangyue* 鄉約); see *The Art of Doing Good: Charity in Late Ming China*, 75–78. The sixth story in *Rocks Nod Their Heads* (*Shi diantou*) offers an amusing snapshot of a "popular" use of the *Six Maxims*: the heroine's father Zhou Liu chants the maxims to the accompaniment of clappers (or a bell) as he goes around door to door peddling mats; see *SDT* 6.138.

2. As Peter Bol has noted, the content and wording of the *Six Maxims* closely follows Zhu Xi's instructions to the villagers on how to comport themselves; Bol, review of *The Troubled Empire: China in the Yuan and Ming Dynasties*, by Timothy Brook. See for example the proclamation issued by Zhu Xi when he was serving as prefect of Zhangzhou in 1190: "Be filial to parents, respectful to elders, cordial to clansmen and relatives, and helpful to neighbors. Each should perform his assigned duty and engage in his primary occupation." 孝順父母, 恭敬長上, 和睦宗姻, 周恤鄉里, 各依本分, 各修本業. Note that Zhu Xi's proclamation is much more detailed in spelling out what constitutes evil deeds: "None should commit adultery or thefts, nor indulge in drinking or gambling, nor fight or sue each other" 莫作姦盜, 莫縱飲博, 莫相鬪打, 莫相論訴. "Quanyu bang," 勸諭榜 in *Hui'an xiansheng Zhu Wengong wenji*, j. 100, 5b–7a; translated in de Bary & Bloom, *Sources of Chinese Tradition*, vol. 1, 749–51. The emphasis on positive

rather than negative injunctions continues in Kangxi's *Sixteen Maxims* of 1670 and Yongzheng's amplifications of 1724.

3. On this point, see Terry Eagleton, "Literature, Virtue and Evil," 51–57.

4. This narrative traces its origin to the May Fourth movement and its attempt to rediscover the native origins of ideas of individual emancipation and critique of political/social/gender hierarchies, but it continued for most of the twentieth century. In the words of Lynn Struve, the late Ming has served as "Modern China's liberal muse"; see Struve, "Modern China's Liberal Muse: The Late Ming."

5. Mote, *Imperial China 900–1800*, 770.

6. Influential studies include Huang, *Desire and Fictional Narrative in Late Imperial China*; Plaks, *The Four Masterworks of the Ming Novel*; and McMahon, *Causality and Containment in Seventeenth-Century Chinese Fiction*.

7. I follow the dates given by Hu Lianyu in "Lu Yunlong shengping kao," 213. These dates are based on the biography of Lu Yunlong written by his son Lu Minshu 陸敏樹 (1616–1675) titled "Account of the Genealogy of Mr. Lu Tui'an" ("Lu Tui'an xiansheng jiazhuan" 陸蛻庵先生家傳), which Hu Lianyu first brought to general attention in an article published in 2001, "Lu Yunlong shengping kaoshu." Tui'an was one of Lu Yunlong's *hao*. The biography is appended to the 1673 reprinted edition of *Opening the Documents of the Mahayana: A Complete Set* (*Qidu dacheng beiti* 啟牘大乘備體), the last known publication associated with Lu Yunlong's name. Copies of this text are preserved at Nanjing Library and Shanghai Library; see Lei, *Wan Ming wenren sixiang tanxi*, 2.

8. Hanan, "The Fiction of Moral Duty: The Vernacular Story in the 1640s."

9. McMahon, *Causality and Containment*, 8–12.

10. Wong, "Morality as Entertainment."

11. Yang, *Appropriation and Representation*, 45, 73.

12. Yang, *Appropriation and Representation*, 73.

13. Lu, *Accidental Incest*.

14. Yang, *Appropriation and Representation*, 79–98; see also his introduction to Feng Menglong, *Stories Old and New*, xxi–xxiii. While the pairing of stories functions as a structuring device in *San Yan*, there were also reactions against this practice. For example, in the "Statement of Principles" ("Fanli" 凡例) section of *Slapping the Table in Amazement* (*Pai'an jingqi*), Ling Mengchu condemns the current practice of rewriting the titles of stories as single lines of matching couplets in order to superficially pair them, a practice he likens to "transforming gold into stone" (*CK*, 2). Against this practice, Ling adopts (probably for the first time) a titular couplet, following the example of chapter titles in long novels. See Yang Shuhui's introduction to Feng, *Stories Old and New*, xxvi and 754–55, fn. 58. However, there does not seem to be a univocal correlation between titular couplet and disregard for pairing the stories, as the case of *Exemplary Words* shows. *Exemplary Words* stories have titular couplets, but the stories still preserve a pairing structure. Further evidence that the stories were often conceived and circulated as pairs is provided by the arrangement of stories in the "Bieke" edi-

tion of *Slapping the Table in Amazement, Second Collection* (*Erke Pai'an jingqi*) and, to a lesser extent, in *Illusion* (*Huanying*).

15. Hanan, "Fiction of Moral Duty," 190 and 410.

16. Jing, *Lu Renlong, Lu Yunlong xiaoshuo chuangzuo yanjiu*, 193.

17. Lei Qingrui's monograph, *Wan Ming wenren sixiang tanxi*, is a study of Lu Yunlong's commentary to *Exemplary Words*. See also Sun Yizhen, "Lu Yunlong de wenyi guan," 146–51.

18. See Chen, "Mingmo Qingchu shishi xiaoshuo de tese," Guo Haofan, "Mingmo Qingchu shishi xiaoshuo sixiang tezheng lunlüe," and Ouyang Jian, "Chaoqian yu shiji bianzuan de xiaoshuo chuangzuo."

19. See Li, "History, Fiction, and Public Opinion."

20. See Hu Lianyu, "Lu Yunlong shengping kao," 217–18.

21. Eyebrow commentaries are found in *San Yan* (Tianqi editions), *Er Pai* (Chongzhen editions), *West Lake Stories, Second Collection* (Chongzhen edition), and *Rocks Nod Their Heads* (late Ming edition). Tail commentaries are found in *Bell in the Still Night* (Southern Ming edition), and *Sobering Stone* (early Qing edition). *Exemplary Words* and *Stories of Figures from the Seventy-Two Domains* (1640s) have both eyebrow and tail commentaries.

22. On Lu Yunlong's authorship of the commentaries in *Exemplary Words*, see Chan Hing-ho [Chen Qinghao]'s preface in *XSYPZ*, vol. 1, 5; Chen Liao, "Xingshi yan xin lun," 2; Chan Hing-ho, "Un recueil de contes retrouvé," 83; Lei, *Wan Ming wenren sixiang tanxi*, 88–89.

23. See Gu Keyong and Wei Ran, "Lu Renlong shi *Xingshi yan* bianzhe er fei zuozhe kaobian," 150–51. Gu and Wei suggest that not only the story arrangement, but the title of the work, are by Lu Yunlong.

24. Zheng Zhenduo's reconstructed dating. For information on this anthology, see the appendix.

25. The original text is corrupted here. I follow the emendation suggested by Zhang Rongqi, the editor of the modern typeset edition: Mengjue daoren and Xihu langzi, *Sanke pai'an jingqi*, 353.

26. Mengjue daoren and Xihu langzi, *Sanke pai'an jingqi*, 353–54.

27. *YSMY*, 1.

28. *JSTY*, 1; Feng, *Stories to Caution the World*, 5.

29. *XSHY*, 1; Feng, *Stories to Awaken the World*, 4.

30. On the central significance that the selection and arrangement of stories has in the practice of anthology-making, see Rainier Lanselle's insightful discussion of *Jingu qiguan* in *Spectacles curieux d'aujourd'hui et d'autrefois*, Introduction, xxxvii–lxii.

31. *QYZ*, 1–7.

32. Tu, "Probing the 'Three Bonds' and 'Five Relationships' in Confucian Humanism."

33. Kutcher, *Mourning in Late Imperial China*, 2.

34. *Wulun quanbei* is attributed to Qiu Jun 邱濬 (1421–1495). For a study of this and other Ming didactic plays, see Situ Xiuying, *Mingdai jiaohua ju qunguan*.

35. For example, the massive compilation *Wulun shu*, compiled during the Xuande era in 1443, follows this canonical order. Further, it dedicates 52 of 62 juan (85 percent of the entire work) to the first relationship, ruler-minister. Alfonso Vagnone's *Dadao jiyan* (1636) also follows the canonical order, except that it inverts the relative placement of brothers and husband-wife relation. It devotes the main bulk of its entries to the first and the last relationships (ruler-subject and friends).

36. Li Zhi was most likely influenced by Jiao Hong's *Jiao's Taxonomical Forest* (*Jiaoshi leilin* 焦氏類林, comp. 1585, pub. 1587), another work in the *Shishuo*-imitation genre that began with the five cardinal relationships. However, instead of preserving the vast number of categories found in Jiao's anthology, Li Zhi used the five relationships as a basis to organize the entire collection. On the late-Ming vogue of works that imitated the *New Accounts of Tales of the World*, and Li Zhi's particular contribution, see Qian, *Spirit and Self in Medieval China*, 253–55.

37. The essay is also included in *A Book to Burn* (*Fenshu*). For an English translation, see Li Zhi, *A Book to Burn and A Book to Keep (Hidden)*, 99–101.

38. The phrase is from *Yijing*, Xugua: 天地, 萬物之本; 夫婦, 人倫之始.

39. Li Zhi, *Chutan ji*, in *Li Zhi quanji zhu*, vol. 12, 1.

40. "Speech and conversation," "affairs of the state," "letters and scholarship," together with "virtuous conduct," are the "four categories" (*sike* 四科) or areas of expertise in which Confucius grouped his disciples (*Lunyu* 11.3). These are also the first four categories in the *New Accounts*. On the *New Accounts* taxonomy, see Qian, *Spirit and Self in Medieval China*, 103–6, 126–32.

41. For example, it is found in the fifteenth-century collection of classical language tales *In the Flowers' Shadow* (*Huaying ji* 花影集) compiled by Tao Fu 陶輔 (inspired by the model of popular collections such as *Jiandeng Xinhua*), where it is cited as premise and justification for the romantic tale; see Tao Fu, *Huaying ji*, 99.

42. Zhanzhan waishi, *Qingshi* (Taibei: Guangwen shuju, 1982), vol. 1, "Xu," 1b. For an alternative English translation and discussion, see Li Mowry, *Chinese Love Stories*, 14–22.

43. For example, see *YSMY* 10, *JSTY* 22, *XSHY* 11 and 15. For a synthetic overview and discussion of the primacy of the husband-and-wife bond in the late Ming, see also Epstein, *Competing Discourses*, 35–37.

44. For Li's letters and essays on the topic of friendship, see Li Zhi, *A Book to Burn*, 122–24, 135–37, 142–45.

45. Gu Dashao, *Bingzhuzhai wenji*, 18b. Cf. English transl. and discussion in Martin Huang, "Male Friendship and *Jiangxue*," 171. This passage is also quoted and discussed in Lü Miaofen, *Yangmingxue shiren shequn*, 323–24. Gu Dashao edited Li Zhi's writings in a monumental collection *Li Wenling ji* 李溫陵集.

46. Gu Dashao, *Bingzhuzhai wenji*, 18b–19a.

47. Gu Dashao, *Bingzhuzhai wenji*, 18b. Here, Gu Dashao comes close to the Aristotelian notion of friendship, whereby the parent-child relation can be seen as a space for the cultivation of friendship.

48. For abbreviated titles of stories from *San Yan* and *Er Pai* I have generally followed those used by Hanan in *The Chinese Vernacular Story*.

49. Gukuangsheng, *Zuixing shi* 12, 441–42.

50. This focus on one ethical principle or relationship is consistent with the presentation of short stories as a genre focused on "a single character in a single action" 一人一事, as expressed in the blurb on the cover page (*fengmian*) of the first edition of *Stories Old and New*. See Hanan, *The Chinese Vernacular Story*, 22–23; Duan Jiangli, "Shanshu yu Ming Qing xiaoshuo zhong de guobao guan," 58.

51. Hanan, *The Chinese Vernacular Story*, 27.

52. See preface to *XSY* 6. "I have seen that in complicated situations superior people find themselves unable to act, while simple men and women remain unperturbed. Superior people may be very insightful about matters of life and death, gain and loss, but simple men and women are just content with doing what is right." 嘗觀事當轇轕之際, 便束能人之手, 而不驚愚夫婦之心。 能人死生利害大明也, 若夫愚夫婦, 則直行其是而已。 *XSY* 6.287; *XSYPZ* 6.94.

53. See for instance *QYZ* 8, *CK* 13.

54. See for instance *XSY* 9, tail commentary and *QYZ* 7, tail commentary. For a discussion of different modes of reading devotional and hagiographical literature in the European Middle Ages and Renaissance, see Constance Furey, "'Intellects Inflamed in Christ': Women and Spiritualized Scholarship in Renaissance Christianity." Furey notes that the literary genre of exempla, for instance, aimed to convey moral lessons rather than literal models for emulation, and that medieval hagiographers often cautioned their readers that saints (and their extraordinary feats) were to be admired rather than imitated.

55. Hanan, *The Chinese Vernacular Story*, 26–27. See also Lauwaert, "Comptes des dieux, calculs des hommes," and Kao, "*Bao* and *Baoying*."

56. See Brokaw, *The Ledgers of Merit and Demerit*; Ogawa Yōichi, *Nichiyō ruisho ni yoru Min-Shin shōsetsu no kenkyū*, and "Mingdai xiaoshuo yu shanshu"; Yang Zonghong, "Lun Mingmo Qingchu huaben xiaoshuo de quanshanxing ji qi wenhua beijing." For a French translation of key morality books, see Vincent Goossaert, ed. and tr., *Livres de morale révélés par les dieux*.

57. For examples of "hidden merit" stories in the two collections, see *XSY* 12, *XSY* 25, *XSY* 31, *QYZ* 5, *QYZ* 13. One of the most famous examples of this story line is Feng Menglong's Lü Dalang story (*JSTY* 5).

58. *XSY* 28.1302; *XSYPZ* 28.495.

59. *XHEJ* 6, 115.

60. "Money and wealth are governed by fate; the superior person will always end up as a superior person, the petty man as a petty man. There is no need to measure them by way of gain and loss. Nevertheless, it may be possible to awaken the mind of the vulgar people by recourse to this logic of gain and loss." 錢財有命, 君子落得為君子, 小人落得為小人, 不必衡之得失之介。然借此得失, 可以醒庸人之心。 *XSY* 25.1144; *XSYPZ* 25.437.

61. See the stories discussed in chapter 4.

Chapter 1

1. See Lu, "Ming Qing Zhongguo wanli xunqin de wenhua shijian"; Fan, "Ming Qing xunqin xiqu qingjie moshi chutan"; Wang Jianke, "Lun Mingdai xiaoshuo xiqu zhong de xunqin zhuti."

2. Huang Zongxi, "Searching for the elder brother over 10,000 miles" ("Wanli xun xiong ji" 萬里尋兄記), in *Huang Lizhou wenji*, 411–12. Also quoted in Lu Miaw-fen, "Ming Qing Zhongguo wanli xunqin de wenhua shijian," 2.

3. Lu, "Ming Qing Zhongguo wanli xunqin de wenhua shijian," 2 (and fn. 8).

4. Lu, "Ming Qing Zhongguo wanli xunqin de wenhua shijian," 1.

5. Cai Baozhen, *Xiaoji*, juan 9 "Xunqin xiaoji."

6. Knapp, *Selfless Offspring*.

7. As Andrew Plaks writes, "the common translation of this term, 'filial piety,' fails to do justice to its significance as the central axis running through all the other cardinal relations, often conceived as a quasi-metaphysical model of vertical continuity at the heart of the cosmic order." *The Four Masterworks*, 171. In their translation of the *Xiaojing*, Roger T. Ames and Henry Rosemont have rendered *xiao* as "family reverence."

8. See introduction.

9. Kutcher, *Mourning in Late Imperial China*, 35.

10. Zhu Di, *Xiaoshun shishi*, 489–623. For a brief discussion of this work, see Lee Cheuk Yin, "Emperor Chengzu and Imperial Filial Piety of the Ming Dynasty," 144–47.

11. See Fisher, *The Chosen One*, 46–106.

12. Wang, *Instructions for Practical Living*, 107–10.

13. On the notion of *ganying*, see Yü Chün-fang, *Kuan-yin*, 153–58; Jimmy Yu, *Sanctity and Self-Inflicted Violence*, 12 and 65.

14. Lu Miaw-fen, "Religious Dimensions of Filial Piety," 1–37. Among the texts she discusses is *Xiaojing jiling* 孝經集靈, a short collection of entries about miracles linked with filial piety, compiled by Yu Chunxi. Yu was a Qiantang native, whose essays Lu Yunlong included in his best-selling anthology *Huang Ming shiliu jia xiaopin* of 1633.

15. Alan Cole, *Mothers and Sons in Chinese Buddhism*, 2–4.

16. Cf. Qiu Zhonglin, "Bu xiao zhi xiao"; Yenna Wu, "Moral Ambivalence in the Portrayals of *gegu* in Late Imperial China"; Chün-fang Yü, *Kuan-yin*, 338–47 (discusses *gegu* in the context of the Miaoshan legend and the larger Guanyin lore); Jimmy Yu, *Sanctity and Self-Inflicted Violence in Chinese Religions, 1500–1700*, 62–88.

17. Kutcher, *Mourning in Late Imperial China*, 35–72.

18. Maram Epstein has noted that filial piety is emphasized as a "central moral and emotional value" in a number of eighteenth- and nineteenth-century novels, such as Xia Jingqu's *Yesou puyan*, Li Lüyuan's *Qilu deng*, Li Ruzhen's *Jinghua yuan*, and Wen Kang's *Ernü yingxiong zhuan*. See Epstein, "Sons and Mothers," 287–88.

19. Ann Waltner has extensively discussed this story in "Writing Her Way Out of Trouble."

20. This story has been discussed by Ann Waltner in *Getting an Heir*, 129–35.

21. See for example *CK* 33, *CK* 38, *EK* 22.

22. "Wang gong," *Xu Cangshu*, in *Li Zhi quanji zhu*, vol. 11, 223–25. Wang Yuan's biography is also found, with slight textual variations, in other compilations, including Jiao Hong, *Guochao xianzheng lu*, juan 112, 86a–89a (vol. 8, 4976–7) and the Wen'an county gazetteer.

23. Shang Wei, *Rulin waishi and Cultural Transformation in Late Imperial China*, 54–55; Lu Miaw-fen, "Ming Qing Zhongguo wanli xunqin," 365–66. The status of Wang Yuan's tale as archetypal filial quest narrative is attested by the frequency with which it is invoked, in biographical and autobiographical accounts such as Huang Xiangjian's 黃向堅 (1609–1673) "Filial Son Huang's Account of the Journey in Search of His Parents" ("Huang xiaozi xunqin jicheng" 黃孝子尋親紀程) and in semifictional anecdote collections such as Ji Yun's 紀昀 *Random Notes at the Cottage of Close Scrutiny* (*Yuewei caotang biji* 閱微草堂筆記), well into the eighteenth century. Huang Xiangjian's travelogues of his "filial trek" from Suzhou to Yunnan and back have been partially translated by Lynn Struve, *Voices from the Ming-Qing Cataclysm*, 162–78; a more recent and full translation is found in Elizabeth Kindall, *Geo-Narratives of a Filial Son*, 343–83. See also Tina Lu's discussion, *Accidental Incest*, 137–41.

24. I am referring here not to the actual historical characters, but rather to the characters as they are constructed in the historical and fictional accounts.

25. *Liji*, "Tan Gong" I.4.

26. In the version of the story included in Yongle's *True Cases of Filial Piety*, Zhu Shouchang resumes his official career immediately after finding his mother. Zhu Di, *Xiaoshun shishi*, juan 7, 578.

27. *Xu Cangshu*, in *Li Zhi quanji zhu*, vol. 11, 223.

28. In fact, earlier versions of the Zhu Shouchang legend, such as the one included in Shen Gua's 沈括 (1031–1095) *Written Chat from Dream Creek* (*Mengxi bitan* 夢溪筆談), mention that Zhu was able to find his mother only after writing the whole text of the Buddhist sutra *Litany of the Compassionate Water of Samādhi* (*Cibei sanmei shuichan* 慈悲三昧水懺) with his own blood, and chanting it day and night. This Buddhist element, however, however, is absent in Guo Jujing's *Twenty-Four Filial Exemplars* version from the Yuan dynasty. See Osawa Akihiro, "Mingdai chuban wenhua zhong de 'Ershisi xiao.'"

29. *Digu yanqin* 滴骨驗親. This method is described in the Song manual of forensic medicine *Xiyuan jilu* 洗冤集錄; see Sung Tz'u, *The Washing Away of Wrongs*.

30. Zhang, *Confucian Image Politics*, 14–15.

31. Lu, *True to Her Word*, 36–40.

32. Brook, *The Confusions of Pleasure*, 139–52.

33. Jing, *Lu Renlong, Lu Yunlong xiaoshuo chuangzuo yanjiu*, 69–70.

34. "Wang gong," *Xu Cangshu*, in *Li Zhi quanji zhu*, vol. 11, 223.

35. *XSY* 9.474–475; *XSYPZ* 9.167.

36. He does so by disparaging the influence of books and classical education and citing the example of a callous scholar who neglected his father to pursue an official career. *SDT* 3.54–55.

37. The "Lu'e" poem (*Shi* 202), translated as "Thick Tarragon" by Waley (*The Book of Songs*, 184–85), is a staple allusion in filial piety stories: see for instance *XSY* 3, *XSY* 9, *CKPA* 13, and *SDT* 3. The poem eulogizes the bounty of one's deceased parents, and emphasizes the idea of "requiting the care debt" that children owe their parents.

38. *SDT* 3.61. The filial son's obliviousness to the natural scenery is one of the topoi of filial quest. As Tina Lu has observed, it can sometime be charged with political significance, as in the case of filial son Huang Xiangjian, whose obliviousness to the cataclysmic events surrounding the Ming fall marks his filial concerns as completely eclipsing political concerns (see Lu, *Accidental Incest*, 137–41).

39. *SDT* 3.74–75.

40. *XSY* 9.477–478; *XSYPZ* 9.168.

41. *SDT* 3.72–73.

42. This mocking attitude seems to be a trademark of Langxian's fiction. In the notorious "Siege of Yangzhou" (*SDT* 11), he has the heroine Zong Erniang publicly declaim a magniloquent piece explaining her self-sacrifice (she sells herself to the butcher so that her husband can collect the money to travel back home to take care of his mother), only to let her be completely misunderstood by the curious onlookers, who do not understand her out-of-town accent.

43. See the final comment at the end of the story, signed by "The Man from Luguo" 魯國男子 (which could also be read as "the upright man"): "There is a biography of Wang Yuan that is similar to this story in its general outline, with some differences on minor details. But when it comes to the description of the village constable's cruelty, and the hardship of being lost along the way, one can really say that the author has spared no effort." 王原有傳，與此大同小異。而其中敘里胥之橫，失路之悲，可云曲至。*XSY* 9.492; *XSYPZ* 9.172. See also Hanan, *The Chinese Vernacular Story*, 127, about the *Rocks* version.

44. For example, he tells his wife that "of the thirty-six stratagems, the best one is running away" 三十六着走為上着 (*XSY* 9.160); the same adage is used by Wang Jin's mother in chapter 2 and by Song Jiang in chapter 18 of *Water Margin*.

45. Cf. Tina Lu's discussion of the token of recognition in parent-children reunion stories. As Lu notes, recognition in these cases is always predicated on inalienable traits, like Yao Ji's single testicle in Li Yu's "Nativity Room." *Accidental Incest*, 135.

46. *XSY* 9.486–87; *XSYPZ* 9.171.

47. *XSY* 9.487; *XSYPZ* 9.171.

48. *XSY* 9.489; *XSYPZ* 9.171.

49. Fan, "Ming Qing xunqin xiqu qingjie moshi chutan;; Wang Jianke, "Lun Mingdai xiaoshuo xiqu zhong de xunqin zhuti."

50. *SDT* 3.68–69. This passage is also translated in Hanan, *The Chinese Vernacular Story*, 135–36.

51. *SDT* 3.68–69. Cf. Hanan, *The Chinese Vernacular Story*, 136.

52. *XSY* 9.491; *XSYPZ* 9.172. The adage is first recorded as a citation from a *Xiaojing* apocrypha, quoted in a memorial by Wei Biao 韋彪 included in his biography in *Hou Han shu* 26.918: "Confucius said: If one serves one's parents with filial piety, then loyalty can thus be transferred to the ruler. For this reason, one should seek a loyal minister in the home of a loyal son." 孔子曰: 事親孝故忠可移於君, 是以求忠臣必於孝子之門。See John Makeham, *Name and Actuality in Early Chinese Thought*, 175–76. See also Knapp, *Selfless Offspring*, 128; Kutcher, *Mourning in Late Imperial China*, 13–14.

53. Kutcher, *Mourning in Late Imperial China*, 2.

54. Li Yu's story "Nativity Room" ("Shengwo lou" 生我樓), included in the *Twelve Towers* (*Shi'er lou* 十二樓) collection of 1658, can be read as a parody and inversion of the filial quest narrative, which is transformed into a "fatherly quest" and reverse adoption. The filial quest narrative continues to be the subject of reworking and parody, most famously in the novels *The Unofficial History of the Scholars* (*Rulin waishi* 儒林外史), as discussed below, and *Flowers in the Mirror* (*Jinghua yuan* 鏡花緣, 1830), where Tang Guichen's quest of her father constitutes the overarching narrative structure of chapters 41–54.

Filial quests also figure marginally in other stories. For example, in the famous *San Yan* story "The Oil Seller" (*XSHY* 3), Qin Zhong, though he does not go into a filial quest proper, writes his family name on the oil jugs in the hopes of finding his long lost father. At the end of the story, he unexpectedly discovers him in a temple, but unlike in the case of Wang Yuan, the father does not move back to live with his son, but instead remains in the temple.

55. Wu Jingzi, *Rulin waishi*, chapters 37–39.

56. Shang, *Rulin waishi and Cultural Transformation in Late Imperial China*, 54–55.

57. See chapter 2 for a discussion of *imitation* and *mimesis*.

Chapter 2

1. Lu Xun famously expressed indignation at Guo Ju in his essay "Ershisi xiao tu" 二十四孝圖 (Picture Book of Twenty-Four Filial Exemplars) included in *Zhaohua xishi* 朝花夕拾 (Dawn Blossoms Plucked at Dusk). *Lu Xun quanji*, vol. 2, 258–68. Yet Lu Xun was hardly the first; already in Ming and Qing times, Fang Xiaoru and Yuan Mei wrote scathing critiques of Guo Ju. See Fang Xiaoru's "Guo Ju" in *Xunzhi zhai ji*, juan 5, 53–54a (also discussed by Tina Lu, *Accidental Incest*, 162–63), and Yuan Mei's "Guo Ju lun" 郭巨論 in *Xiaocang shanfang wenji*, vol. 778, juan 20, 23a–b. The latter piece, written when Yuan Mei was merely thirteen years old, was "highly praised by Yuan Mei's teachers, and one of his

twentieth-century biographers thought that it was the beginning of his love for overturning old conventions." Jerry Schmidt, *Harmony Garden*, 9.

2. Knapp, *Selfless Offspring*, 117, 126–28.

3. Fang Xiaoru and Yuan Mei's critiques of Guo Ju obey a similar logic, by turning the attention to the mother's perspective. Lu Xun takes instead the point of view of the son. For a cross-cultural comparison, see Kierkegaard's discussion of Abraham's story from Isaac's point of view in *Fear and Trembling*.

4. The tale is found in the collection *Jiuyue qianji* 九籥前集, juan 11, 5b–7b. This collection includes Song's early works, composed up to about 1596. See Hanan, "The Making of *The Pearl-Sewn Shirt*," 126. Tina Lu also briefly discusses this story in *Accidental Incest*, 144–45.

5. These are *YSMY* 1 and *JSTY* 32. The relationship between the two sets has been thoroughly studied by Patrick Hanan in his "The Making of *The Pearl-Sewn Shirt*."

6. *XSY* 3.150; *XSYPZ* 3.40. For the origin of this adage, cf. Knapp, *Selfless Offspring*, 17, 126, and footnotes.

7. Ling Mengchu's story "The Parricide" (*CKPA* 13) is just such a cautionary tale about an uxorious son who replaces the affection he owes his parents with an infatuation for his less-than-virtuous wife.

8. Lu, *Accidental Incest*, 145.

9. *XSY* 3.195–96; *XSYPZ* 3.54.

10. *XSY* 3.152; *XSYPZ* 3.41. Zhai Zhong's wife said: "All men can be husbands, but there is only one father" 人盡夫也, 父一而已. The irony, though, is that Zhai Zhong's wife said this to protect her husband. *Chunqiu Zuozhuan zhu*, Huan 15.2, vol. 1, 143.

11. Lu, *Accidental Incest*, 145. Lu only discusses the classical tale.

12. *XSY* 3.147–48; *XSYPZ* 3.39.

13. *XSY* 3.201; *XSY* 3.55. Here Lu Yunlong echoes the final commentary to "The Filial Son from Suzhou," where Song Maocheng writes: "I, the useless one, find pleasure in telling this story. It must be because of the way in which he [the filial son] was able to handle the predicament without losing his composure." 廢人喜述此事, 蓋以其處變不擾也。 *Jiuyue qianji*, juan 11, 7b.

14. *XSY* 3.151; *XSYPZ* 3.40.

15. *XSY* 3.151; *XSYPZ* 3.40–41.

16. *XSY* 6.291; *XSYPZ* 6.95–96.

17. Song, *Jiuyue qianji*, juan 11, 5b.

18. The decision of the husband to embark on a trading venture that will take him away from home is depicted as baleful in other stories; see for example "The Pearl-Sewn Shirt" (*YSMY* 1).

19. *XSY* 3.201; *XSYPZ* 3.55.

20. See Xiao Feng, "*Xingshi yan* di san hui sucai laiyuan." The tale is included in *Huadangge congtan* 花當閣叢談 (published in 1627), juan 5, 8b–10b. Rpt. in *Xuxiu siku quanshu*, vol. 1175, 86–87.

21. "Cui xiaotong" 崔孝童, *Xu Cangshu*, in *Li Zhi quanji zhu*, vol. 11, 232–33. "Cui Jian zhuan" 崔鑒傳, in Jiao Hong, *Guochao xianzheng lu*, j. 112, 68a–69b (vol. 8, 4967).

22. "Cui Jian xiao lie" 崔鑒孝烈, in Shen, *Wanli yehuo bian*, j. 18, vol. 1, 516. Cf. Lévy, *Inventaire*, vol. VIII-4, 362.

23. Shen, *Wanli yehuo bian*, juan 18, vol. 1, 516.

24. QYZ 7.214.

25. QYZ 7.224.

26. QYZ 7.225–26.

27. QYZ 7.228.

28. QYZ 7.236–37.

29. QYZ 7.238.

30. QYZ 7.228.

31. QYZ 7.247–48.

32. QYZ 7.256.

33. QYZ 7.257.

34. Epstein, "Making a Case," 27–43.

35. It could be argued, however, that imperial pardon simply bypasses (momentarily invalidates) the law by espousing ritual duty.

36. The direct source, which is quoted at the end of the story, is the biography of Wang Shiming written by Zhang Fengyi 張鳳翼 (1527–1613), included in Jiao Hong, *Guochao xianzheng lu*, juan 112. See also Shen Guoyuan 沉國元, *Huang Ming congxin lu* 皇明從信錄, *Xu*, juan 1.

37. XSY 2.113–14; XSYPZ 2.27.

38. See Anne Cheng, "Filial Piety with a Vengeance." As Cheng puts it, filial vengeance is predicated on a paradox, in that while it proceeds from ritual duty, which normally rules social relationships a priori, it "nonetheless strikes a posteriori, just as penal sanction would do" (29).

39. Dalby, "Revenge and the Law in Traditional China," 292–94.

40. This story offers first-rate material for the examination of the diffusion of legal, and more specifically forensic, knowledge. See Hegel, "Introduction: Writing and Law," 10–17; Pierre-Étienne Will, "Developing Forensic Knowledge through Cases in the Qing Dynasty."

41. The method of "steaming the bones" (*zhenggu* 蒸骨) was already in use during the Song, and it is described in detail in the thirteenth-century handbook *Xiyuan jilu* (Washing Away of Wrongs): "First, use water to wash the bones. Using hemp twine, string them together to form a skeleton. Next, lay them out on a mat. Then, dig a pit in the ground measuring five feet long, three feet wide, and two feet deep. Burn wood and charcoal in it until the ground is red hot. Clear out the coals, and pour in two pints (*sheng*) of good wine and five pints of strong vinegar. While it is steaming, lay the bones in the pit and cover them with straw mats. Let them remain there for two to four hours. When the ground has cooled, remove the mats and take the skeleton to a level,

well-lighted place where it can be examined under a red oiled umbrella. If there are places on the bones that have been struck, then there will be traces of red color. The two ends of the place where the bones were broken will have a blood red halo. Moreover, if on holding the injured bone up to the light it shows a vivid red color, then the injuries were clearly inflicted before death." Sung Tz'u, *The Washing Away of Wrongs*, 102.

42. *XSY* 2.121–22; *XSYPZ* 2.29.
43. *XSY* 2.123; *XSYPZ* 2.29.
44. *QYZ* 8.291–93.
45. Liu, *The Chinese Knight-Errant*.
46. Altenburger, "The Avenger's Coldness."
47. *XSY* 2.130–31; *XSYPZ* 2.32. While Altenburger's notion of "syndrome of coldness" is inspiring, his analysis does not seem to take into account the authorial manipulations of focalization (in Genette's sense). For example, in Pu Songling's famous tale "Xianü," the protagonist's "icy" demeanor is, to a large extent, the result of the withholding of information on the part of the author.
48. Ironsmiths and goldsmiths regularly make for colorful minor characters in *Exemplary Words* stories. They are characterized by Boeotian ignorance (as in this story) or cunning and deceit (in "Injustice to Tang Guimei," *XSY* 6).
49. James Liu describes the "supermoral" behavior in these terms: "to bestow a kindness and not to expect a reward is moral; to bestow a kindness and to reject any reward is supermoral." *The Chinese Knight-Errant*, 4.
50. *XSY* 2.143; *XSYPZ* 2.35.
51. *XSY* 2.144; *XSYPZ* 2.36.
52. *XSY* 2.109; *XSYPZ* 2.25.
53. *XSY* 2.113; *XSYPZ* 2.27.
54. *XSY* 2.146; *XSYPZ* 2.36. The last sentence is different from the original text, which reads: "in order to instruct the people on the value of filial piety" 以教民孝也. See Jiao Hong, *Guochao xianzheng lu*, juan 112, 88a.
55. *XSY* 2.140; *XSYPZ* 2.34.
56. *XSY* 2.143; *XSYPZ* 2.35.
57. *XSY* 2.146; *XSYPZ* 2.36. The dichotomy between *jing* 經 (constant norm, standard) and *quan* 權 (expedient assessment, discretion) is found in the Gongyang commentary to *Chunqiu*; see Lewis, *Writing and Authority in Early China*, 143. The *loci classici* on *quan* are *Analects* 9.30, and *Mengzi* 4A.17, where *quan* is contrasted with *li* (ritual propriety) rather than *jing*. See also Qian Zhongshu's note on *Zuozhuan*, Cheng 15, in *Guanzhui bian*, vol. 1, 340–43; and Wei, "Chu Hsi on the Standard and the Expedient."
58. *XSY* 2.139; *XSYPZ* 2.34.
59. *XSY* 2.142; *XSYPZ* 2.35.
60. This is true of both the vernacular story and the classical language account by Zhang Fengyi.
61. The "Bieben" edition of *Slapping the Table in Amazement, Second Collection* preserved at the Bibliothèque nationale, which includes ten stories from Ling

Mengchu's *Second Collection* and twenty-four stories from *Exemplary Words*, reproduces the version in *Exemplary Words* for the story of Wang Shiming. Another story that appears in both collections is the story of the fox spirit of Dabie mountain (*XSY* 38 and *EK* 29)—this however is not included in the "Bieben" edition. It is possible that Feng Menglong's *Qingshi* might have been the common source or inspiration for both Wang Shiming's story and the fox of Dabie mountain, at least as far as Ling Mengchu's collection is concerned.

62. *EK* 31.352.

63. This may be due to the fact that Ling Mengchu's story is based on a different source from *Exemplary Words*: Tan Zhengbi and other scholars indicate Wang Tonggui's (fl. 1530–1608) *Tales Overheard* (*Ertan* 耳談, 1602) as a probable source for both this story and the *Qingshi* version, which is titled "Wang Shiming qi" 王世名妻. See *Ertan*, juan 2, entry "Wang Shiming Yushi" 王世名俞氏, 27–28.

64. This is nowhere spelled out more clearly than in the final commentary of the *Qingshi* version of this story (also probably based on *Ertan*): "She was the only one who could see through his intentions, while all the others failed to see it. Thus she must have been extremely intimate with him. Yet, even though she knew his intentions, she did not stop him, which testifies to her ability to understand the principle of right and wrong, without letting her attachment to her husband obfuscate her mind. Her husband endured for five [sic] years before sacrificing himself to filial piety, while the wife endured for three years before dying for her husband. In both cases, their ardent resolution was fulfilled in a serene way. How amazing!" 他人不知, 俞獨知之, 俞必可與為密者. 俞知之而不止之, 是能明大義, 不為情掩者也. 夫忍五載而死孝, 婦忍三歲而死節, 慷慨之誼俱以從容成之. 卓哉！ The penultimate sentence, which I have translated somewhat freely, alludes to the ability of both husband and wife to encompass the dichotomy *kangkai* 慷慨 (vehement, fervent) and *congrong* 從容 (serene, impassive) often used to describe opposite attitudes toward self-sacrifice and death. Zhanzhan waishi, *Qingshi*, vol. 1, 9–10. See also chapter 3, note 75.

65. *XSY* 2.144; *XSYPZ* 2.36.

66. Lu, *True to Her Word*, 21.

67. Song Lian, *Wenxian ji*, juan 16, 73a–75a. Rpt. in *Siku quanshu*, vol. 1224, 63–64. For a comparison of the classical source and the vernacular story, see Wu Yanna [Yenna Wu], "Lijiao, qinggan, he zongjiao zhi hudong."

68. *XSY* 2.140; *XSYPZ* 2.34.

69. See the "Lu'e" lines in James Legge's translation: "Father, from whose loins I sprung, / Mother, on whose breast I hung" 父兮生我、母兮鞠我, *The She King*, 242. See also chapter 1, note 37.

70. *XSY* 2.140; *XSYPZ* 2.34.

71. Gu Dashao, *Bingzhuzhai wenji*, 18b. See English transl. in Martin Huang, "Male Friendship and *Jiangxue*," 171. This passage is also quoted in Lü Miaofen, *Yangmingxue shiren shequn*, 323–24. See also chapter 6.

72. Lu, *Accidental Incest*, 153.

73. *XSY* 2.205–206; *XSYPZ* 4.62.

74. Cf. the critique of chastity plaques: Chen Miaozhen's mother is originally set against remarriage, but she is gradually persuaded by her brother to reconsider. Her brother argues that even if the magistrate confers chastity plaques, they will only go to the rich and influential families, and that other women from the village have remarried and nobody criticized their conduct. *XSY* 4.212; *XSYPZ* 4.64.

75. "Why should we always muse over the lines: 'If it were not for my grandmother, I would not be here today; if my grandmother did not have me, she would have no means to live to the end of her days.' This is considering the issue in terms of mere reciprocation, it does not stem from the pure principle (of filiality)." 何必低回于「臣無祖母, 無以有今日; 祖母無臣, 無以終餘年」哉！是猶在報復作想, 而未純也. *XSY* 4.204; *XSYPZ* 4.61.

76. "Your physical person with its hair and skin are received from your parents. Vigilance in not allowing anything to do injury to your person is where filial piety begins." Translation adapted from Ames and Rosemont, *The Chinese Classic of Family Reverence*, 105. Ames and Rosemont translate *xiao* as "family reverence" instead of the more common rendering "filial piety," which I have opted to follow.

77. According to an alternative punctuation, the text would read: "Those who think that protecting one's body to preserve one's body is not right will say, 'I won't do it.' But those who sacrifice their body to loyalty and filiality will say: 'If one sticks to this argument, then there is no difference between loyalty and filiality.'"

78. *XSY* 4.206; *XSYPZ* 4.62.

79. In fact, the circle of people that Lu dubs "pedants" (*yufu* 迂腐) historically included such eminent figures as Han Yu 韓愈 and Pi Rixiu 皮日休 in the Tang. Han Yu in particular denounced the practice of *gegu* in his essay "Huren dui" 鄠人對 by arguing that if the act resulted in death, it would compromise the continuation of the family line—in other words, it would constitute a most unfilial act. Cf. Chün-fang Yü, *Kuan-yin*, 339; Yenna Wu, "Moral Ambivalence," 249.

80. Song Lian, *Wenxian ji*, juan 16, 75a; rpt. in *Siku quanshu*, vol. 1224, 64. Song Lian concludes that Han Yu's essay "Huren dui" must be a forgery. In this he is following the conclusion of his predecessor, the Southern Song-Yuan literatus Huang Zhen 黃震 (Dongfa 東發) (1213–1280), who had most vehemently argued in favor of *gegu*.

81. Roger T. Ames and Henry Rosemont, *The Chinese Classic of Family Reverence*, 113 (with slight modification). This idea was later reformulated by Yongle as "transferring filial piety to loyalty" (*yi xiao wei zhong* 移孝為忠) in *True Cases of Filial Piety*. See Lee Cheuk Yin, "Emperor Chengzu and Imperial Filial Piety of the Ming Dynasty," 151.

82. On the darker side, this argument echoes the escalation of physical violence and cruelty noted, among others, by Zhao Yuan (*Ming Qing zhi ji shidaifu yanjiu*, 5–22): the increasingly violent forms of corporal punishment, torture, and execution implemented by the Ming emperors can be seen as linked with the increasingly gruesome acts of self-inflicted violence among the officialdom.

The graphic images used by both Lu Renlong and Song Lian are quite telling in this respect.

83. Bartoli, *La Cina*, 91–92.

84. In recent scholarship, *gegu* is often translated as "filial cannibalism" and constructed as a cannibalistic act (see for example Keith Knapp and Tina Lu). However provocative the parallel between cannibalism and *gegu* may be, I find it problematic. The discourse of cannibalism as a cultural construct focuses on the subject who is eating human flesh, and on the shared beliefs surrounding the consumption of human flesh. While *gegu* undoubtedly implies a shared set of beliefs on the medicinal properties of human flesh, the focus in late imperial narratives is not on the parent consuming the child's flesh, but rather on the child offering his or her flesh for the parent's survival. Moreover, the cutting is supposedly done in secret, unbeknown to the parent. Of course, the paradox is that the act is then publicly celebrated in biographies and historical records. See Jimmy Yu, *Sanctity and Self-Inflicted Violence in Chinese Religions, 1500–1700*, 62–88. Yu uses the term "filial slicing," which I find preferable.

85. This is the case of filial son Shen 沈 from Renhe, Hangzhou, who cut his heart in an attempt to save his father.

86. XSY 4.226; XSYPZ 4.68.

87. On the legend of Miaoshan, who donated her arms and eyes to cure her father's illness, even after he had repudiated and executed her, see Dudbridge, *The Legend of Miaoshan*; Idema, *Personal Salvation and Filial Piety*; Yü, *Kuan-yin*, 293–350.

88. XSY 4.219–20; XSYPZ 4.66.

89. XSY 4.220; XSYPZ 4.66.

90. Ibid.

91. Rigolot, "The Renaissance Crisis of Exemplarity," 558. Medieval *imitatio* "posited fictional texts as extensions of a unique source of undifferentiated truth: the Holy Scriptures, an infinitely expendable master text." Renaissance *imitatio*, by contrast, became increasingly metaphoric, the dominion of analogy, similitude, and so on.

92. See for example Lyons, *Exemplum*; Hampton, *Writing from History*.

93. XSY 4.224; XSYPZ 4.67–68.

94. *Selfless Offspring*, 169–74.

95. On the pairing of stories as structuring device in story collections, see the introduction.

96. See for instance the study by Lin Liyue, "Xiaodao yu fudao."

Chapter 3

1. For a discussion of the construction of *erchen* as a historiographical category during the Qianlong period, see Crossley, *A Translucent Mirror*, 290–96; and Lin, "In the Name of Honor."

2. Tu, "Probing the 'Three Bonds' and 'Five Relationships' in Confucian Humanism," 125–26.

3. Qian Zhongshu locates the original articulation of this concept in the poem "Four Steeds" (Shi 162). Qian, *Guanzhui bian*, "Maoshi zhengyi," no. 49 "Si mu," vol. 1, 226–29.

4. These two moments were also the focus of the catalog of Ming martyrs commissioned by the Qianlong emperor, *Shengchao xunjie zhuchen lu* 勝朝殉節諸臣錄. See Lin, "In the Name of Honor," 331–35.

5. Zhu Yunwen, who reigned with the era name Jianwen 建文 from 1398 to 1402, was the legitimate heir as the eldest surviving son of the eldest son of Zhu Yuanzhang, the Ming dynasty founder.

6. See Zhao Yuan 趙園, *Ming Qing zhi ji shidaifu yanjiu*, 165–91; Benjamin Elman, "The Formation of 'Dao Learning' as Imperial Ideology during the Early Ming Dynasty," 58–82; Hok-lam Chan, "Legitimating Usurpation," 118–25.

7. *CHC*, 202–4. Hok-Lam Chan has traced the history of the slow lifting of imperial proscriptions against Jianwen and his ministers, and showed how this process was periodically slowed down by other episodes of irregular succession, e.g. Jingtai (1449–1457) and Jiajing (1522–1567). Chan, "Legitimating Usurpation," 115–18. See also Ditmanson, "Venerating the Martyrs of the 1402 Usurpation." Zhu Qiyu (Jingtai) was a younger half-brother of Zhu Qizhen (Zhengtong), and chosen as his successor after Zhu Qizhen was captured by the Oirat Mongols after the Tumu bao debacle. Zhu Houcong (Jiajing) was a younger cousin of Zhu Houzhao (Zhengde) who had died without issue.

8. See Lei Qingrui, *Wan Ming wenren sixiang tanxi*, 102–5; Liu, "Diwang huanhun: Mingdai Jianwendi liuwang xushi de yanyi" and "Ren, tian, mo: *Nüxian waishi* zhong de lishi quehan yu ta jie xiangxiang." The fascination with the Jianwen loyalists continued in the early Qing, as shown for instance in Lü Xiong's novel *Nüxian waishi* (Unofficial History of Female Immortals), and it resurfaced again in the late Qing. Figures such as Fang Xiaoru and Tie Xuan were the object of a fervent popular cult at the local level, as depicted in fictional texts. In chapter 2 of *Lao Can youji*, Liu E describes the eponymous hero's visit to Tie Xuan's shrine, which is presented as one of the "must see" places in Jinan.

9. Chan, "Legitimating Usurpation," 119–21.

10. In the roughly contemporary collection of classical language stories *Samsara Tales to Awaken the World* (*Lunhui xingshi* 輪迴醒世), Fang Xiaoru is the only Ming figure in the section dedicated to cases of loyalty and treachery. He is portrayed as an exemplar of loyalty together with his entire clan. His tragic fate is inscribed within a scheme of retribution, which is the emphasis of the collection. In the story, Fang Xiaoru was guilty of destroying a nest of snakes buried beneath the site he had chosen to serve as an ancestral grave, hence his whole family was later executed by the emperor. *Lunhui xingshi*, juan 14, 462–64. A similar retribution scheme revolving around snakes is found in *Taowu xianping*, one of the Wei Zhongxian novels published in the aftermath of the eunuch's

downfall; H. Laura Wu, "Corpses on Display: Representations of Torture and Pain in the Wei Zhongxian Novels," 51.

11. A commentated edition of the apocryphal *Zhongjing* 忠經 (Classic of Loyalty) published in the Tianqi or Chongzhen era includes a list of brief biographies of loyal exemplars—all of which are martial figures (from Jiang Taigong and Sun Wuzi, to Guo Ziyi, Yue Fei, and the Mongol general Bayan of the Mergid). For an illuminating study of the circulation and reception of the *Zhongjing* in the Ming, see Liu, "Tiandao, zhishu, shangpin: *Zhongjing* zhi chuban yu Mingdai zhong wenhua."

12. Xu Kui (1482/4–1517/9) was a high-ranking official in Jiangxi at the time of the rebellion of the Prince of Ning. He refused to follow the prince and was eventually killed by his men.

Sun Sui (1460–1519) was the governor of Jiangxi. He submitted several unheeded reports on the Prince of Ning's treason. He was finally executed by the Prince of Ning in July 1519. See *CHC*, 426–29. Both Sun Sui and Xu Kui are recorded in the "Biographies of the Loyal and Righteous Officials" section (*Zhongyi zhuan*) in *Mingshi*.

Hu Guang (1370–1418), learned scholar and Hanlin academician, switched his allegiance to Yongle, and quickly became one of his most trusted advisors. The entry in *DMB* (compiled by Angela Hsi and L. Carrington Goodrich) describes him as a moderate and upright adviser who played a role in dissuading Yongle from exterminating the remaining partisans of Jianwen (*DMB*, 628). In the *Exemplary Words* story, however, Hu Guang cuts a less noble figure. The anecdote related in the prologue tells of how Hu Guang's daughter had been betrothed to the son of Xie Jin 解縉 (1369–1415), another influential adviser of Yongle and a close friend of Hu Guang. After Xie's downfall, Hu Guang intended to break the engagement, but his daughter showed her mettle by cutting her ears and swearing she would marry no one else but Xie Jin's son.

Li Shishi (?–1520) had been in good terms with the Prince of Ning, yet he intended to commit suicide when the rebellion broke out, to avoid becoming marked as a traitor. However, his children, coveting riches and honors, dissuaded him from doing so. In the end he died an ignominious death (he was beaten to death by the Nanchang populace) and brought infamy to his whole family. See *XSYPZ*, 20 fn. 13.

13. Hanan, *The Chinese Vernacular Story*, 114.

14. Huang, *China: A Macro-History*, 165. In popular literature, the Zhengde emperor is typically depicted as a foolish and debauched ruler. See Idema, "Prosimetric and Verse Narrative," 360–61.

15. Wang Shuying was a Hanlin academician under Jianwen. He raised an army in the attempt to resist the Prince of Yan's invasion, and he committed suicide when the capital fell. In the early sixteenth century a commemorating shrine was erected to honor his memory in his hometown. The shrine was built with wing shrines to commemorate Wang's wife and daughters. See Katherine

Carlitz, "Shrines, Governing-Class Identity, and the Cult of Widow Fidelity in Mid-Ming Jiangnan," 634–35.

Huang Guan ranked first in the Hongwu 24 (1391) palace examination. He also raised an army to attempt to oppose the advance of the Prince of Yan, and he drowned himself when the latter entered the capital. His story is also dramatized in *West Lake Stories, Second Collection* (see note 45 below).

Hu Run served as vice-minister at the Court of Judicial Review under Jianwen. He was brutally executed by Yongle.

16. Gu Yingtai, *Mingshi jishi benmo* (1658), j. 18.

17. Zhang, *Confucian Image Politics*, 14–15, 51–60, and passim. For a comparative philosophical approach to the idea of transgenerational virtue, see Erin Cline, *Families of Virtue*.

18. *XSY* 1.45; *XSYPZ* 1.1. Cf. *Sanguo yanyi*, chapter 68, 564: "The Lord feeds you, you serve the Lord" 食君之祿, 忠君之事. The probable source of this adage is a passage from the *Zuozhuan*, in which Zilu proclaims his loyalty to the lord who "fed" him: "Having received a salary from him, I will not avoid him now that he is in a difficult situation" 食焉, 不辟其難, *Chunqiu Zuozhuan zhu*, Ai 15.5, vol. 4, 1696. I am grateful to professor Wai-yee Li for this reference.

19. *XSY* 1.45; *XSYPZ* 1.1.

20. Li Jinglong is the particular target of the interlineal commentator's venom. When Jianwen decides to reinstate Li even after he had repeatedly lost to Zhu Di's armies, the commentator bursts out: "Why not kill this hopeless idiot?" 孺子何以不殺? *XSY* 1.63; *XSYPZ* 1.6. Li Jinglong later surrendered to Yongle (he was said to be responsible for opening the gates of Nanjing to his army, thus causing the fall of the city), but he eventually ran afoul of the new emperor, who stripped him of his title and threw him in jail. See *DMB*, 886–87.

21. Yongle had all official documents and histories concerning Jianwen destroyed, artificially extending the Hongwu era from 32 to 35 years. Ever since, the Jianwen period has been referred to as the "expunged period" *gechu* 革除. Cf. *CHC*, 202.

22. *XSY* 1.107–108; *XSYPZ* 1.19. In the woodblock edition, there is a reverential blank space (*jing kong* 敬空) before the name of Jianwen, while Chengzu's name is placed at the head of a new line. In the text of the story proper, a reverential space is uniformly used before the era names of all the emperors mentioned in the story, Hongwu, Jianwen, and Yongle.

23. Indeed, the accusation of being "impractical and unrealistic" was voiced by many historians. Cf. Frederick Mote's entry on Fang Xiaoru in *DMB*, 428. Cf. the disparaging remarks against Fang Xiaoru by one character in *Rulin waishi*, chapter 29 (where Fang is also seen as an "impractical pedant" 迂而無當 who deserved to die). See Stephen Roddy's analysis of the passage, *Literati Identity*, 95–96, and footnotes 260–61.

24. Cf. *CHC*, 187–89.

25. See Bu Shichang and Tu Heng, *Huang Ming tongji shuyi*, 3.66a–b. (This work, published in 1605, is an expanded edition of Chen Jian's *Huang Ming tongji*

皇明通記 of 1555). See also Li Zhi, *Xu Cangshu*, j. 5, in *Li Zhi quanji zhu*, vol. 9, 210 (Li Zhi's version stops short and does not mention the commutation of penalty from ninth to tenth degree of kinship). For an English translation and discussion of the incident, see Benjamin Elman, "Where Is King Ch'eng?," also *A Cultural History of Civil Examinations in Late Imperial China*, 97–100. For a discussion of how Fang Xiaoru's image as thinker and martyr was perceived throughout the dynasty, see Peter Ditmanson, "Death in Fidelity," 114–43.

26. Huang, *Mingru xue'an*, juan 43, 1a–2b. For an English translation, see Huang Tsung-hsi, *The Records of Ming Scholars*, 208–10.

27. Zhao Yuan has eloquently argued about the close link between the ruler's cruelty and the subject's self-destructive attitude—the two can be seen as two sides of the same coin. Brutality calls for increasingly extreme forms of self-mutilation, and vice versa, in a crescendo of violence, suffered and inflicted with seemingly equal relish. Zhao Yuan, *Ming Qing zhi ji shidaifu yanjiu*, 5–22.

28. Lu Renlong's account of Tie Xuan was probably based on the entry in Li Zhi's *Xu Cangshu*, j. 5, in *Li Zhi quanji zhu*, vol. 9, 228–29. See Zhang Anfeng, "Xingshi yan sucai laiyuan (1)," 187. According to some sources, the emperor had Tie Xuan's ears and nose cut off, before he was executed by slow slicing. His body parts were then deep-fried until they were completely burnt. See *DMB*, 1,285. See also Gu Yingtai's narration of the deaths of the Jianwen martyrs in *Mingshi jishi benmo*.

29. *XSY* 1.74–75; *XSYPZ* 1.9.

30. *XSY* 1.67, 104; *XSYPZ* 1.7, 18. The Orphan of Zhao saga was made popular by Ji Junxiang's 紀君祥 *zaju* play *Zhao shi gu'er* 趙氏孤兒 (The Orphan of the House of Zhao). The play is based on *Zuozhuan* Xuan 2 (although the orphan is not mentioned here) and Sima Qian's *Shiji* 43.

31. In Sima Qian's account (but not in either Yuan or Ming version of the play), after the orphan of Zhao has taken his revenge against Tu'an Gu, Cheng Ying commits suicide to fulfill the pledge he had made to Gongsun Chujiu twenty years earlier.

32. This is reminiscent of the appreciative attitude of another notorious usurper, Empress Wu Zetian, toward Luo Binwang's essay written to indict her.

33. The proverbial phrase originates from a passage in the biography of Yu Xu 虞詡, an early second-century military governor, in *Hou Han shu*.

34. *XSY* 1.90; *XSYPZ* 1.14. The phrase *pifu xiaoliang* is an allusion from *Lunyu* 14.17, a passage in which Confucius extols the Qi minister Guan Zhong, who lived on to serve Duke Huan, the murderer of his former lord.

35. The commentator draws an analogy with Jizi 箕子, a Shang nobleman who was imprisoned by the evil last ruler, King Zhòu, and faked madness to escape execution. He was later released by King Wu of Zhou and, according to some versions of the legend, he went to Korea along with 5,000 followers and became the first ruler of the Kija (Jizi) Chosŏn.

36. Tie Xuan and his daughters are mentioned in two essays originally published in 1934, "Miscellaneous Talks after Illness" (*Bing hou zatan* 病後雜談)

and "More Miscellaneous Talks after Illness" (*Bing hou zatan zhi yu* 病後雜談之餘). See *Lu Xun quanji*, vol. 6, 167–204. These passages are also discussed by Ban Wang in *Illuminations from the Past*, 74–76.

37. *Lu Xun quanji*, vol. 6, 176. Lu Xun quotes from Yu Zhengxie's *Guisi leigao* a piece of evidence that throws doubt on the very existence of the Tie daughters. He writes:

"Suppose that Tie Xuan in fact had no daughters, or that they indeed had committed suicide; from this trumped-up story it is possible for us to get a glimpse of a larger psychological pattern in society. Namely, it is much more appealing that the households of those fallen on hard times should have daughters rather than not; likewise, it is much more appealing that said daughters should end up in the brothel rather than commit suicide; and yet, since Tie Xuan is after all a loyal minister, having his daughters end up their lives in the brothel would surely cause discomfort [in the readers]. Therefore they should enjoy a different fate from that of ordinary women, and by offering their poetry they should be married off to officials." 倘使鐵鉉真的並無女兒, 或有而實已自殺, 則由這虛構的故事, 也可以窺見社會心理之一斑。就是: 在受難者家族中, 無女不如其有之有趣, 自殺又不如其落教坊之有趣, 但鐵鉉究竟是忠臣, 使其女永淪教坊, 終覺于心不安, 所以還是和尋常女子不同, 因獻詩而配了士子. *Lu Xun quanji*, vol. 6, 197.

38. Two poems attributed to Tie's daughters are quoted in the *Exemplary Words* story, where they are both attributed to the younger sister, *XSY* 1.96, 100; *XSYPZ*.1.16–17. In his *Liechao shiji* 列朝詩集 (Collected Poems of the Successive Reigns), Qian Qianyi writes that the poem attributed to the elder sister is in fact a personal composition written by an early Ming poet, Fan Changqi 范昌期, in the voice of an aging courtesan. It is especially the poem ending with the couplet: "When spring comes dew descends in rainy profusion abundant as an ocean, Marrying Liu Chen would be better even than marrying Ruan Zhao!" 春來雨露深如海, 嫁得劉郎勝阮郎, which elicits Qian Qianyi's ire. Qian judged the poem as vulgar and unbecoming for a supposedly chaste girl of good family. Qian Qianyi, *Liechao shiji xiaozhuan*, vol. 2, 740.

39. Chu Renhuo said that the records he consulted only mention one girl aged four *sui* at the time of Tie Xuan's execution. See *Jianhu ji* 堅瓠集 (Hard Gourds), quoted in Zhang Anfeng, "*Xingshi yan* sucai laiyuan (1)," 189, 198.

40. On Fang Xiaoru's daughters, see Ditmanson, "Death in Fidelity," 132–33.

41. In the story, Tie Xuan and Sheng Yong use rockets (*pentong* 噴筒) or "spurting tubes" (according to Needham's translation), "magic firelances" (*shenji chong* 神機銃), and "Frankish machines" (*Folang ji* 佛狼機). *XSY* 1.58; *XSYPZ* 1.4–5. The "magic firelances" are mentioned in a famous and controversial passage in the *Mingshi*, according to which the weapons were imported from Vietnam during the Yongle reign. The Dai Viet had first obtained the firearms from the Chinese a couple of centuries earlier, but they were able to significantly improve them. As a result, the most skilled Vietnamese weapon artisans were brought to China by Yongle. See Sun Laichen, "Chinese Military Technology and Dai Viet." The "Frankish machines" (Timothy Brook's translation) were in fact cannons made by the Spanish and Portuguese; see Andrade, *The Gunpowder Age*,

135–43. On the use of firearms in the battles with the Manchu, see Nicola Di Cosmo, "Did Guns Matter?"

42. Lu Renlong, *Liaohai danzhong lu*, 26.

43. *XSY* 1.92–93; *XSYPZ* 1.15.

44. *XSY* 1.97; *XSYPZ* 1.16.

45. The prologue story in *West Lake Stories, Second Collection* 18 "Shang Lu ensures victory and captures Man Si" (商文毅決勝擒滿四) is also concerned with the celebration of a Jianwen loyalist, Huang Guan 黃觀. In this story, the narrator introduces a supernatural element to justify Yongle's irresistible ascent. Yongle is said to be the reincarnation of the Dark Warrior (Xuanwu), deity of the North, and his final victory is obtained through the help of various deities. Physical violence is here displaced by way of synecdoche: Yongle vents his anger at Huang's ceremonial headdress, which is all that the imperial guards were able to fish out from the river after Huang had drowned himself. Yongle orders an effigy of Huang Guan made out of straw, and his headdress placed on top. He then has the effigy chopped into pieces as an emblem of lingering death (*linchi* 凌遲). See *XHEJ* 18.379–82.

46. Shen Lian, like Yang Jisheng, another major model of selfless martyrdom in the Yan Song era, acquired a reputation for outspokenness mixed with a certain intransigent naiveté. See Dietrich Tschanz, "History and Meaning in the Late Ming Drama *Ming feng ji*," 8–9.

47. *YSMY* 40.710; Feng Menglong, *Stories Old and New*, 724, with slight modification. On the exploits of Jia Fuxi (1590–1674) as a literatus turned storyteller, see Strassberg, *The World of K'ung Shang-jen*, 33–40; Volpp, *Worldly Stage*, 233–35; Zhao, "Literati Use of Oral or Oral-Related Genres to Talk about History in the Late Ming and Early Qing," 89–106.

48. *YSMY* 40.710; Feng, *Stories Old and New*, 724.

49. See *CHC*, 730; also Shih-Shan Henry Tsai, *Perpetual Happiness*, 70; Chan, "Legitimating Usurpation," 121–25. For fictional renditions, see for instance *West Lake Stories, Second Collection* 25; *Nüxian waishi* 女仙外史; *Xu Yinglie zhuan* 續英烈傳. For a dramatic adaptation, see Li Yu's 李玉 (ca. 1586–ca. 1667) play *Qianzhong lu* 千忠戮 (later renamed 千鐘錄).

50. Li Zhi, *Xu Cangshu*, j. 7, in *Li Zhi quanji zhu*, vol. 9, 313–15. See Zhang Anfeng, "*Xingshi yan* sucai laiyuan (1)," 193–95.

51. *XSY* 8.394; *XSYPZ* 8. 137. In *Zuozhuan*, Jie Zhitui refused to take any credit, hence did not expect any reward, for what he believed to be entirely heaven's merit. He said that one should not greedily "appropriate heaven's merit as one's own effort" 貪天之功以為己力; *Chunqiu Zuozhuan zhu*, Xi 24.1, 417–19.

52. *XSY* 8.395; *XSYPZ* 8.137.

53. Ibid. This sarcastic treatment of Jie Zhitui foreshadows the more radical debunking in the first story of the postconquest collection *Idle Talk under the Bean Arbor*.

54. The exemplarity of the survivor is also celebrated in *XSY* 17. The main hero of this story, Xiang Zhong, makes a conscious decision not to commit suicide once he has been captured by the Oirats, but rather to find a way to

escape. In this story too, the commentator rejects the idea of dying for the sake of it.

55. *XSY* 8.398; *XSYPZ* 8.138.

56. *Chunqiu Zuozhuan zhu*, Xi 28.8, 472; Durrant, Li, and Schaberg, *Zuo Tradition*, vol. 1, 426–27.

57. Hanan, *The Chinese Vernacular Story*, 83–84.

58. See Jing Yugui's discussion of *zhi* in Lu Yunlong's other works in his monograph *Lu Renlong, Lu Yunlong xiaoshuo chuangzuo yanjiu*, 50–53. Xiang Zhong in Story 17 also is described as a notably sagacious (*zhi*) official in the story title.

59. *XSY* 8.399–400, 410–17; *XSYPZ* 8.138, 142–43. Cf. *XHEJ* 25.527–31; *Li Zhi quanji zhu*, vol. 9, 313–15.

60. "Clear away disaster" (*jingnan* 靖難) is the phrase used to retroactively refer to the campaign of the Prince of Yan in official accounts. See Chan, "Legitimating Usurpation," 87 and 136n.

61. *XSY* 8.434; *XSYPZ* 8.149. Cf. *Li Zhi quanji zhu*, vol. 9, 315.

62. See Xu Zhiping, "Qingchu duanpian shishi xiaoshuo xilun," 242–45, for a brief discussion of *QYZ* 1, 4, and 14.

63. Jizi 箕子 (the Viscount of Ji) and Bi Gan were both Shang noblemen who lived during the reign of the notorious last Shang ruler, King Zhou. For Jizi, see n. 33 above. Bi Gan 比幹 remonstrated with the king (who was actually his nephew) and was therefore executed and eviscerated.

64. Xu You 許由 and Bo Yi 伯夷 were both famous recluses of antiquity, often invoked as models of incorruptible integrity and purity. Xu You refused to take the throne offered to him by the sage King Yao, and he is said to have washed his ears lest they be contaminated by the talk of holding office. Bo Yi together with his brother Shu Qi retreated to Mount Shouyang when the Shang fell and refused to "eat the grain of the Zhou," thereby starving to death. Mencius praises Bo Yi as "the sage who was unsullied" (*sheng zhi qing zhe* 聖之清者); he also calls him "too straitlaced" (*ai* 隘) in another passage. *Mengzi yi zhu* 5B.1 and 2A.9, 233 and 84; *Mencius*, 111 and 40.

65. *QYZ*, 1.14.

66. Lu Yunlong, *Cuiyuge jinyan*, juan 2, 133.

67. For Yang Lian's biography, see *ECCP*, 892–93.

68. Jing Yugui, *Lu Renlong, Lu Yunlong xiaoshuo chuangzuo yanjiu*, 182–83.

69. Plaks, *The Four Masterworks of the Ming Novel*, 279.

70. Lu Yunlong, *Wei Zhongxian xiaoshuo chijian shu*, 774, 776–77. Note that the *Mingshi* also records a similar anecdote: when Yang Lian was arrested to be brought to the capital "tens of thousands of people, gentry and commoners, lined up on the road, grabbed the police and shouted at them, trying to stop them from taking him away. All along the way, cities and villages burned incense and held sacrifices to pray for Yang Lian's safe return." Quoted in Lu, *True to Her Words*, 44.

71. *QYZ*, 1.26–27.

72. This is in contrast with Ji Liuqi's account of Wang Wei in *Mingji bei lüe*, where Geng-shi is given more agency as she explicitly requests to follow her husband in death should things take a turn for the worse. Ji, *Mingji bei lüe*, j. 21.
73. This detail is also in Ji Liuqi's account.
74. See Seligman et al., *Ritual and Its Consequences*.
75. On the dichotomy *kangkai* vs. *congrong*, see He Guanbiao, *Sheng yu si*, 140–45. Cf. Wang Fuzhi's remarks on the topic discussed in Zhao Yuan, *Ming Qing zhi ji shidaifu yanjiu*, 44. The proverb "To kill oneself impetuously is easy, to serenely die for the sake of justice is difficult" *kangkai shashen yi, congrong jiuyi nan* 慷慨殺身易, 從容就義難 (and similar variants) seems to have first gained currency during the Southern Song, and is found in the writings of the Cheng brothers, Zhu Xi, Xie Fangde, and others.
76. *QYZ*, 1.33.
77. A brief biographical entry on Yang Yipeng is included in *Mingshi*, j. 260, 6,745–46.
78. *QYZ* 14.336–38.

Chapter 4

1. Raphals, *Sharing the Light*.
2. The phrase *fu yi fu ting* originally comes from *Liji*, "Liyun," 18. For the role of remonstrance in the father-child and ruler-minister relationship, see *Analects* 4.18, 19.10; *Liji*, "Quli" II.113 and "Neize," 18; *Xiaojing*, chapter 15. For an English translation and discussion of the term *jian* 諫 in *Xiaojing*, see Ames and Rosemont, *The Chinese Classic of Family Reverence*, 113–14 and 71–72.
3. Bossler, *Courtesans, Concubines, and the Cult of Female Fidelity*, 130.
4. Attempts to redefine the meaning of chastity beyond merely corporeal (sexual) terms may be seen as a reaction or response to this kind of semantic narrowing. In late Ming literary anthologies, courtesans could also be characterized as *zhen* or *jie*. Mei Dingzuo's 梅鼎祚 (1549–1615) collection of the lives of courtesans *Qingni lianhua ji* 青泥蓮花記 has a section on *jie*. Feng Menglong's *Qingshi* 情史 includes a number of entries on "faithful courtesans" (*zhenji* 貞妓) in the first section titled "Qingzhen" 情貞. The exchange between Yu Huai 余懷 (1616–1696) and the courtesan Li Shiniang/Zhenmei 李十娘/貞美 in *Banqiao zaji* 板橋雜記 also points to such a reinterpretation of *zhen*; the passage is discussed in Wai-yee Li, *Women and National Trauma*, 301–2. In *Exemplary Words*, Wang Cuiqiao (*XSY* 7) may be considered one such virtuous courtesan (if we exclude the Tie daughters in Story 1, who are very atypical courtesans); but, in line with the conservative approach of the collection regarding female virtue, she is characterized as *yi* 義, rather than *zhen* or *jie*.
5. *Yi*, a notoriously ambiguous term that covered a range of meanings including "rightness," "moral appropriateness," and "honor-bound sense of duty,"

was often used in reference to women who took care of other people's children (typically at the expense of their own). *Lie* 烈, which itself could be seen as a semantic narrowing of the related and much broader *lie* 列 (arrayed, exemplary), had been used to describe women who died to resist rape or to avenge a wrong done to the family or the state in earlier sources, but the former meaning came to be used almost exclusively in later sources. Similarly, *xian* 賢 had been used to describe women who advised family members on sociopolitical issues, but it became restricted to the domestic sphere in later sources. Qian, "*Lienü* versus *Xianyuan*," 81–82.

6. Scholars have drawn on sources as varied as official biographies, gazetteer entries, literary compilations, records of court cases, and visual and architectural vestiges—including woodblock illustrations, memorial arches, and shrines. Among the most influential studies are Mark Elvin, "Female Virtue and the State in China"; T'ien Ju-k'ang, *Male Anxiety and Female Chastity*; Paola Paderni, "Between Formal and Informal Justice: A Case of Wife-Selling in Eighteenth-century China"; Katherine Carlitz, "Shrines, Governing-Class Identity, and the Cult of Widow Fidelity in Mid-Ming Jiangnan"; Susan Mann and Fangqin Du, "Competing Claims on Womanly Virtue in Late Imperial China"; Paul Ropp et al., *Passionate Women: Female Suicide in Late Imperial China*; Janet Theiss, *Disgraceful Matters*; Weijing Lu, *True to Her Word*.

7. Lu, *True to Her Word*. After the fall of the Ming, the figure of the "faithful maiden" becomes an even more compelling symbol of a scholar who has passed his exams and registered to become an official, but has never entered office, and commits suicide for the sake of the fallen dynasty, although this kind of analogy was already articulated before the fall. See Jiang Yingke, "Xu Lienü jie," quoted in Huang, *Negotiating Masculinities*, 73–74.

8. Huang, *Negotiating Masculinities in Late Imperial China*, 73.

9. See, for example, Gui Youguang 歸有光 (1507–1571), discussed in Huang, *Negotiating Masculinities in Late Imperial China*, 72–73.

10. For instances of exemplary female characters in *San Yan* and *Er Pai*, see "Chen Duoshou" (*XSHY* 9), "Against Autopsy" (*EK* 31), and "Mother Jia Wrongly Upbraids Her Daughter" (*EK* 35). The latter features female suicide as its central theme.

11. These observations are consistent with the differences between classical and vernacular texts noted by Patrick Hanan and Allan Barr. See Hanan, *The Chinese Vernacular Story*, 23–25, and Barr, "*Liaozhai zhiyi* and Chinese Vernacular Fiction," 3.

12. Elvin, "Female Virtue and the State in China," 129–33.

13. Carlitz, "Three Ming Dynasty Martyrs and Their Monstrous Mothers-in-Law."

14. For a history of editions of the play, see West, "A Study in Appropriation: Zang Maoxun's Injustice to Dou E."

15. See Carlitz, "Three Ming Dynasty Martyrs and Their Monstrous Mothers-in-Law," 11.

16. Yang Shen, "Biography of the Filial and Heroic Tang Guimei" 孝烈婦唐貴梅傳, in *Sheng'an quanji*, j. 11, 122–23; included, with slight modification, in Li Zhi, *Fenshu*, j. 5, in *Li Zhi quanji zhu*, vol. 2, 179–180. The story of Tang Guimei is also found in a variety of compilations. Although Li Zhi's account emphasizes the filial piety component, elsewhere the story of Tang Guimei is listed under the rubric of chastity. For example, in the sixteenth-century didactic tract for women *Nüfan jielu* 女範捷錄, Tang Guimei is listed under "chaste and heroic women" (*zhenlie* 貞烈), rather than under the filial piety section. *Nüfan jielu*, comp. by Chaste Widow Wang (aka Lady Liu), chapter 5, in Huang Yanli, ed., *Nü sishu jizhu yizheng*. The Wanli illustrated edition of *Nüfan bian* 女範編, compiled by Huang Shangwen 黃尚文, includes Tang Guimei under the "heroic women" (*lienü* 烈女) category (j. 4).

For an insightful analysis of Yang Shen's biography and Li Zhi's commentary, see Barbara Bisetto, "La tradizione biografica femminile in epoca Ming." Yang Shen's biography has been translated into English by Qitao Guo, *Ritual Opera and Mercantile Lineage*, 175–76, and the abridged *Mingshi* version by Katherine Carlitz, "Three Ming Dynasty Martyrs and Their Monstrous Mothers-in-Law," 7–8, 10. Carlitz compares the abridged *Mingshi* version with the original biographical account, and insightfully analyzes Tang Guimei's case in the context of other biographies of daughters-in-law victimized by their corrupt mothers-in-law.

17. Yang Shen, *Sheng'an quanji*, j. 11, 122–23. For an alternative English translation, see Guo, *Ritual Opera and Mercantile Lineage*, 175–76.

18. See Lu Yunlong's preface to Story 6, XSY 6.287–88; XSYPZ 6.94.

19. Li Zhi, *Fenshu*, in *Li Zhi quanji zhu*, vol. 2, 179–80.

20. See, for example, Idema and Grant, *The Red Brush: Writing Women of Imperial China*, 85.

21. XSY 6.293; XSYPZ 6.96. Zhu Yan's name itself points to his face.

22. XSY 6.311; XSYPZ 6.102.

23. Carlitz, "Three Ming Dynasty Martyrs and Their Monstrous Mothers-in-Law."

24. McMahon, *Causality and Containment in Seventeenth-Century Chinese Fiction*, 93.

25. Yang Shen, *Sheng'an quanji*, juan 11, 122.

26. XSY 6.293–309; XSYPZ 6.96–101.

27. XSY 6.317, 319, 325; XSYPZ 6.103, 104, 106.

28. XSY 6.336; XSYPZ 6.109.

29. XSY 6.337; XSYPZ 6.110. Original source is Li Zhi, *Fenshu*, in *Li Zhi quanji zhu*, vol. 2, 180.

30. A similar conundrum occurs in Story 27 of *Constant Words*, where Li Yuying (a reputedly historical character who lived in the early sixteenth century) is accused by her corrupted stepmother of being lecherous and unfilial for having written some poems. Like Tang Guimei, Li Yuying is thrown into jail, but she does not dare to exculpate herself in order to avoid compounding the crime of unfiliality. Unlike Guimei, however, Li Yuying pours out her story in a long and

astutely crafted memorial to the Jiajing emperor, who had solicited memorials from wrongly accused prisoners in the summer of 1525. As a result, she was pardoned, and her persecutors executed. See Ann Waltner's discussion of this story "Writing Her Way Out of Trouble," 231 in particular. Story 17 in *Slapping the Table in Amazement* also provides interesting material for comparison. In the story, lady Wu, a widow, accuses her virtuous son of unfiliality in a plot to get rid of him to enjoy a life of debauchery with a Daoist abbot. But unlike the story of Tang Guimei, the boy is rescued and the mother redeems herself in the end.

31. *XSY* 6.332–33; *XSYPZ* 6.108.

32. *XSY* 6.323; *XSYPZ* 6.105. We may detect here also the pressure of a literary motif that Katherine Carlitz has described as the "monstrous–feminine": this is the chaste-turned-insatiable young wife typified by the woman from Hejian in Liu Zongyuan's *chuanqi* tale. Carlitz, "Three Ming Dynasty Martyrs and Their Monstrous Mothers-in-Law," 16–18.

33. *XSY* 6.333–34; *XSYPZ* 6.108–9.

34. On this point see Binbin Yang, *Heroines of the Qing*, 8.

35. See Li Zhi's commentary, *XSY* 6.337–38; *XSYPZ* 6.110. Originally in *Li Zhi quanji zhu*, vol. 2, 180.

36. The heroism of Tang Guimei, her "clever" embodiment of chastity and filial piety, undoubtedly had a special grip on the Lu brothers' imagination. Lu Yunlong cites Tang Guimei in his commentary to a biography of Cheng Juying by Tu Long 屠隆 (1542–1605), included in his best-selling anthology *Informal Essays by Sixteen Eminent Authors of the August Ming*. This is "Cheng lienü zhuan," in Lu Yunlong, *Huang Ming shiliu mingjia xiaopin*, Ji bu, vol. 378, 180–81; biography originally in Tu Long's *Youquan ji* 由拳集, juan 19. Cheng Juying 程菊英 had been betrothed to a Zhang, but the rich and powerful Xu family tried to persuade her father to break the earlier engagement and marry her to their son. Cheng's father adamantly refused and on his deathbed asked his daughter not to renege. Cheng thereupon committed suicide by strangling herself in the bridal palanquin. The author praises Cheng, her father, mother, and brother, while blaming the Xu family and the corrupted local officials. Story 4 in the early Qing collection *Sobering Stone* is based on this anecdote.

37. The final commentary, which appears to be truncated in the extant edition, reads: "In the past, I have written a vernacular rendition (*yanyi*) of Tang Guimei, which can be considered as a remarkable tale. But the story of these two women, who were able to act in unison, is even more remarkable. In the present reign everyone harbors different intention, how can one hope for fervent examples . . ." 常作唐貴梅演義。可足為世奇。此兩女流而能同，更事之奇。今在朝人各一心。又安望有烈烈 . . . *QYZ* 2.72. See Jing Yugui, *Lu Renlong, Lu Yunlong xiaoshuo chuangzuo yanjiu*, 193; Li Xiaolong, "Qingye zhong zuozhe buzheng," 232.

38. *XSY* 6.311; *XSYPZ* 6.101–2.

39. Jing Yugui has identified Zhu Ziqiang as Zhu Jian 朱健, a relatively prominent late Ming literatus, and possibly a personal acquaintance of Lu Yunlong. Jing, *Lu Renlong, Lu Yunlong xiaoshuo chuangzuo yanjiu*, 204–6. A poem "Shuanglie

shi" attributed to Zhu Ziqiang is printed on the back of the illustration for this story (although its doggerel-like quality hardly matches the narrator's hyperbolic praise at the end of the story). *QYZ* 4.

40. The term *rensi* 忍死 in the titular couplet seems to be used in the meaning of "enduring death," rather than "holding on to life for the sake of a higher principle" as in the case of the loyalty stories discussed in chapter 3.

41. Lu Yunlong included this biography in his anthology *Mingwen qiyan* 明文奇艷 (1636), juan 9. Quoted in Gu Keyong and Wei Ran, "Lu Renlong shi *Xingshi yan* bianzhe er fei zuozhe kaobian," 151–53. The biography is also recorded in the Kunshan county gazetteer, in the section on Gui Zimu, and in the Suzhou prefecture gazetteer, in the "Lienü zhuan" section; see Zhang Anfeng, "*Xingshi yan* sucai laiyuan (1)," 197; Quan Ning'ai, "*Xingshi yan* yanjiu," 92. Lu Renlong follows closely the literary source, with one notable insertion: the amusing episode of the visit to the Tianzhu temple and other temples in Hangzhou, which gives the author the chance to satirize the monks' greed.

42. *XSY* 10.498; *XSYPZ* 10.180.

43. *XSY* 10.513–14; *XSYPZ* 10.184–85.

44. Theiss, *Disgraceful Matters*, 177–91.

45. Elvin, "Female Virtue and the State in China," 127–29; Mann and Du, "Competing Claims on Womanly Virtue in Late Imperial China," 234–35; Theiss, *Disgraceful Matters*, 30–38.

46. Yang Jisheng, "Yang Zhongmin gong yibi" 楊忠愍公遺筆, quoted in Hu Lianyu, "Wu'ai de huangliang," 72; Lei Qingrui, *Wan Ming wenren sixiang tanxi*, 180. For an English translation and discussion of Yang's letter see "*Final Instructions* by Yang Jisheng," translated by Beverly Bossler, in Mann and Cheng, *Under Confucian Eyes*, 119–33. These instructions were addressed to Yang's wife Zhang Zhen, who, according to some sources, committed suicide on the day of Yang's execution. (For an alternative version, according to which Yang's wife did *not* commit suicide, see Hammond, "Virtuous Surrogates"). In the final commentary to this story, Lu Yunlong uses the same image of the swan's down to describe Chen Zhi'er's attitude toward death, but with the opposite meaning, that is, he praises Zhi'er for treating death as lightly as a swan's down to describe her insouciance when facing death. *XSY* 10.524; *XSYPZ* 10.188. (The tail commentary appears truncated in the Kyujanggak edition.)

47. There is a literary language version of this story in *Qingshi*, under the title "Li Miaohui." Zhanzhan waishi, *Qingshi*, vol. 1, 5–7. Other versions are also found in *Yanshan biji*, entry "Jinshan si." In the classical Chinese versions, the story is set in the Song, whereas it is moved to the Chenghua reign in *Rocks*.

48. *SDT* 2.37–38.

49. *XSY* 10.518; *XSYPZ* 10.186.

50. The original biography reads: 人各有幸不幸, 兩大人皆老, 新婦年少, 歲月遙遙, 事變難料。新婦何敢望從大母, 死決矣. Chen and Shen, *Huang Ming congxin lu*, j. 38, 54b.

51. I thank professor Rainier Lanselle for this insight.

52. See for example the prologue of *XSY* 4 (discussed in chapter 2). This would seem to contradict the general "democratization" trend discussed by Elvin. "Female Virtue and the State in China," 114.

53. *XSY* 10.524; *XSYPZ* 10.187–88.

54. The sound made by the girl who has just hanged herself and is overheard, typically by a parent or parent-in-law, is a motif present in other tales of suicide. See for example "Chen Duoshou and His Wife Bound in Life and Death" 陳多壽生死夫妻, *XSHY* 9.112.

55. *XSY* 10.520; *XSYPZ* 10.186.

56. See for example Theiss, *Disgraceful Matters*; Lu, *True to Her Word*.

57. This is an allusion to the adage "to sacrifice one's life with ardent passion is easier than going to one's death with serene composure" (*kangkai juan sheng yi, congrong jiu yi nan* 慷慨捐生易, 從容就義難). On the dichotomy *kangkai* vs. *congrong*, see chapter 3, note 75.

58. *XSY* 10.496–97; *XSYPZ* 10.179.

59. *XSY* 10.493–94; *XSYPZ* 10.178.

60. This biography is itself based on a prior biography by a Li Bangzhi 李邦直. In *Exemplary Words* he is erroneously referred to as a *shaoqing* of Nanzhou 南洲 (*XSYPZ* 16.282), while Yang Shen writes that he is an official in Dongzhou 東洲. *Sheng'an quanji*, juan 4, 65. See Chen Yiyuan, *Cong* Jiao Hong ji *dao* Hongloumeng, 274.

61. *XSY* 16.744; *XSYPZ* 16.276.

62. *XSY* 16.757; *XSYPZ* 16.280.

63. *XSY* 16.766; *XSYPZ* 16.283.

64. This contradicts the satirical passages on the rampant corruption at the provincial-level bureaus of the ministry of personnel, which are referred to the present of the narration, that is, the same Jiajing reign. *XSY* 16.762; *XSYPZ* 16.281.

65. For an example of both kinds of reading, see Hu, "Wu'ai de huangliang," 70–71, 73. See also Jing, *Lu Renlong, Lu Yunlong xiaoshuo chuangzuo yanjiu*, 59–65.

Chapter 5

1. For a discussion of how *Jingu qiguan* recasts *San Yan* stories, see Lanselle, "Introduction," in *Spectacle curieux d'aujourd'hui et d'autrefois*, ix–xlvi; and Patricia Sieber, chapter 2 of her forthcoming book *How to Wage Peace with A Dictionary: Print Culture, Class, and Chinese Studies in Nineteenth-Century Britain*.

2. For a discussion of the vulnerability of the brotherly bond and its literary representations in the early medieval period, see Keith Knapp, "Brother, Can You Spare a Dime? Siblings in Early Medieval Accounts of Filial Children."

3. *Mengzi* 3A.4, in *Mengzi yi zhu*, 125; *Mencius*, 60.

4. The *locus classicus* is *Lunyu* 1.6, "A young person should be filial when at home and respectful of his elders when in public." 弟子入則孝, 出則弟 (悌).

Lunyu yi zhu, 4–5; *Analects*, 3. This idea is reiterated in *Mengzi* 3B.4, in *Mengzi yi zhu*, 146; *Mencius*, 67. The phrase "parallel conception of society" is borrowed from Kutcher, *Mourning in Late Imperial China*, 2.

5. Adrian Davis proposes the translation "loving fraternity." Davis, "Fraternity and Fratricide in Late Imperial China," 1,630.

6. Davis, "Fraternity and Fratricide in Late Imperial China," 1,631.

7. As in the *Great Ming Commandment* (Da Ming ling): "A family's property and land are to be divided equally among sons of the wife or others according to their number without regard to whether they were born of the wife, a concubine, or a slave." In De Bary and Bloom, *Sources of Chinese Tradition*, vol. 1, 785. Also cited in Li and Meynard, *Jesuit Chreia in Late Ming China*, 114.

8. Vagnone's *Illustrations* devotes thirty-one entries, corresponding to 9 percent of the total work, to the *kun di* 昆弟 category. As a comparison, the mid-fifteenth-century monumental imperial compilation *Wulun shu* 五倫書 (62 juan) devotes 2 percent to this category. See Li and Meynard, *Jesuit Chreia in Late Ming China*, 143, 146. Li Zhi's *Chutan ji* devotes 2 juans, or 6.6 percent of the total work, to the brotherly bond.

9. Li and Meynard, *Jesuit Chreia in Late Ming China*, 264–68.

10. In her article on the Ming loyalist Huang Chunyao 黃淳耀, Lynn Struve notes that Huang treated his younger brother as a friend, while he become quickly weary of the club meetings with his actual friends: "rather than pattern his extrafamilial friendships on the brotherly bond, he related as a friend to his much-younger full brother, Yuanyao, the one true intimate in his life." Struve, "Self-Struggles of a Martyr: Memories, Dreams, and Obsessions in the Extant Diary of Huang Chunyao," 359.

11. In the tale "Raising One's Brother as One's Son" 育弟為子, Mao Ju 毛矩 raises as a son his half-brother Zhen 珍, who had been born of a concubine forced to leave the house by Ju's shrewish mother. Even after Ju reveals his real identity to Zhen, who has by now become a high official, Zhen continues to revere him as a father, and even obtains a special permission from the Jiajing emperor to do so! *Lunhui xingshi*, 317–21. Another tale, "Brothers Stay Loyal" 手足不二, represents the younger brother as a prodigal-son figure, who squanders his own as well as a large part of his brother's share of patrimony, before eventually repenting. *Lunhui xingshi*, 321–23.

12. *Samsara Tales* (*Lunhui xingshi*) again offers more examples of this story type: the tale "The Dutiful Ones Obtain Progeny" 義氣得後 tells of three brothers whose harmonious and complementary activities as farmers, traders, and housekeepers turn their family into a sort of ideal Confucian microcosm. *Lunhui xingshi*, 323–25.

13. An exception is found in *YSMY* 39, "Wang Xinzhi Dies to Save the Family" (汪信之一死救全家), where the estrangement between the protagonist Wang Ge and his older brother leads to the hero's decision to leave the house and set up his own "kingdom." The story ends with a posthumous reconcilia-

tion, and with the elder brother Wang Fu yielding his estate (*rangchan* 讓產) to his brother's offspring. However, beyond serving as basic plot, the brotherly relationship is not explored in this story.

14. *XSY* 13.618–19; *XSYPZ* 13.228.

15. Sima Guang, who showed unwavering devotion and deference to his older brother even after he had became a top official, is also the figure selected to illustrate the second maxim of the *Sacred Edict* in Zhong, *Illustrated Explanation of the Sacred Edict*; see introduction, note 1.

16. In the original story (a variant of the "eat me when I am fatter" folktale type) it is actually the elder brother Zhao Xiao 趙孝 who offers himself up to save his younger brother Li. See the biography of Zhao Xiao in *Hou Hanshu*, juan 39. The Yuan play attributed to Qin Jianfu *Zhao Li Yields to [His Brother's] Plumpness* (*Zhao Li rang fei* 趙禮讓肥) is based on this story. In the play not only the elder brother Xiao but also Li and their mother (who has also hurried to the scene to save her sons) all argue that each of them is the plumpest, with the result that the bandit leader decides to release all three of them. For an annotated French translation of the play, see Isabella Falaschi, *Trois pièces du théâtre des Yuan*, lxxxv–civ (introduction) and 162–214 (translation).

17. Wang Xiang is best remembered as one of the twenty-four filial exemplars.

18. *XSY* 13.615; *XSYPZ* 13.226.

19. *XSY* 13.610–11; *XSYPZ* 13.225.

20. *XSY* 13.615–16; *XSYPZ* 13.227.

21. *XSHY* 2.18; Feng, *Stories to Awaken the World*, 35.

22. Two cautionary stories of evil brothers in *Samsara Tales* concern fratricide originated by fights over property, though here it is the younger brother or brothers who kill the elder, abusive brother. See *Lunhui xingshi*, 343–46.

23. Full title is 遲取券毛烈賴原錢, 失還魂牙僧索剩命 (Mao Lie holds on to the mortgage receipt to fraudulently keep the bailment money; the broker-monk who had missed his chance to reincarnate demands the remainder of his allotted lifespan).

24. *EK* 16.197.

25. *YSMY* 10.152; Feng, *Stories Old and New*, 173.

26. *QYZ* 8.263–64.

27. *QYZ* 8.265–66.

28. *QYZ* 8.271.

29. Cf. Lévy, *Inventaire*, vol. 4, 367.

30. *QYZ* 8.285.

31. For Zhang Gongyi, see Knapp, *Selfless Offspring*, 17. The ideal of "hundred forbearances" 百忍 and "nine generations living under the same roof" 九世同居 was criticized later in the seventeenth century as analogous to practices such as *gegu* 割股 (filial slicing) and *lumu* 廬墓 (living in a shed by the parents' grave), which should be seen as extreme forms of virtuous behavior under duress, and

not upheld as general norms. Zhang Chao, *Youmeng ying* 幽夢影 (Quiet Dream Shadows); cited in Lu, "Reviving an Ancient Filial Ideal," 178.

32. *QYZ* 8.296.

33. Davis, "Fraternity and Fratricide in Late Imperial China," 1,640.

Chapter 6

1. Rivi Handler-Spitz, Pauline Lee, and Haun Saussy, "Introduction," in *A Book to Burn*, xxvii. Translating the term *you* 友 as "friendship" is not without its problems. *You* is often used to designate a range of private associations between men, from club membership (*sheyou* 社友 or *huiyou* 會友) to something akin to the close friendship that is the object of the stories discussed in this chapter. The problem is also compounded by the fact that in the West, too, the notion of friendship underwent significant changes. For a discussion of the etymology of this term, see Shields, *One Who Knows Me*, 32–37.

2. For a discussion of the medieval genres of *juejiao shu* and *juejiao lun*, see Jansen, "The Art of Severing Relationships (*juejiao*) in Early Medieval China," and Asselin, "'A Significant Season.'"

3. Tu, "Probing the 'Three Bonds' and 'Five Relationships' in Confucian Humanism," 129.

4. Mann, "The Male Bond in Chinese History and Culture," 1,605.

5. Kutcher, "The Fifth Relationship," 1,615n.

6. This is in contrast with the Aristotelian notion of friendship. In the *Nicomachean Ethic* (Book VIII, 132–34), Aristotle talks about friendship between parent and child as natural, though he does posit it as a case of friendship between nonequals.

7. See McDermott, "Friendship and Its Friends in the Late Ming"; Lai, "Friendship in Confucian China: Classical and Late Ming"; Mann, "The Male Bond in Chinese History and Culture"; Kutcher, "The Fifth Relationship"; Lu Miaw-fen, *Yangmingxue shiren shequn*, 295–325. See also the special issue of *Nan Nü* (9, 2007) devoted to the topic of male bonding in the Ming, with contributions by Martin Huang, Kimberly Besio, Anne Gerritsen, and Joseph Lam.

8. See for example Joanna Handlin Smith, *The Art of Doing Good*; Wang Fansen, "Mingmo Qingchu de renpu yu xingguohui."

9. Huang, "Male Friendship and *Jiangxue*"; Lu, *Yangmingxue shiren shequn*, 295–325. For an overview of the major figures and activities of the Neo-Confucian movement during the latter half of the Ming, see Willard Peterson, "Confucian Learning in Late Ming Thought," in *CHC* 8.2, 708–88. See also Theodore de Bary, "Individualism and Humanitarianism in Late Ming Thought," 145–247.

10. Lu, *Yangmingxue shiren shequn*, 304–11. The phrase *you tianxia zhi shanshi* is found, for example, in a letter of Luo Hongxian's 羅洪先 (1504–1564), quoted in Lu, 304. See also Huang, "Male Friendship and *Jiangxue*," 152.

11. *He Xinyin ji*, 28. Translation based on Lo Yuet Keung's, "My Second Self," 238.

12. *He Xinyin ji*, 66.

13. Li Zhi, "He Xinyin lun," *Fenshu*, j. 3, in *Li Zhi quanji zhu*, vol. 1, 246. In the text, the quotation is attributed to He Xinyin's detractors. The author judges this and other accusations against He not worthy of being refuted.

14. de Bary, "Individualism and Humanitarianism," 199.

15. Li Zhi, *Chutan ji*, in *Li Zhi quanji zhu*, vols. 12–13. 10 juans are devoted to the *shi you* 師友 (Teacher-Friend) category, or 33 percent of the total work.

16. See introduction.

17. As Mencius argues, fathers and sons should not demand goodness of each other, that is, they should not expect flawless behavior or criticize each other's moral conduct, as that would inevitably lead to an estrangement between them. *Mengzi yi zhu*, 4A.18 and 4B.30, 178–79 and 200–201; *Mencius*, 84–85 and 95–96.

18. When asked to comment on the characteristics of a true scholar-official, Confucius replied, "he must be earnest and critical with his friends, and affable with his brothers." 朋友切切、偲偲, 兄弟怡怡. *Lunyu yi zhu* 13.28, 143–44; *Analects*, 151–52.

19. Lü Kun, *Shenyin yu* (Groaning Words, 1593), "Lunli," in *Lü Kun quanji*, vol. 2, 632. For the English translation I have consulted Martin Huang, "Male Friendship and *Jiangxue*," 168–69. See also Lu, *Yangmingxue shiren shequn*, 322–23.

20. According to Ricci's proem, the composition of *Jiaoyou lun* was prompted by his friendship with the Prince of Jian'an Commandery. See Billings's discussion of this proem in Ricci, *On Friendship*, 7–10.

21. Famed literati such as Feng Yingjing 馮應京 and Chen Jiru 陳繼儒 wrote prefaces for it. Li Zhi also played a role in circulating the work among his wide network of disciples and friends. The work was included in several late Ming anthologies. It even earned an entry in the eighteenth-century *Siku quanshu zongmu tiyao* 四庫全書總目提要, and its full text was included in the encyclopedia *Gujin tushu jicheng* 古今圖書集成 of 1726.

22. The impetus for this flourishing of literature on friendship was provided by the rediscovery of Cicero's treatise *De amicitia*, first printed in English translation in 1481. Friendship became a dominant component of the humanist tradition. See for example Thomas Breme's *Mirror of Friendship* (1584), Thomas Churchyard, *A Sparke of Friendship* (1588), and Walter Dorke, *A Type or Figure of Friendship*, 1589. For a discussion of these and other treatises, see for instance Harriette Andreadis, "Re-Configuring Early Modern Friendship," 523–42.

23. The term *chreia* to refer to this particular type of anecdotal *exempla* has been used by scholars Sher-shiueh Li [Li Shixue] and Thierry Meynard; see Li and Meynard, *Jesuit Chreia in Late Ming China*, 11–18 passim. Scholars have long established that the proximate source used by Ricci was a bestselling compilation by the Portuguese Latinist Andreas Eborensis (Andrea de Rèsende 1498–1573), *Sententiae et exempla, ex probatissimis quibusque scriptoribus collecta et per locos com-

munes digesta. Cf. Pasquale M. d'Elia, "Il trattato sull'amicizia," 425–515. Ricci apparently owned a copy of the fifth edition of this book, published in 1590.

24. One hundred twenty-two entries, or 34 percent of the total work. However, only forty-two entries in this section are devoted to expounding the meaning of true friendship; other entries are in the subcategories of flattery, favoritism, and reprimanding. See Li and Meynard, *Jesuit Chreia in the Late Ming*, 143, 176.

25. Besio, "A Friendship of Metal and Stone," 113.

26. The source for both anecdotes is Huang Zongxi, *Mingru xue'an*, quoted in Theodore de Bary, "Individualism and Humanitarianism in Late Ming Thought," 179.

27. Hanan, *The Chinese Vernacular Story*, 110–11; Wong, "Morality as Entertainment," 62; Shuhui Yang, *Appropriation and Representation*, 79–85. See also Besio, "A Friendship of Metal and Stone," 137.

28. Reprinted in Tan Zhengbi, *San Yan Liang Pai ziliao*, vol. 1, 42–46. Cyril Birch has translated the tale in his anthology *Stories from a Ming Collection*, 121–28. Patrick Hanan, who has dated this story as "late, by Feng Menglong" (*The Chinese Short Story*, 237), believes that the immediate source is the entry "Qi nanzi zhuan" 奇男子傳 in *Heke Sanzhi* 合刻三志 (*The Chinese Short Story*, 77n). This version, however, as Hanan writes, is "minimally different from the *Taiping guangji* version."

29. See Hanan, *The Chinese Short Story*, 75; Lévy, *Inventaire*, vol. 1.2, 356. The story is included in the collection *Xiaoshuo chuanqi* (1619 ca.) and is reprinted in Lu Gong, ed., *Guben pinghua xiaoshuo ji*, vol. 1, 95–106.

30. The legend of Fan Juqing in particular features the notion of *siyou* 死友 "friend unto death" or "friend-in-death," as opposed to ordinary friends (*shengyou* 生友 "friend in this life"). *Siyou* can also be read as "dying for the sake of a friend," parallel to *sijie* 死節, *sixiao* 死孝, *sizhong* 死忠, etc. The ideal of life-and-death friendship celebrated in these widely popular stories contradicts Norman Kutcher's contention that the subversive potential of friendship was often contained by ways of understanding intense relationships between friends as temporally limited, as a life stage. Kutcher argues that the ideal of friendship in which friends were willing to share property or even die for each other had all but disappeared since the Song, and that even the paradigmatic friendship between Guan Zhong and Bao Shu was understood as a bonding between young men. See his article "The Fifth Relationship," 1,620, 1,626–27.

31. Other friendship stories from the mid seventeenth century are the ninth story in *Bell in the Still Night*, which is unfortunately missing in the existing editions, and Story 6 in the post-Conquest collection *Sobering Stone*, which features an exemplary friend who takes care of a poet's wife and son after the poet's metamorphosis into a tiger (the story is actually a reworking of a Tang classical tale, "Li Zheng" 李徵).

32. The idea of "gang morality" and the rhetorical appropriation of the ideals of *xin* 信 (trust, or good faith), *tongzhi* 同志 (sharing aspirations, or being of the same mind), and *yiqi* 義氣 (sense of honor and duty, personal loyalty toward

one's friend or leader) by "outlaws of the margins" have been explored by C. T. Hsia, *The Classic Chinese Novel*, 85–96. For friendship as sexualized male bonding, see Vitiello, *The Libertine's Friend*; Volpp, "The Discourse on Male Marriage"; Jie Guo, "Confusing Desires," 71–126.

33. The main episode of Wang Mian rescuing Lu Tai's daughters is probably based on Song Lian's 宋濂 (1310–1381) biography of Wang Mian—and Song Lian is also the probable source of the story of Du Huan included in the prologue, discussed below. Song Lian, "Wang Mian zhuan" 王冕傳, in *Song xueshi wenji* 宋學士文集, *Zhiyuan houji* 芝園後集, juan 10; "Du Huan xiao zhuan" 杜環小傳, in *Zhiyuan xuji* 芝園續集, juan 2, also reprinted. in Zhao Botao, ed., *Ming wenxuan*, 1–5. Song's biography of Wang Mian is included in *Guochao xianzheng lu*, juan 116. The same compilation also includes a biography of Du Huan by Huang Zuo 黃佐, "Luling Du gong zhuan" 廬陵杜公傳, in *Guochao xianzheng lu*, juan 70. See Zhang Anfeng, "*Xingshi yan* sucai laiyuan (2)," 177–78; and Lévy, *Inventaire*, vol. 5, 48.

34. On Liu Ji (Liu Bowen) see Hok-Lam Chan's essays, "Liu Chi (1311–1375) and His Models" and "Liu Chi (1311–1175) in the *Ying-Lieh Chuan*." Liu Ji acquired an aura of a wizard-like advisor in popular culture, which continues to the present day. There is a Taiwanese TV drama (with an astounding run of 404 episodes) titled *Shenji miaoshuan Liu Bowen* 神機妙算劉伯溫 (Divine witted and marvelous predictor Liu Bowen), starring Huang Shaoqi (Eric Huang) in the lead role.

35. *XSY* 14.653; *XSYPZ* 14.241.

36. Ricci, *On Friendship*, 90–91.

37. Cicero, *Laelius*, 17.64. W. A. Falconer's wordier English translation "When Fortune's fickle the faithful friend is found" likewise aims to render the alliterations and consonances of the Latin original. Cicero, *De senectute, De amicitia, De divinatione*, 174–75.

38. On the ambiguity of the modern usage of the proverb "A friend in need is a friend indeed/in deed," see Barbara Kirshenblatt-Gimblett, "Toward a Theory of Proverb Meaning," 113–15.

39. Lu Renlong here follows Song Lian's "partisan" biography, which had coopted the famous recluse to the cause of the Ming. This is in sharp contrast with the characterization in *Rulin waishi*: here the author changes Wang Mian's actual dates by making him die after the Ming founding, and by having him choose to go into reclusion *after* the Ming founding. For a discussion of the different versions of Wang Mian's espousal of the cause of the Ming founding, as well as Wu Jingzi's fictional rewriting and rebuttal of the historical sources, see Stephen Roddy, *Literati Identity*, 113–16.

40. For an account of a real case of friendship among three men of differing political, regional, and ethnic backgrounds during the Yuan-Ming transition, see Anne Gerritsen's article "Friendship through Fourteenth-Century Fissures: Dai Liang, Wu Sidao and Ding Henian."

41. Zhang Shicheng was a powerful regional leader who lorded over Jiangsu and northern Zhejiang. He alternatively surrendered to and betrayed the Yuan several times, before being defeated by the Ming founder Zhu Yuanzhang. *CHC*, 30–36.

42. *XSY* 14.671; *XSYPZ* 14.246–47.

43. See note 33 above.

44. *XSY* 14.659; *XSYPZ* 14.243. This detail is also in Du Huan's biography by Song Lian. In Song's text Du Huan's forbearance is emphasized even more, as he instructs his servants to put up with the lady's bad temper: "The woman was quick-tempered and irascible. If the slightest thing displeased her, she would immediately burst out in anger. Huan secretly instructed the servants and family members to give in to her, forbidding them to belittle her on account of her reduced circumstances" 母性褊急, 少不愜意, 輒詬怒。 瓛私戒其家人, 順其所為, 勿以困故, 輕慢與較. At the end, however, the old lady is given a moment of redemption (unlike in the vernacular story): on her deathbed, she acknowledges her great debt toward Huan, and she wishes that his progeny will be every bit as filial as him. This deathbed wish is a topos in narratives of filial daughters-in-law. Zhao Botao, ed., *Ming wenxuan*, 2–3.

45. This proverb is quoted for example by Liu Bei in *Sanguo yanyi*, chapter 15.

46. "Wu Tianyou tried to snatch away the bamboo basket, claiming that his parents' bones should, by rights, be carried by him, but Zhongxiang would not hear of it. Tearfully, he said, 'Yonggu devoted ten years of his life for my ransom. By carrying his bones for a little while, I am doing what little I can to show my gratitude.'" 吳天祐道, 是他父母的骸骨, 理合他馱, 來奪那竹籠。 仲翔那肯放下, 哭曰:「永固為我奔走十年, 今我暫時為之負骨, 少盡我心而已。」 *YSMY* 8.134; Feng, *Stories Old and New*, 155.

47. Ricci, *On Friendship*, 90–91.

48. The source is a maxim from Andreas Eborensis, *Sententiae et exempla*, 1590 (5th edition), which reads: "Filius sicut in substantia derelicta, ita in paterna amicitia succedere debet" (The son must succeed to his father's property and friendships alike). "Filius" is quoted without attributes. Ricci, *Dell'amicizia*, 148. However, the Italian autographed version preserved in the British Library is coherent with the Chinese text: "Il figliuolo obediente continua le amicitie di suo padre morto insieme con la heredità di esso" (The obedient son continues to cultivate his deceased father's friendships in the same way as he succeeds to his inheritance). Ricci, *Dell'amicizia*, 110. This indicates that the addition was consciously made by Ricci. The original source of the saying is not known.

49. Ricci, *On Friendship*, 110–11. The source of this maxim is Cicero, *Laelius de amicitia* V.19. Ricci, *Dell'amicizia*, 167. The only notable change made by Ricci is the added emphasis on "only" 惟, absent from the original Latin text.

50. *Mengzi yi zhu*, 4A.18 and 4B.30, 178–79 and 200–201; *Mencius*, 84–85 and 95–96.

51. On the friendship between Wang Shizhen and Yang Jisheng, as well as the role played by Yang's wife in his martyrdom, see Hammond, "Virtuous Surrogates," 117–33.

52. Zhang Anfeng, "*Xingshi yan* sucai laiyuan (2)," 182.

53. In popular literature Liuxia Hui and the man from Lu are often conflated into one figure.

54. The story is translated by Patrick Hanan in *Falling in Love*, 180–214.

55. See for example *XSY* 11. The story "Wang Youdao Harbors Suspicion and Discards His Wife" (王有道疑心棄妻子, *Huanxi yuanjia* 18), tells of a young man who escorts a woman who had been caught in a storm back home, without taking advantage of her. Her husband does not believe that, and he divorces her. Later, the young man performs spectacularly well at the exams. By a coincidence, the husband gets to learn the truth from the young man. He reunites with his wife, and he marries his sister to the young man. In this story, the young man confesses to be a devotee of the moral tract *Taishang ganying pian*, and to abide by the dictum that "there is no worse sin than lust." Xihu yuyin zhuren, *Huanxi yuanjia*, v. 2, 249–53.

56. *XSY* 20.904–5; *XSYPZ* 20.339.

Concluding Note

1. Hanan, *The Chinese Vernacular Story*, 195.
2. *Mengzi* 4A.19.
3. Aina jushi, *Doupeng xianhua*, 56–67. A complete English translation of the collection has just appeared: see Robert E. Hegel, ed., *Idle Talk under the Bean Arbor*; Jing Zhang's translation of this story is on pp. 72–85.
4. Aina jushi, *Doupeng xianhua*, 83.
5. Ibid., 86–7.
6. Ibid., 93. See Hanan's translation and discussion of passages from this story in *The Chinese Vernacular Story*, 201–3; Yenna Wu, "The Debunking of Historical Heroes in *Idle Talk under the Bean Arbor*," 8–9; and Li Wai-yee, in *The Cambridge History of Chinese Literature*, edited by Chang and Owen, vol. 2, 201–3. For a complete English translation of this story by Mei Chun and Lane J. Harris, see Hegel, *Idle Talk under the Bean Arbor*, 101–16.
7. See, for example, Andrew Jacobs and Adam Century, "As China Ages, Beijing Turns to Morality Tales to Spur Filial Devotion," *New York Times*, September 5, 2012, accessed April 5, 2017, http://www.nytimes.com/2012/09/06/world/asia/beijing-updates-parables-the-24-paragons-of-filial-piety.html; Shreeya Sinha and John Niedermeyer, "Filial Piety: From Strangling Tigers to Taming the Internet," *New York Times*, September 5, 2012, accessed April 5, 2017, http://www.nytimes.com/interactive/2012/09/06/world/asia/20120905_parables.html. Angela Zito is writing a book-length study of the new *Twenty-Four Filial Exemplars*.

Appendix

1. See for example Qi Yukun, *Mingdai xiaoshuo shi*, 390; Ouyang Daifa, *Huaben xiaoshuo shi*, 290. In general, there is a tendency to conflate the two categories of "minor" and "later" collections.

2. Chen Liao, "Xingshi yan xin lun," 2.

3. Chen Qinghao, "*Xingshi yan* xiaozhu ben xu," in *XSYPZ*, vol. 1, 5.

4. An incomplete edition of *Ilusion* consisting of seven stories was discovered by Zheng Zhenduo in the 1930s. This edition is now preserved at the National Library of China. *Slapping the Table in Amazement, Third Collection* was discovered by Ma Lian 馬廉 in 1929 and it is now preserved at the library of Beijing University. This edition includes all but three of thirty stories (Stories 13 through 15 are missing). The preface is signed by Mengjue daoren 夢覺道人 (The person of the Way awakened from dreams). The stories are ascribed to Mengjue daoren and Xihu langzi 西湖浪子 (The Loafer of West Lake). Zheng Zhenduo, on the basis of the preface, has dated this edition to 1643. Not only are all the stories in *Illusion* found in *Slapping the Table in Amazement, Third Collection*, but also the typographical appearance of the two editions is virtually identical, which has led scholars to believe that the same woodblocks were used for both editions. For all practical purposes, we can then treat the two collections as one.

5. This collection is preserved in two exemplars at the Bibliothèque nationale in Paris and the Saeki Bunko in Japan. It includes thirty-four stories. The first ten come from Ling Mengchu's *Slapping the Table in Amazement, Second Collection*, while the remaining twenty-four are from *Exemplary Words*. This edition also contains illustrations of fourteen stories from *Exemplary Words*. These are reprinted in Lu Renlong, *Xingshi yan*, edited by Chan Hing-ho (Taibei: Zhongyang yanjiuyuan, 1992), vol. 1, 27–54. This edition has been dated to the early Qing, on the basis of internal evidence. For information on *Huanying, Sanke pai'an jingqi* and "Bieke," see Chan Hing-ho, "Daoyan" (Taibei: Zhongyang yanjiuyuan, 1992), Vol. 1, 12–36; and Chan, "*Xing shi yan* yanjiu bulun"; Jing Yugui, *Lu Yunlong, Lu Renlong xiaoshuo chuangzuo yanjiu*, 105–23; Gu Keyong, *Shufangzhu zuojia Lu Yunlong xiongdi yanjiu*, 110–31.

6. It should be noted that some modern editions of *Exemplary Words* (e.g., the 1995 Huaxia chubanshe edition) use the title *Slapping the Table in Amazement, Third Collection*. This is done, no doubt, to capitalize on the popularity of Ling Mengchu's collections, today as in the seventeenth century; however, the two collections ought not to be confused.

7. Compare, for example, the first and last page of story 16 in *Bieben erke pai'an jingqi*, vol. 5, 1a and 25b; the first and last page of story 6 in Mengjue daoren and Xihu langzi, *Sanke pai'an jingqi*, vol. 1, 217 and 266; and the corresponding story in *Exemplary Words*, *XSY* 6.289 and 6.338.

8. The facsimile reprint in the *Guben xiaoshuo jicheng* (Shanghai: Shanghai guji chubanshe, 1990) series reproduces Stories 1–8 and 13–14 from Lu Gong's edition (formerly owned by Zheng Zhenduo) and the edition preserved at the Anhui Provincial Museum. This edition also includes sixteen fine woodblock illustrations followed by descriptive verse in a variety of typographic styles. Two of the illustrations are signed by noted Huizhou carvers Huang Zihe 黃子和 and Liu Qixian 劉啟先 (see Hegel, *Reading Illustrated Fiction in Late Imperial*

China, 201). A modern typeset reprint can be found in Lu Gong, ed., *Guben pinghua xiaoshuo ji*, Vol. 1.

9. Scholars who are in favor of Lu Yunlong's authorship include Lu Gong, Hu Lianyu, Ōtsuka Hidetaka, Jing Yugui, and Li Xiaolong. Gu Keyong and Wei Ran on the other hand have argued against this attribution on the basis of stylistic evidence. They argue that the author must be some obscure literatus from the Zhejiang area. See Jing, *Lu Renlong, Lu Yunlong xiaoshuo chuangzuo yanjiu*, 191–208; Gu, *Shufangzhu zuojia Lu Yunlong xiongdi yanjiu*, 260–78.

10. See Ōtsuka Hidetaka, "*Xingshi yan* yanjiu pingshu," 6–7; Li Xiaolong, "*Qingye zhong* zuozhe buzheng," 231–37.

11. See Gu, *Shufangzhu zuojia Lu Yunlong xiongdi yanjiu*, 260–61.

12. Jing, *Lu Renlong, Lu Yunlong xiaoshuo chuangzuo yanjiu*, 193.

13. For a list of collaborators and various people involved in the Zhengxiaoguan, see Gu Keyong, *Shufangzhu zuojia Lu Yunlong xiongdi yanjiu*, 28–32.

14. Chan Hing-ho gives Li Qing's dates as 1591–1673; see "Un recueil de contes retrouvé," 90.

15. See Qian Nanxiu, *Spirit and Self in Medieval China*, 283–318, for a discussion of Li Qing's work and Lu Minshu's preface.

16. See David Wang's *The Monster That Is History*, 200–12 for a discussion of this novel.

17. Gu Keyong argues that *Exemplary Words* is the earliest collection of short stories to have been compiled using a call for submission method. *Shufangzhu zuojia Lu Yunlong xiongdi yanjiu*, 71–72.

18. The notice calls for "unusual events heard from all over the world" (*yunei yiwen* 宇內異聞), to be sent directly to Lu Renlong's house. Quoted in Gu Keyong, *Shufangzhu zuojia Lu Yunlong xiongdi yanjiu*, 71.

19. "For the publication of *Exemplary Words for the World, Second Collection*, please submit [records of] unusual events heard from across the empire" (*kan "Xingshi yan erji" zheng hainei yiwen* 刊《型世言二集》徵海內異聞). Quoted in Gu Keyong, *Shufangzhu zuojia Lu Yunlong xiongdi yanjiu*, 71.

20. On the practice of calls for submission as part of the prefatory materials, see Kai-wing Chow, *Publishing, Culture, and Power*, 75–77; Zhang Xiumin, *Zhongguo yinshua shi*, 325 (Zhang gives the date of 1336 as the earliest case of solicitation for manuscripts in a poetry anthology). Shang Wei notes that guidebooks would often include a notice for submissions. Shang, "'Jin Ping Mei' and Late Ming Print Culture," 191. Patrick Hanan writes that the earliest of Li Yu's compilation is *Chidu chuzheng* (A First Collection of Letters, 1660), where he solicits readers' contributions in the "universally practiced genre of letter-writing." Hanan, *The Invention of Li Yu*, 24–25. See also Widmer, "The Huanduzhai of Hangzhou and Suzhou," 93 and 105.

Bibliography

Aina jushi 艾衲居士, and Zhuoyuan ting zhuren 酌元亭主人, comp. *Doupeng xianhua* 豆棚閒話. *Zhaoshi bei* 照世盃. Edited by Chen Dakang 陳大康 and Wang Guanshi 王關仕. Taipei: Sanmin shuju, 1998.

Altenburger, Roland. "The Avenger's Coldness: On the Emotional Condition of Revenge as Represented in Pre-Modern Chinese Fictional Narrative." In *Love, Hatred, and Other Passions: Questions and Themes on Emotions in Chinese Civilization*, edited by Paolo Santangelo and Donatella Guida, 356–69. Leiden: Brill, 2006.

Ames, Roger T., and Henry Rosemont, trans. and eds. *The Chinese Classic of Family Reverence: A Philosophical Translation of the* Xiaojing. Honolulu: University of Hawai'i Press, 2009.

Andrade, Tonio. *The Gunpowder Age: China, Military Innovation, and the Rise of the West in World History*. Princeton, NJ: Princeton University Press, 2016.

Andreadis, Harriette. "Re-Configuring Early Modern Friendship: Katherine Philips and Homoerotic Desire." *Studies in English Literature 1500–1900* 46, no. 3 (Summer 2006): 523–42.

Aristotle. *Nichomachean Ethics*. Translated and edited by Terence Irwin. 2nd edition. Indianapolis, IN: Hackett, 1999.

Asselin, Mark Laurent. "'A Significant Season'—Literature in a Time of Endings: Cai Yong and a Few Contemporaries." PhD diss., University of Washington, 1997.

Barr, Allan H. "*Liaozhai zhiyi* and Chinese Vernacular Fiction." In *Reading China: Fiction, History and the Dynamics of Discourse. Essays in Honour of Professor Glen Dudbridge*, edited by Daria Berg, 3–36. Leiden: Brill, 2007.

———. "The Wanli Context of the 'Courtesan's Jewel Box' Story." *Harvard Journal of Asiatic Studies* 57 (1997): 107–41.

Bartoli, Daniello. *La Cina*. Milano: Bompiani, 1975.

Besio, Kimberly. "A Friendship of Metal and Stone: Representations of Fan Juqing and Zhang Yuanbo in the Ming Dynasty." *Nan Nü* 9 (2007): 111–45.

Bieben erke pai'an jingqi 別本二刻拍案驚奇. 8 vols. Taipei: Tianyi chubanshe, 1985.

Birch, Cyril, ed. and trans. *Stories from a Ming Collection: Translations of Chinese Short Stories Published in the Seventeenth Century*. New York: Grove Press, 1958.

Bisetto, Barbara. "La tradizione biografica femminile in epoca Ming: il caso di Tang Guimei." In *Caro Maestro . . . Scritti in onore di Lionello Lanciotti per l'ottantesimo compleanno*, edited by Maurizio Scarpari and Tiziana Lippiello, 133–44. Venezia: Cafoscarina, 2005.

Bol, Peter. Review of *The Troubled Empire: China in the Yuan and Ming Dynasties*, by Timothy Brook. *Journal of Song-Yuan Studies* 41 (2011): 405–10.

Breuer, Rüdiger. *Vorbilder für die Welt: Zwei Novellen aus der Sammlung* Xing Shi Yan *(um 1632)*. Dortmund: Project Verlag, 1997.

Brokaw, Cynthia. *The Ledgers of Merit and Demerit: Social Change and Moral Order in Late Imperial China*. Princeton, NJ: Princeton University Press, 1991.

Brook, Timothy. *The Confusions of Pleasure: Commerce and Culture in Ming China*. Berkeley: University of California Press, 1998.

Bu Shichang 卜世昌 and Tu Heng 屠衡, comp. *Huang Ming tongji shuyi* 皇明通記述遺. Rpt. in *Zhongguo yeshi jicheng xubian* 中國野史集成續編. Vol. 9. Chengdu: Ba Shu shushe, 2000.

Cai Baozhen 蔡保禎. *Xiaoji* 孝紀. Rpt. in *Siku quanshu cunmu congshu* 四庫全書存目叢書. Ser. 2. Vol. 88. Jinan: Qi Lu shushe, 1997.

Carlitz, Katherine. "Shrines, Governing-Class Identity, and the Cult of Widow Fidelity in Mid-Ming Jiangnan." *Journal of Asian Studies* 56, no. 3 (August 1997): 612–40.

———. "Three Ming Dynasty Martyrs and Their Monstrous Mothers-in-Law." *Ming Studies* 68 (2013): 5–32.

Chan Hing-ho. "Un recueil de contes retrouvé après trois cents ans: le *Xing shi yan*." *T'oung Pao* LXXXI (1995): 81–107.

Chan Hing-ho 陳慶浩. "*Xing shi yan* yanjiu bulun 型世言研究補論." In *'93 Zhongguo gudai xiaoshuo guoji yantaohui lunwen ji '93* 中國古代小說國際研討會論文集, 309–28. Beijing: Kaiming chubanshe, 1996.

Chan, Hok-lam. "Liu Chi (1311–75) and His Models: The Image-Building of a Chinese Imperial Adviser." *Oriens Extremus* 15, no. 1 (1968): 34–55. Rpt. in *China and the Mongols: History and Legend under the Yüan and Ming*, VII. Aldershot, UK: Ashgate, 1999.

———. "Liu Chi (1311–75) in the *Ying-Lieh Chuan*: The Fictionalization of a Scholar-Hero." *Journal of the Oriental Society of Australia* 5, 1–2 (1967): 26–42. Rpt. in *China and the Mongols: History and Legend under the Yüan and Ming*, VIII. Aldershot, UK: Ashgate, 1999.

———. "Legitimating Usurpation: Historical Revisions under the Ming Yongle Emperor (r. 1402–1424)." In *The Legitimation of New Orders: Case Studies in World History*, edited by Philip Yuen-sang Leung, 75–158. Hong Kong: Chinese University Press, 2007.

Chang, Kang-i Sun, and Stephen Owen, eds. *The Cambridge History of Chinese Literature*. Vol. II. Cambridge, UK: Cambridge University Press, 2010.

Chavannes, Édouard. "Les saintes instructions de l'empereur Hong-Wou (1368–1398), publiées en 1587 et illustrées par Tchong Houa-min." *Bulletin de l'Ecole Française d'Extrême-Orient* 3 (1903): 549–62.

Chen Dadao 陳大道. "Mingmo Qingchu shishi xiaoshuo de tese" 明末清初時事小說的特色. *Xiaoshuo xiqu yanjiu* 小說戲曲研究 3 (1987): 181–220.

Chen Jian 陳建 and Shen Guoyuan 沉國元. *Huang Ming congxin lu* 皇明從信錄. Rpt. in *Xuxiu siku quanshu* 續修四庫全書. Vol. 355. Shanghai: Shanghai guji chubanshe, [1995–1999].

Chen Liao 陳遼. "Xingshi yan xin lun" 型世言新論. *Neijiang shifan xueyuan xuebao* 3, no. 29 (2014): 1–5.

Cheng, Anne. "Filial Piety with a Vengeance: The Tension Between Rites and Law in the Han." In *Filial Piety in Chinese Thought and History*, edited by Alan K. L. Chan and Sor-hoon Tan, 29–43. London: RoutledgeCurzon, 2004.

Chow, Kai-wing. *Publishing, Culture, and Power in Early Modern China*. Stanford, CA: Stanford University Press, 2004.

———. *The Rise of Confucian Ritualism in Late Imperial China: Ethics, Classics, and Lineage Discorse*. Stanford, CA: Stanford University Press, 1994.

Chunqiu Zuozhuan zhu 春秋左傳注. Edited by Yang Bojun 楊伯峻. Rev. ed. 4 vols. Beijing: Zhonghua, 1990.

Cicero, Marcus Tullius. *De senectute, De amicitia, De divinatione*. Translated by W. A. Falconer. Loeb Classical Library 20. Cambridge, MA: Harvard University Press; London: W. Heinemann, 1923.

Cline, Erin M. *Families of Virtue: Confucian and Western Views on Childhood Development*. New York: Columbia University Press, 2015.

Cole, Alan. *Mothers and Sons in Chinese Buddhism*. Stanford, CA: Stanford University Press, 1998.

Confucius. *Analects. With Selections from Traditional Commentaries*. Translated by Edward Slingerland. Indianapolis, IN: Hackett, 2003.

Crossley, Pamela Kyle. *A Translucent Mirror: History and Identity in Qing Imperial Ideology*. Berkeley: University of California Press, 1999.

Dalby, Michael. "Revenge and the Law in Traditional China." *The American Journal of Legal History* 25 (1981): 267–307.

Davis, Adrian. "Fraternity and Fratricide in Late Imperial China." *The American Historical Review* 105, no. 5 (Dec. 2000): 1,630–40.

de Bary, Wm. Theodore. "Individualism and Humanitarianism in Late Ming Thought." In *Self and Society in Ming Thought*, 145–248. New York: Columbia University Press, 1970.

de Bary, Wm. Theodore, and Irene Bloom, eds. *Sources of Chinese Tradition*. Vol. 1: *From Earliest Times to 1600*. 2nd ed. New York: Columbia University Press, 1999.

d'Elia, Pasquale M. "Il trattato sull'amicizia: primo libro scritto in cinese da Matteo Ricci S. I. (1595). Testo cinese, Traduzione antica (Ricci) e moderna (D'Elia), Fonti, Introduzione e Note." *Studia Missionalia* 7 (1952): 425–515.

Di Cosmo, Nicola. "Did Guns Matter? Firearms and the Qing Formation." In *The Qing Formation in World-Historical Time*, edited by Lynn Struve, 121–166. Cambridge, MA: Harvard University Asia Center, 2004.

Ditmanson, Peter. "Death in Fidelity: Mid- and Late-Ming Reconstructions of Fang Xiaoru." *Ming Studies* 45–46 (2002): 114–43.

———. "Venerating the Martyrs of the 1402 Usurpation: History and Memory in the Mid and Late Ming Dynasty." *T'oung Pao* 93 (2007): 110–58.

Dudbrige, Glen. *The Legend of Miaoshan*. Rev. ed. Oxford, UK: Oxford University Press, 2004.

Durrant, Stephen, Wai-yee Li, and David Schaberg, eds. and trans. *Zuo Tradition. Zuozhuan: Commentary on the "Spring and Autumn Annals."* 3 vols. Seattle: University of Washington Press, 2016.

Eagleton, Terry. "Literature, Virtue and Evil." In *Il bene e il male: L'etica nel romanzo modern*, edited by Paolo Tortonese, 49–57. Roma: Bulzoni, 2007.

Elman, Benjamin. *A Cultural History of Civil Examinations in Late Imperial China*. Berkeley: University of California Press, 2000.

———. "The Formation of 'Dao Learning' as Imperial Ideology during the Early Ming Dynasty." In *Culture and State in Chinese History: Conventions, Accommodations, and Critiques*, edited by Theodore Huters, R. Bin Wong, and Pauline Yu, 58–82. Stanford, CA: Stanford University, 1997.

———. "Where Is King Ch'eng? Civil Examinations & Confucian Ideology During the Early Ming, 1368–1415." *T'oung Pao* 79 (1993): 23–68.

Elvin, Mark. "Female Virtue and the State in China." *Past and Present* 104 (Aug 1984): 111–52.

Epstein, Maram. *Competing Discourses: Orthodoxy, Authenticity, and Engendered Meanings in Late Imperial Chinese Fiction*. Cambridge, MA: Harvard University Asia Center, 2001.

———. "Making a Case: Characterizing the Filial Son." In *Writing and Law in Late Imperial China: Crime, Conflict, and Judgment*, edited by Robert E. Hegel and Katherine Carlitz, 27–43. Seattle: University of Washington Press, 2007.

———. "Sons and Mothers: The Social Construction of Filial Piety in Late-Imperial China." In *Love, Hatred, and Other Passions: Questions and Themes on Emotions in Chinese Civilization*, edited by Paolo Santangelo and Donatella Guida, 285–300. Leiden: Brill, 2006.

Falaschi, Isabella, ed. and trans. *Trois pièces du théâtre des Yuan*. Paris: Les Belles Lettres, 2015.

Fan Hongjuan 范紅娟. "Ming Qing xunqin xiqu qingjie moshi chutan" 明清尋親戲曲情節模式初探. *Qiushi xuekan* 38.3 (2011): 107–12.

Fang Ruhao 方汝浩. *Chanzhen houshi* 禪真後史. Hangzhou: Zhejiang guji chubanshe, 1987.

Fang Xiaoru 方孝孺. *Xunzhi zhai ji* 遜志齋集. Rpt. in *Siku quanshu* 四庫全書. Vol. 1235. Taipei: Taiwan shangwu yinshu guan, 1983.

Feng Menglong 馮夢龍. *Jingshi tongyan xinzhu quanben* 警世通言新注全本. Edited by Wu Shuyin 吳書蔭. Beijing: Beijing shiyue wenyi chubanshe, 1994.

———. *Xingshi hengyan xinzhu quanben* 醒世恆言新注全本. Edited by Zhang Minggao 張明高. Beijing: Beijing shiyue wenyi chubanshe, 1994.

———. *Yushi mingyan xinzhu quanben* 喻世明言新注全本. Edited by Chen Xizhong 陳曦鐘. Beijing: Beijing shiyue wenyi chubanshe, 1994.
Feng Menglong, comp. *Stories Old and New: A Ming Dynasty Collection*. Translated by Shuhui Yang and Yunqin Yang. Seattle: University of Washington Press, 2000.
———, comp. *Stories to Awaken the World: A Ming Dynasty Collection*. Vol. 3. Translated by Shuhui Yang and Yunqin Yang. Seattle: University of Washington Press, 2009.
———, comp. *Stories to Caution the World: A Ming Dynasty Collection*. Vol. 2. Translated by Shuhui Yang and Yunqin Yang. Seattle: University of Washington Press, 2005.
Fisher, Carney T. *The Chosen One: Succession and Adoption in the Court of Ming Shizong*. Boston: Allen & Unwin, 1990.
Furey, Constance. " 'Intellects Inflamed in Christ': Women and Spiritualized Scholarship in Renaissance Christianity." *The Journal of Religion* 84, no. 1 (January 2004): 1–22.
Gerritsen, Anne. "Friendship through Fourteenth-Century Fissures: Dai Liang, Wu Sidao and Ding Henian." *Nan Nü* 9 (2007): 34–69.
Goodrich, L. Carrington, and Chao-ying Fang, eds. *Dictionary of Ming Biography 1368–1644*. New York: Columbia University Press, 1976.
Goossaert, Vincent, ed. and trans. *Livres de morale révélés par les dieux (Shanshu ba zhong)*. Paris: Les Belles Lettres, 2012.
Gu Dashao 顧大韶. *Bingzhuzhai wenji* 炳燭齋文集. Shanghai: Guoxue fulunshe, 1909.
Gu Keyong 顧克勇. *Shufangzhu zuojia Lu Yunlong xiongdi yanjiu* 書坊主作家陸雲龍兄弟研究. Beijing: Zhongguo shehui kexue chubanshe, 2010.
Gu Keyong 顧克勇, and Wei Ran 蔚然. "Lu Renlong shi *Xingshi yan* bianzhe er fei zuozhe kaobian" 陸人龍是型世言編者而非作者考辨. *Ming Qing xiaoshuo yanjiu* 明清小說研究 2003.3: 146–53.
———. "*Xingshi yan* de nüxing guan—yu *San Yan Er Pai* bijiao" 型世言的女性觀—與三言二拍比較. *Wuhan keji daxue xuebao* 武漢科技大學學報 2006.3: 78–81.
Gukuangsheng 古狂生, comp. *Zuixing shi* 醉醒石. *Guben xiaoshuo jicheng* 古本小說集成 series. Shanghai: Shanghai guji chubanshe, 1990.
Gu Yingtai 谷應泰. *Mingshi jishi benmo* 明史紀事本末. Shanghai: Shangwu yinshuguan, 1934.
Guo Haofan 郭浩帆. "Mingmo Qingchu shishi xiaoshuo sixiang tezheng lunlüe" 明末清初時事小說思想特徵論略. *Xiamen jiaoyu xueyuan xuebao* 夏門教育學院學報 3 (2007.9): 12–14.
Guo Jie. "Confusing Desires: Representations of Male Same-Sex Relationships in Late Ming and Early Qing Literature." PhD diss., Johns Hopkins University, 2008.
Guo Qitao. *Ritual Opera and Mercantile Lineage: The Confucian Transformation of Popular Culture in Late Imperial Huizhou*. Stanford: Stanford University Press, 2005.

Hammond, Kenneth. "Virtuous Surrogates: Moral Action and Substitution in the Case of Yang Jisheng." In *The Quest for Gentility in China*, edited by Daria Berg and Chloë Starr, 117–33. London: Routledge, 2007.

Hampton, Timothy. *Writing from History: The Rhetoric of Exemplarity in Renaissance Literature*. Ithaca: Cornell University Press, 1990.

Hanan, Patrick. *The Chinese Short Story: Studies in Dating, Authorship, and Composition*. Cambridge, MA: Harvard University Press, 1973.

———. *The Chinese Vernacular Story*. Cambridge, MA: Harvard University Press, 1981.

———, trans. *Falling in Love. Stories from Ming China*. Honolulu: University of Hawai'i Press, 2008.

———. "The Fiction of Moral Duty: The Vernacular Story in the 1640s." In *Expressions of Self in Chinese Literature*, edited by Robert E. Hegel and Richard C. Hessney, 189–213. New York: Columbia University Press, 1985.

———. *The Invention of Li Yu*. Cambridge, MA: Harvard University Press, 1988.

———. "The Making of *The Pearl-Sewn Shirt* and *The Courtesan's Jewel Box*." *Harvard Journal of Asiatic Studies* 33 (1973): 124–53.

———. "The Nature of Ling Meng-ch'u's Fiction." In *Chinese Narrative: Critical and Theoretical Essays*, edited by Andrew H. Plaks, 85–114. Princeton, NJ: Princeton University Press, 1977.

He Guanbiao 何冠彪. *Sheng yu si: Ming ji shidaifu de jueze* 生與死: 明季士大夫的抉擇. Taibei: Lianjing chuban shiye gongsi, 1997.

He Xinyin 何心隱. *He Xinyin ji* 何心隱集. Beijing: Zhonghua shuju, 1960.

Hegel, Robert E., ed. *Idle Talk under the Bean Arbor: A Seventeenth-Century Chinese Story Collection*. Compiled by Aina the Layman, with commentary by Ziran the Eccentric Wanderer. Seattle: University of Washington Press, 2017.

———. "Introduction: Writing and Law." In *Writing and Law in Late Imperial China: Crime, Conflict, and Judgment*, edited by Robert E. Hegel and Katherine Carlitz, 3–23. Seattle: University of Washington Press, 2007.

Hsia, C. T. "Society and Self in the Chinese Short Story." In *The Classic Chinese Novel: A Critical Introduction*, 299–321. New York: Columbia University Press, 1968.

Hsu Dau-lin. "The Myth of the Five Human Relationships of Confucius." *Monumenta Serica* 29 (1970–71): 27–37.

Hu Lianyu 胡蓮玉. "Lu Yunlong shengping kaoshu" 陸雲龍生平考述. *Ming Qing xiaoshuo yanjiu* 61, no. 3 (2001): 213–22.

———. "Wu'ai de huangliang—*Xingshi yan* zhi nüxing shijie" 無愛的荒涼—型世言之女性世界. *Tongji daxue xuebao* 同濟大學學報 (Shehui kexue ban 社會科學版) 2002.1: 70–76, 90.

Hu Shiying 胡士瑩. *Huaben xiaoshuo gailun* 話本小說概論. 2 vols. Beijing: Zhonghua shuju, 1980.

Huang, Martin W. "Karmic Retribution and Didactic Dilemma in *Xingshi yinyuan zhuan*." *Hanxue yanjiu* 15, no. 1 (1997): 397–440.

———. "Male Friendship and *Jiangxue* (Philosophical Debates) in Sixteenth-Century China." *Nan Nü* 9 (2007): 146–78.
———. *Negotiating Masculinities in Late Imperial China*. Honolulu: University of Hawai'i Press, 2006.
Huang, Ray. *China: A Macro-History*. Armonk, NY: Sharpe, 1997.
Huang Tsung-hsi. *The Records of Ming Scholars*. Translated by Julia Ching and Chaoying Fang. Honolulu: University of Hawaii Press, 1987.
Huang Zongxi 黃宗羲. *Mingru xue'an* 明儒學案. Beijing: Zhongguo shudian, 1990.
———. *Huang Lizhou wenji* 黃梨洲文集. Edited by Chen Naiqian 陳乃乾. Beijing: Zhonghua shuju, 1959.
Hummel, Arthur W., ed. *Eminent Chinese of the Ch'ing Period (1644–1912)*. 2 vols. Washington, DC: Government Printing Office, 1943.
Idema, Wilt L. *Chinese Vernacular Fiction: The Formative Period*. Leiden: Brill, 1974.
———. *Personal Salvation and Filial Piety: Two Precious Scroll Narratives of Guanyin and Her Acolytes*. Honolulu: University of Hawai'i Press, 2008.
———. "Prosimetric and Verse Narrative." In *The Cambridge History of Chinese Literature*, edited by Kang-i Sun Chang and Stephen Owen. Vol. II, 343–412. Cambridge, UK: Cambridge University Press, 2010.
Idema, Wilt, and Beata Grant, eds. *The Red Brush: Writing Women of Imperial China*. Cambridge, MA: Harvard University Asia Center, 2004.
Idema, Wilt, Wai-yee Li, and Ellen Widmer, eds. *Trauma and Transcendence in Early Qing Literature*. Cambridge, MA: Harvard University Asia Center, 2006.
Jansen, Thomas. "The Art of Severing Relationships (*juejiao*) in Early Medieval China." *The Journal of the American Oriental Society* 126 (2006): 347–65.
Jiao Hong 焦竑. *Guochao xianzheng lu* 國朝獻徵錄. 8 vols. Taibei: Taiwan xuesheng shuju, 1964.
Jing Yugui 井玉貴. *Lu Renlong, Lu Yunlong xiaoshuo chuangzuo yanjiu* 陸人龍、陸雲龍小說創作研究. Beijing: Zhongguo shehui kexue chubanshe, 2008.
Jinmu sanren 金木散人. *Guzhang juechen* 鼓絕塵. Edited by Liu Wei 劉蔵. Nanjing: Jiangsu guji chubanshe, 1990.
Kao, Karl S. Y. "*Bao* and *Baoying*: Narrative Causality and External Motivation in Chinese Fiction." *Chinese Literature: Essays, Articles, Reviews (CLEAR)* 11 (1989): 115–38.
Kindall, Elizabeth. *Geo-Narratives of a Filial Son: The Paintings and Travel Diaries of Huang Xiangjian (1609–1673)*. Cambridge, MA: Harvard University Asia Center, 2016.
Kirshenblatt-Gimblett, Barbara. "Toward a Theory of Proverb Meaning." In *The Wisdom of Many: Essays on the Proverb*, edited by Wolfgang Mieder and Alan Dundes, 111–21. New York: Garland, 1981.
Knapp, Keith. "Brother, Can You Spare a Dime? Siblings in Early Medieval Accounts of Filial Children." Unpublished paper.
———. *Selfless Offspring: Filial Children and Social Order in Medieval China*. Honolulu: University of Hawai'i Press, 2005.

Kutcher, Norman. "The Fifth Relationship: Dangerous Friendships in the Confucian Context." *American Historical Review* 105, no. 5 (Dec., 2000): 1,615–29.

———. *Mourning in Late Imperial China: Filial Piety and the State*. Cambridge, UK: Cambridge University Press, 1999.

Lai, Whalen. "Friendship in Confucian China: Classical and Late Ming." In *Friendship East and West: Philosophical Perspectives*, edited by Oliver Leaman, 215–50. Richmond, UK: Curzon, 1996.

Lanselle, Rainier, trans. and ed. *Spectacles curieux d'aujourd'hui et d'autrefois (Jingu qiguan)*. Paris: Gallimard, 1996.

Lauwaert, Françoise. "Comptes des dieux, calculs des hommes: essai sur la rétribution dans les contes en langue vulgaire du 17e siècle." *T'oung Pao* 76 (1990): 62–94.

Lee Cheuk Yin (Li Zhuoran). "Emperor Chengzu and Imperial Filial Piety of the Ming Dynasty: From the *Classic of Filial Piety* to the *Biographical Accounts of Filial Piety*." In *Filial Piety in Chinese Thought and History*, edited by Alan K. L. Chan and Sor-hoon Tan, 141–53. London: RoutledgeCurzon, 2004.

Legge, James. *The She King; Or, The Book of Ancient Poetry, Translated in English Verse, With Essays and Notes*. London: Trübner, 1876.

Lei Qingrui 雷慶銳. *Le conte en langue vulgaire du XVIIe siècle*. Paris: Collège de France, Institut des Hautes Études Chinoises, 1981.

———. *Wan Ming wenren sixiang tanxi: Xingshi yan pingdian yu Lu Yunlong sixiang yanjiu* 晚明文人思想探析：《型世言》評點與陸雲龍思想研究. Beijing: Zhongguo shehui kexue chubanshe, 2006.

Lévy, André. *Études sur le conte et le roman chinois*. Paris: École française d'Extrême-Orient, 1971.

Lévy, André, et al. *Inventaire analytique et critique du conte chinois en langue vulgaire*. 5 vols. Paris: Collège de France, Institut des Hautes Études Chinoises, 1978–2006.

Lewis, Mark Edward. *Writing and Authority in Early China*. Albany: State University of New York Press, 1999.

Li Han. "History, Fiction, and Public Opinion: Writings on Mao Wenlong in the Early Seventeenth Century." *Journal of the American Oriental Society* 134, no. 1 (Spring 2014): 69–88.

Li Ruzhen 李汝珍. *Jinghua yuan* 鏡花緣. Edited by Zhang Youhe 張友鶴. 2 vols. Beijing: Renmin wenxue chubanshe, 1996.

Li, Sher-shiueh, and Thierry Meynard. *Jesuit Chreia in Late Ming China: Two Studies with an Annotated Translation of Alfonso Vagnone's* Illustrations of the Grand Dao. Bern: Peter Lang, 2014.

Li Wai-yee. *The Readability of the Past in Early Chinese Historiography*. Cambridge, MA: Harvard University Asia Center, 2007.

———. *Women and National Trauma in Late Imperial China*. Cambridge, MA: Harvard University Asia Center, 2014.

Li Xiaolong 李小龍. "Qingye zhong zuozhe buzheng" 清夜鐘作者補徵. *Ming Qing xiaoshuo yanjiu* 87 (2008.1): 231–37.

Li Yu 李漁. *Li Yu quanji* 李漁全集. 20 vols. Hangzhou: Zhejiang guji chubanshe, 1991.
Li Zhi 李贄. *Li Zhi quanji zhu* 李贄全集注. Edited by Zhang Jianye 張建業. 26 vols. Beijing: Shehui kexue wenxian chubanshe, 2010.
———. *A Book to Burn and a Book to Keep (Hidden): Selected Writings of Li Zhi*. Edited and translated by Rivi Handler-Spitz, Pauline C. Lee, and Haun Saussy. New York: Columbia University Press, 2016.
Liji zhushu 禮記註疏. Commentaries by Zheng Xuan 鄭玄, Kong Yingda 孔穎達, and glosses by Lu Deming 陸德明. 2 vols. Taibei: Taiwan Shangwu yinshuguan, 1983.
Lin Hsüeh-yi. "In the Name of Honor: Qian Qianyi (1582–1664) and the Politics of Loyalty in Late Imperial China." PhD diss., Princeton University, 2010.
Lin Liyue 林麗月. "Xiaodao yu fudao: Mingdai xiaofu de wenhua shi kaocha," 孝道與婦道: 明代孝婦的文化史考察. *Jindai Zhongguo funü shi yanjiu* 6 (1998): 1–29.
Ling Mengchu 凌濛初. *Pai'an jingqi* 拍案驚奇. Edited by Chen Erdong 陳邇冬 and Guo Junjie 郭雋傑. Beijing: Renmin wenxue chubanshe, 1991.
———. *Erke pai'an jingqi* 二刻拍案驚奇. Edited by Chen Erdong 陳邇冬 and Guo Junjie 郭雋傑. Beijing: Renmin wenxue chubanshe, 1996.
Ling Xiaoqiao. "Law, Deities, and Beyond: From the *Sanyan* Stories to *Xingshi yinyuan zhuan*." *Harvard Journal of Asiatic Studies* 74 (2014): 1–42.
Liu Chiung-yun [Qiongyun] 劉瓊云. "Diwang huanhun: Mingdai Jianwendi liuwang xushi de yanyi." 帝王還魂－明代建文帝流亡敘事的衍異. *Xin shixue* 新史學 23, no. 4 (December 2012): 61–117.
———. "Ren, tian, mo: *Nüxian waishi* zhong de lishi quehan yu ta jie xiangxiang" 人、天、魔: 女仙外史中的歷史缺憾與〔她〕界想像. *Zhongguo wenzhe yanjiu jikan* 中國文哲研究集刊 (March 2011): 43–94.
———. "Tiandao, zhishu, shangpin: *Zhongjing* zhi chuban yu Mingdai zhong wenhua" 天道、治術、商品:《忠經》之出版與明代忠文化. *Zhongguo wenzhe yanjiu tongxun* 24, no. 2 (June 2014): 73–120.
Liu, James. *The Chinese Knight-Errant*. London: Routledge and K. Paul, 1967.
Lo Yuet Keung (Lao Yueqiang), "My Second Self: Matteo Ricci's Friendship in China," *Monumenta Serica* 54 (2006): 221–41.
Lu Gong 路工 and Tan Tian 譚天, eds. *Guben pinghua xiaoshuo ji* 古本平話小說集. 2 vols. Beijing: Renmin wenxue chubanshe, 2006.
Lü Kun 呂坤. *Lü Kun quanji* 呂坤全集. 3 vols. Beijing: Zhonghua shuju, 2008.
Lu Miaw-fen. "Religious Dimensions of Filial Piety as Developed in Late Ming Interpretations of the *Xiaojing*." *Late Imperial China* 27, no. 2 (December 2006): 1–37.
Lu Miaw-fen (Lü Miaofen) 呂妙芬. "Ming Qing Zhongguo wanli xunqin de wenhua shijian" 明清中國萬里尋親的文化實踐. *Zhongyang yanjiuyuan lishi yuyan yanjiusuo jikan* 中央研究院歷史語言研究所集刊 78 (2007): 359–406.
———. *Yangmingxue shiren shequn: lishi, sixiang yu shijian* 陽明學士人社群: 歷史, 思想與實踐. Taipei: Zhongyang yanjiu yuan jindai shi yanjiu suo, 2003.

Lu Renlong 陸人龍. *Liaohai danzhong lu* 遼海丹忠錄. Beijing: Dazhong wenyi chubanshe, 1999.

———. *Xingshi yan* 型世言. Edited by Chan Hing-ho 陳慶浩. 3 vols. Taibei: Zhongyang yanjiuyuan, Zhongguo wen zhe yanjiusuo 中央研究院中國文哲研究所, 1992.

———. *Xingshi yan pingzhu* 型世言評注. Edited by Chan Hing-ho, Wu Shuyin 吳書蔭, and Wang Ying 王鍈. 2 vols. Beijing: Xinhua chubanshe, 1999.

Lu, Tina. *Accidental Incest, Filial Cannibalism, and Other Peculiar Encounters in Late Imperial Chinese Literature*. Cambridge, MA: Harvard University Asia Center, 2008.

Lu Weijing. "Reviving an Ancient Filial Ideal: The Seventeenth-Century Practice of *Lumu* 廬墓." *The Chinese Historical Review* 20, no. 2 (November 1, 2013): 159–79.

———. *True to Her Word: The Faithful Maiden Cult in Late Imperial China*. Stanford, CA: Stanford University Press, 2008.

Lu Xun 魯迅. *Lu Xun quanji* 魯迅全集. 18 vols. Beijing: Renmin wenxue chubanshe, 2005.

Lu Yunlong 陸雲龍, He Weiran 何偉然, and Ding Yunhe 丁允和. *Huang Ming shiliu mingjia xiaopin* 皇明十六名家小品. Rpt. in *Siku quanshu cunmu congshu* 四庫全書存目叢書. Ser. 4. Vol. 378. Jinan: Qi Lu shushe, 1997.

Lunhui xingshi 輪迴醒世. Edited by Cheng Yizhong 程毅中. Beijing: Zhonghua shuju, 2008.

Lunyu yi zhu 論語譯注. Edited by Yang Bojun 楊伯峻. Beijing: Zhonghua shuju, 1980.

Lyons, John. *Exemplum: The Rhetoric of Example in Early Modern France and Italy*. Princeton, NJ: Princeton University Press, 1989.

Mair, Victor H. "Language and Ideology in the Written Popularizations of the *Sacred Edict*." In *Popular Culture in Late Imperial China*, edited by David Johnson, Andrew J. Nathan, and Evelyn S. Rawski, 325–59. Berkeley: University of California Press, 1985.

Makeham, John. *Name and Actuality in Early Chinese Thought*. Albany: State University of New York Press, 1994.

Mann, Susan. "The Male Bond in Chinese History and Culture." *American Historical Review* 105, no. 5 (Dec., 2000): 1,600–14.

Mann, Susan, and Fangqin Du. "Competing Claims on Womanly Virtue in Late Imperial China." In *Women and Confucian Cultures in Premodern China, Korean, and Japan*, edited by Dorothy Ko et al., 219–47. Berkeley: University of California Press, 2003.

Mann, Susan, and Yu-yin Cheng, eds. *Under Confucian Eyes: Writings on Gender in Chinese History*. Berkeley: University of California Press, 2001.

McDermott, Joseph P. "Friendship and Its Friends in the Late Ming." In Institute of Modern History, Academia Sinica, *Jinshi jiazu yu zhengzhi bijiao lishi lunwen ji* 近世家族與政治比較史論文集 (Family Process and Political Process in Chinese History), 67–96. Taibei: Academia Sinica, 1992.

McMahon, Keith. *Causality and Containment in Seventeenth-Century Chinese Fiction.* Leiden: Brill, 1988.

Mengjue daoren 夢覺道人, and Xihu langzi 西湖浪子. *Sanke pai'an jingqi* 三刻拍案驚奇. Original title: *Huanying* 幻影. Edited by Zhang Rongqi 張榮起. Beijing: Beijing daxue chubanshe, 1987.

———. *Sanke pai'an jingqi* 三刻拍案驚奇. *Guben xiaoshuo jicheng* series. 2 vols. Shanghai: Shanghai guji, 1990.

Mengzi yi zhu 孟子譯注. Edited by Yang Bojun 楊伯峻. Beijing: Zhonghua shuju, 1960.

Mote, Frederick W., and Denis Twitchett, eds. *The Cambridge History of China.* Vol. 7: *The Ming Dynasty, 1368–1644.* Part 1. Cambridge, UK: Cambridge University Press, 1988.

———. *The Cambridge History of China.* Vol. 8: *The Ming Dynasty, 1368–1644.* Part 2. Cambridge, UK: Cambridge University Press, 1998.

Mowry, Hua-yuan Li. *Chinese Love Stories from "Ch'ing-shih."* Hamden, CT: Archon, 1983.

Murray, Julia K. "Didactic Picturebooks for Late Ming Emperors and Princes." In *Culture, Courtiers, and Competition: The Ming Court (1368–1644),* edited by David M. Robinson, 231–268. Cambridge, MA: Harvard University Asia Center, 2008.

Ogawa Yōichi 小川陽一. "Mingdai xiaoshuo yu shanshu" 明代小說與善書. *Hanxue yanjiu,* 6, no. 1 (1988): 331–40.

———. *Nichiyō ruisho ni yoru Min-Shin shōsetsu no kenkyū* 日用類書による 明清小說の研究. Tokyo: Kenbun shuppan, 1995.

Osawa Akihiro 大澤顯浩, "Mingdai chuban wenhua zhong de 'Ershisi xiao'—Lun xiaozi xingxiang de jianli yu fazhan" 明代出版文化中的「二十四孝」—論孝子形象的建立與發展. *Mingdai yanjiu tongxun* (2002.12): 11–33.

Ōtsuka Hidetaka 大塚秀高. "*Xingshi yan* yanjiu pingshu" 型世言研究評述. Translated by Yan Jiaren 閻家仁 and Dong Hao 董皓. *Baoding shifan zhuanke xuexiao xuebao* 保定師範專科學校學報 2006.3: 1–7.

Ouyang Daifa 歐陽代發. *Huaben xiaoshuo shi* 話本小說史. Wuhan: Wuhan chubanshe, 1994.

Ouyang Jian 歐陽健. "Chaoqian yu shiji bianzuan de xiaoshuo chuangzuo—Ming Qing shishi xiaoshuo xinlun" 超前于史籍編纂的小說創作- 明清時事小說新論. *Wenxue yichan* (1992.5): 80–90.

Paderni, Paola. "Between Formal and Informal Justice: A Case of Wife-Selling in Eighteenth-Century China." *Ming Qing yanjiu* (1996): 139–56.

Pino, Angel. "Sur les éditions disponibles du *Xing shi yan* et les premières recherches consacrées à l'œuvre de Lu Renlong." *Revue bibliographique de sinologie* XIII (1995): 375–82.

Plaks, Andrew H. "After the Fall: *Hsing-shih yin-yuan chuan* and the Seventeenth-Century Chinese Novel." *Harvard Journal of Asiatic Studies* 45 (December 1985): 543–80.

———. *The Four Masterworks of the Ming Novel.* Princeton, NJ: Princeton University Press, 1987.

Pu Songling 蒲松齡. *Quanben xinzhu Liaozhai zhiyi* 全本新注聊齋誌異. Edited by Zhu Qikai 朱其鎧 et al. 3 vols. Beijing: Renmin wenxue chubanshe, 1989.

Qishi'er chao renwu yanyi 七十二朝人物演義. *Guben xiaoshuo jicheng* 古本小說集成 series. Shanghai: Shanghai guji chubanshe, 1990.

Qi Yukun 齊裕焜. *Mingdai xiaoshuo shi* 明代小說史. Hangzhou: Zhejiang guji chubanshe, 1997.

Qian Nanxiu. *Spirit and Self in Medieval China: The Shih-shuo hsin-yü and Its Legacy*. Honolulu: University of Hawai'i Press, 2001.

Qian Qianyi 錢謙益. *Liechao shiji xiaozhuan* 列朝詩集小傳. 2 vols. Shanghai: Shanghai guji chubanshe, 1983.

Qian Zhongshu 錢鍾書. *Guanzhui bian* 管錐編. 4 vols. Beijing: Sanlian shudian, 2007.

Qiu Zhonglin 邱仲麟. "Bu xiao zhi xiao: Tang yilai gegu liaoqin xianxiang de shehui shi chutan" 不孝之孝：唐以來割股療親現象的社會史初探. *Xin shi xue* 新史學 6, no. 1 (1995): 49–94.

Quan Ning'ai (Kwŏn Yŏng-ae) 權寧愛. "*Xingshi yan* yanjiu" 型世言研究. PhD diss., Dongwu daxue 東吳大學 (Soochow University), Taipei, 1993.

Ricci, Matteo. *Dell'amicizia*. Edited by Filippo Mignini. Macerata: Quodlibet, 2005.

———. *On Friendship: One Hundred Maxims for a Chinese Prince*. Edited and translated by Timothy Billings. New York: Columbia University Press, 2009.

Rigolot, François. "The Renaissance Crisis of Exemplarity." *Journal of the History of Ideas* 59, no. 4 (October 1998): 557–63.

Roddy, Stephen. *Literati Identity and Its Fictional Representations in Late Imperial China*. Stanford, CA: Stanford University Press, 1998.

Rolston, David L. *Traditional Chinese Fiction and Fiction Commentary: Reading and Writing Between the Lines*. Stanford, CA: Stanford University Press, 1997.

Ropp, Paul, Paola Zamperini, and Harriet Zurndorfer, eds. *Passionate Women: Female Suicide in Late Imperial China*. Leiden: Brill, 2001.

Schmidt, Jerry D. *Harmony Garden: The Life, Literary Criticism, and Poetry of Yuan Mei (1716–1798)*. London: RoutledgeCurzon, 2003.

Seligman, Adam B., Robert P. Weller, Michael J. Puett, and Bennet Simon. *Ritual and Its Consequences: An Essay on the Limits of Sincerity*. New York: Oxford University Press, 2008.

Shang Wei. *Rulin waishi and Cultural Transformation in Late Imperial China*. Cambridge, MA: Harvard University Asia Center, 2003.

Shen Defu 沈德符. *Wanli yehuo bian* 萬曆野獲編. 2 vols. Beijing: Wenhua yishu chubanshe, 1998.

Shi Lin 石麟. *Huaben xiaoshuo tonglun* 話本小說通論. Wuchang: Huazhong ligong daxue chubanshe, 1998.

Shields, Anna M. *One Who Knows Me: Friendship and Literary Culture in Mid-Tang China*. Cambridge, MA: Harvard University Asia Center, 2015.

Situ Xiuying 司徒秀英. *Mingdai jiaohua ju qunguan* 明代教化劇群觀. Shanghai: Shanghai guji, 2009.

Smith, Joanna Handlin. *The Art of Doing Good: Charity in Late Ming China*. Berkeley: University of California Press, 2009.

Song Lian 宋濂. *Wenxian ji* 文憲集. Rpt. in *Siku quanshu*. Vols. 1,223–1,224. Taipei: Taiwan shangwu yinshuguan, 1983.

Song Maocheng 宋楙澄. *Jiuyue qianji* 九籥前集. Rpt. in *Xuxiu siku quanshu* 續修四庫全書. Vol. 1,373. Shanghai: Shanghai guji chubanshe [1995–1999].

Struve, Lynn A. "Self-Struggles of a Martyr: Memories, Dreams, and Obsessions in the Extant Diary of Huang Chunyao." *Harvard Journal of Asiatic Studies* 69, no. 2 (2009): 343–94.

———, ed. and trans. *Voices from the Ming-Qing Cataclysm: China in Tigers' Jaw*. New Haven, CT: Yale University Press, 1993.

Sun Laichen. "Chinese Military Technology and Dai Viet: c. 1390–1497." *Asia Research Institute Working Paper Series* (National University of Singapore) 11 (September 2003): 1–28. Web. <http://www.ari.nus.edu.sg/docs/wps/wps03_011.pdf>.

Sung Tz'u [Song Ci]. *The Washing Away of Wrongs: Forensic Medicine in Thirteenth-Century China*. Translated by Brian E. McKnight. Ann Arbor: Center for Chinese Studies, University of Michigan, 1981.

Tan Zhengbi 譚正璧. *San Yan Liang Pai ziliao* 三言兩拍資料. 2 vols. Shanghai: Shanghai guji chubanshe, 1980.

Tao Fu 陶輔. *Huaying ji* 花影集. Edited by Cheng Yizhong 程毅中. Zhou Shaolian 周紹濂. *Yuanzhu zhiyu xuechuang tanyi* 鴛渚誌餘雪窗談異. Edited by Yu Wenzao. Beijing: Zhonghua shuju, 2008.

Theiss, Janet. *Disgraceful Matters: The Politics of Chastity in Eighteenth-Century China*. Berkeley: University of California Press, 2004.

Tianran chisou 天然癡叟. *Shi diantou* 石點頭. Edited by Li Zhongming 李忠明 and Wang Guanshi 王關仕. Taipei: Sanmin shuju, 1998.

T'ien Ju-k'ang. *Male Anxiety and Female Chastity: A Comparative Study of Chinese Ethical Values in Ming-Ch'ing Times*. Leiden: Brill, 1988.

Tsai, Shih-Shan Henry. *Perpetual Happiness: The Ming Emperor Yongle*. Seattle: University of Washington Press, 2001.

Tschanz, Dietrich. "History and Meaning in the Late Ming Drama *Ming feng ji*." *Ming Studies* 35 (1995): 1–31.

Tu Wei-ming. "Probing the 'Three Bonds' and 'Five Relationships' in Confucian Humanism." In *Confucianism and the Family*, edited by Walter H. Slote and George A. de Vos, 121–36. Albany: State University of New York Press, 1998.

Vitiello, Giovanni. *The Libertine's Friend: Homosexuality and Masculinity in Late Imperial China*. Chicago: University of Chicago Press, 2011.

Volpp, Sophie. "The Discourse on Male Marriage: Li Yu's 'A Male Mencius's Mother.'" *positions* 2, no. 1 (Spring 1994): 113–32.

Waley, Arthur, trans. *The Book of Songs*. Edited with additional translations by Joseph R. Allen. New York: Grove, 1996.

Waltner, Ann. *Getting an Heir: Adoption and the Construction of Kinship in Late Imperial China*. Honolulu: University of Hawaii Press, 1990.

———. "Writing Her Way Out of Trouble: Li Yuying in History and Fiction." In *Writing Women in Late Imperial China*, edited by Ellen Widmer and Kang-i Sun Chang, 221–41. Stanford, CA: Stanford University Press, 1997.

Wang, David. *The Monster That Is History: History, Violence, and Fictional Writing in Twentieth-Century China.* Berkeley: University of California Press, 2004.
Wang Fansen 王汎森. "Mingmo Qingchu de renpu yu xingguohui" 明末清初的人譜與省過會. *Zhongyang yanjiuyuan lishi yuyan yanjiusuo jikan* 中央研究院歷史語言研究所集刊 63, no. 3 (1993.7): 679–712.
Wang Tonggui 王同軌. *Ertan* 耳談. Taibei: Weiwen tushu chubanshe, 1977.
Wang Yang-ming. *Instructions for Practical Living and Other Neo-Confucian Writings.* Translated and edited by Wing-tsit Chan. New York: Columbia University Press, 1963.
Wei, Cheng-t'ung. "Chu Hsi on the Standard and the Expedient." In *Chu Hsi and Neo-Confucianism*, edited by Wing-tsit Chan, 255–72. Honolulu: University of Hawaii Press, 1986.
Weiyuan zhuren 薇園主人. *Qingye zhong* 清夜鐘. Rpt. in *Guben xiaoshuo jicheng* 古本小說集成. Ser. 4. Vol. 13. Shanghai: Shanghai guji chubanshe, 1990.
West, Stephen H. "A Study in Appropriation: Zang Maoxun's Injustice to Dou E." *Journal of the American Oriental Society* 111, no. 2 (April-June 1991): 283–302.
Widmer, Ellen. "The Huanduzhai of Hangzhou and Suzhou: A Study in Seventeenth-Century Publishing." *Harvard Journal of Asiatic Studies* 56, no. 1 (June 1996): 77–122.
Will, Pierre-Étienne. "Developing Forensic Knowledge through Cases in the Qing Dynasty." In *Thinking With Cases: Specialist Knowledge in Chinese Cultural History*, edited by Charlotte Furth, Judith T. Zeitlin, and Ping-Chen Hsiung, 62–100. Honolulu: University of Hawai'i Press, 2007.
Wivell, Charles Joseph. "Adaptation and Coherence in Late Ming Short Vernacular Fiction: A Study of the *Second West Lake Collection*." PhD diss., University of Washington, 1975.
Wong, Timothy. "Entertainment as Art: An Approach to *Ku-chin hsiao-shuo*." *Chinese Literature: Essays, Articles, Reviews (CLEAR)* 3, no. 2 (July 1981): 235–55.
———. "Morality as Entertainment: Altruistic Friendship in *Ku-chin hsiao-shuo*." *Tamkang Review* 13, no. 1 (1982): 55–69.
Wu, H. Laura. "Corpses on Display: Representations of Torture and Pain in the Wei Zhongxian Novels." *Ming Studies* 59 (2009): 42–55.
Wu Jingzi 吳敬梓. *Rulin waishi* 儒林外史. Edited by Hong Jiang 洪江. Shanghai: Shanghai guji chubanshe, 2000.
Wu Yanna 吳燕娜 [Wu Yenna]. "Lijiao, qinggan, he zongjiao zhi hudong: Fenxi bijiao *Xingshi yan* di si hui he 'Lishui Chen xiaonü zhuanbei' dui gegu liaoqin de chengxian" 禮教、情感、和宗教之互動：分析比較《型世言》第四回和〈麗水陳孝女傳碑〉對割股療親的呈現. *Wen yu zhe* 文與哲 12 (2008): 413–54.
Wu, Yenna. "The Debunking of Historical Heroes in *Idle Talk Under the Bean Arbor*." *Selected Papers in Asian Studies* n.s. 43 (1992): 1–27.
Wu, Yenna. "Moral Ambivalence in the Portrayal of *gegu* in Late Imperial Chinese Literature." In *Ming Qing wenhua xinlun* 明清文化新論, edited by Wang Chengmian 王成勉, 247–74. Taipei: Wenjin chubanshe 文津出版社, 2000.
Xiao Feng 肖峰. "*Xingshi yan* di san hui sucai laiyuan" 型世言第三回素材來源. *Wenjiao ziliao* 2001.3: 142–43.

Bibliography

Xiao Xinqiao 蕭欣橋 and Liu Fuyuan 劉福元. *Huaben xiaoshuo shi* 話本小說史. Hangzhou: Zhejiang guji chubanshe, 2003.

Xihu yuyin zhuren 西湖漁隱主人. *Huanxi yuanjia* 歡喜冤家. 2 vols. *Guben xiaoshuo jicheng* 古本小說集成 series. Shanghai: Shanghai guji chubanshe, 1990.

Xu Fuzuo 徐復祚. *Huadangge congtan* 花當閣叢談. Rpt. in *Xuxiu siku quanshu* 續修四庫全書. Vol. 1175. Shanghai: Shanghai guji chubanshe, [1995–1999].

Xu Zhiping 徐志平. "Qingchu duanpian 'shishi xiaoshuo' xilun" 清初短篇時事小說析論. *Dalu zazhi* 大陸雜誌 99, no. 6 (1999): 241–47.

Yang Binbin. *Heroines of the Qing: Exemplary Women Tell Their Stories*. Seattle: University of Washington Press, 2016.

Yang Shen 楊慎. *Sheng'an quanji* 升庵全集. Shanghai: Shangwu yinshuguan, 1935.

Yang Shuhui. *Appropriation and Representation: Feng Menglong and the Chinese Vernacular Story*. Ann Arbor: Center for Chinese Studies, University of Michigan, 1998.

Yang Zonghong 楊宗紅. "Lun Mingmo Qingchu huaben xiaoshuo de quanshanxing ji qi wenhua beijing—yi qi yu shanshu guanxi wei kaocha zhongxin" 論明末清初話本小說的勸善性及其文化背景－以其與善書關係為考察中心. *Anhui daxue xuebao (zhexue shehuike xueban)* 2 (2013): 48–54.

Yü Chün-fang. *The Renewal of Buddhism in China: Chu-hung and the Late Ming Synthesis*. New York: Columbia University Press, 1981.

———. *Kuan-yin: The Chinese Transformation of Avalokiteśvara*. New York: Columbia University Press, 2001.

Yu Chunxi 虞淳熙. *Xiaojing jiling* 孝經集靈. Rpt. in *Siku quanshu cunmu congshu* 四庫全書存目叢書. Ser. 3. Vol. 247. Jinan: Qi Lu shushe, 1997.

Yu, Jimmy. *Sanctity and Self-Inflicted Violence in Chinese Religions, 1500–1700*. Oxford, UK: Oxford University Press, 2012.

Yuan Mei 袁枚. *Xiaocang shanfang wenji* 小蒼山房文集. 6 vols. (775–780). Taipei: Wenhai chubanshe, 1981.

Zhanzhan waishi 詹詹外史 (aka Feng Menglong). *Qingshi* 情史. 2 vols. Taibei: Guangwen shuju, 1982.

Zhang Anfeng 張安峰. "*Xingshi yan* sucai laiyuan" 型世言素材來源 (一,二,三). *Ming Qing xiaoshuo yanjiu* 明清小說研究 1998.1: 187–98; 1998.2: 175–84; 1998.3: 187–97.

Zhang Jing. "Playing with Desire: Reading Short Vernacular Fiction in 16th- and 17th-Century China." PhD diss., Washington University, 2006.

Zhang Tingyu 張廷玉 et al., eds. *Mingshi* 明史. 28 vols. Beijing: Zhonghua shuju, 1974.

Zhang Xiumin 張秀民. *Zhongguo yinshua shi* 中國印刷史. Shanghai: Shanghai Renmin chubanshe, 1989.

Zhang Ying. *Confucian Image Politics: Masculine Morality in Seventeenth-Century China*. Seattle: University of Washington Press, 2017.

Zhao Botao 趙伯陶, ed. *Ming wenxuan* 明文選. Beijing: Renmin wenxue chubanshe, 2006.

Zhao Yingzhi. "Literati Use of Oral or Oral-Related Genres to Talk about History in the Late Ming and Early Qing: From Yang Shen to Jia Fuxi and

Gui Zhuang, and from Education (*Jiaohua*) to Cursing the World (*Mashi*)." *CHINOPERL*, 34.2 (2015): 81–114.

Zhao Yuan 趙園. *Ming Qing zhi ji shidaifu yanjiu* 明清之際士大夫研究. Beijing: Beijing daxue chubanshe, 1999.

Zheng Zhenduo 鄭振鐸. "Ming Qing er dai de pinghua ji" 明清二代的平話集. Rpt. in *Zhongguo wenxue yanjiu*. Beijing: Zuojia chubanshe, 1957, vol. 1.

Zhou Ji 周楫. *Xihu erji* 西湖二集. Edited by Chen Meilin 陳美林. Taipei: Sanmin shuju, 1998.

Zhu Di 朱棣. *Xiaoshun shishi* 孝順事實. Rpt. in *Beijing tushuguan guji zhenben congkan* 北京圖書館古籍珍本叢刊. Vol. 14. Beijing: Shumu wenxian chubanshe, 1988.

Zhu Xi 朱熹. *Hui'an xiansheng Zhu Wengong wenji* 晦庵先生朱文公文集. Published by Tu Zongying 涂宗瀛. Lu'an: Qiuwo zhai 求我齋, Tongzhi 12 [1873]. 100 juan. Accessed on ctext.org: http://ctext.org/library.pl?if=gb&res=79916&by_title=朱熹.

Zhuoyuanting zhuren 酌元亭主人. *Zhaoshi bei* 照世盃. Edited by Chen Dakang 陳大康 and Wang Guanshi 王關仕. Taipei: Sanmin shuju, 1998.

Index

Page numbers in italic indicate a figure.

adoptive relationships, 32–33
"Against Autopsy," 68–69, 181n63, 181n64
Aina jushi. See *Idle Talk under the Bean Arbor* (*Doupeng xianhua*)
Alternative Edition of Slapping the Table in Amazement, Second Collection (Bieben erke), 166, 205n5
Analects, 37
ancestral rites, 30
autopsy, 63–65, 68, 137

bao, 4, 22–25, 160; autopsy and, 68; in "The Beauties and the Bumpkins," 117; in friendship stories, 156–58; loyalty and, 96
Bartoli, Daniello, 74–75
"Beauties and the Bumpkins, The," 107–108, 116–18, 194n37, 194–95n39
Bell in the Still Night (*Qingye zhong*), 3; commentaries to, 167; models of loyalty in, 84; preface to, 17; text and authorship of, 5, 167, 168, 205–206n8, 206n9; virtue in, 24. *See also* "Beauties and the Bumpkins, The"; "Chongzhen's Loyal Minister and His Wife"; "Cui Jian the Filial Boy"; "Divine Instructor Warned Him Three Times, The Director of Grain Transport Did Not Escape Death, The"; "Fratricide in the Rear Garden"
Bieben erke. See *Alternative Edition of Slapping the Table in Amazement, Second Collection* (Bieben erke)
Bi Gan, 100, 190n63
biography, 116; and female exemplarity, 107; of Lu Yunlong, 7; as source for "The Faithful Widows of the Xiao Family," 123–24, 196n60; as source for "The Heroic Woman and Her Mother," 118, 195n41; as source for "Injustice to Tang Guimei," 109–17; as source for "A Slice of Liver for Grandma," 70, 73; as source for "Wang Shiming the Filial Avenger," 66–67; as source for Wang Yuan stories, 33–36, 40, 46
"Biography of the Filial and Heroic Tang Guimei," 109–11, 113
body, 70–71; and filial piety, 182n76. *See also* autopsy; filial dilemmas: filial murder; filial piety: female; flesh slicing (*gegu*); "steaming the bones" (*zhenggu*)
Bo Yi, 100, 162–63, 190n64
brotherly bond, 26, 127–29, 138, 197n11, 197n12; estrangement and, 133–38; exemplarity and, 129–33

Index

Buddhism, 16, 30–31

Cai Baozhen. See *Filial Records (Xiaoji)*
cannibalism, 4, 75, 183n84
chastity (*jie, zhen*), 80, 105–106; in conflict with heroism, 122; defined by women, 122; female compared to male, 157; male, 154–58, 204n55; as related to filial piety, 114–15, 121, 193–94n30; shifting meaning of, 191n4; in "Tie Xuan and His Daughters," 92–93, 105–106
chastity plaques, 72, 182n74
"Cheng Ji and the Jianwen Emperor," 84–85, 95–99
"Chicken-and-Millet Dinner for Fan Juqing, Friend in Life and Death, The," 145–46
Chongzhen emperor, 125, 167
"Chongzhen's Loyal Minister and His Wife," 99–100, 102–103
Cicero, 144, 148, 200n22
Classic of Filial Piety (Xiaojing), 22, 28–30, 37, 73–74, 111, 182n76
commentaries, 4: attribution of, 3, 166–67; eyebrow, 7, 171n21; interlineal, 113; tail, 7, 53, 88–89, 93, 125, 171n21. *See also* prefaces
Common Words to Warn the World (Jingshi tongyan), 145–46
concubines, 34, 41, 53, 102, 107, 130; as heroines, 123–25; and male chastity, 154–56; murder of, 57–58, 61–62
Confucianism: in "Cheng Ji and the Jianwen Emperor," 99; in *Illusion*, 16; and filial piety, 35, 177n52; in filial quest narratives, 41, 45; and late Ming reader, 161; in *San Yan*, 16; in twenty-first century, 163; and *xia*, 65
Confucius, 142, 200n18. See also *Analects*; Confucianism

Constant Words to Awaken the World (Xingshi hengyan), 31–32. *See also* "Three Devoted Brothers Win Honor by Yielding Family Property to One Another"
corruption: in the examination system, 102, 157; in "The Filial Quest of Wang Yuan,» 35; of friendship, 140; Lu Renlong on, 124–25, 196n64. *See also* autopsy
"Cui Jian the Filial Boy," 50, 57–61
Cuiyuge Jinyan. See *Recent Words by Cuiyuge (Cuiyuge Jinyan)*

"Deceitful Accomplice, The," 133–34
discursive frame, 49, 107–108, 115, 118, 124–26
"Divine Instructor Warned Him Three Times, The Director of Grain Transport Did Not Escape Death," 103–104
Donglin party, 6, 100–101
Dou E yuan. See *Injustice to Dou E (Dou E yuan)*
Doupeng xianhua. See *Idle Talk under the Bean Arbor (Doupeng xianhua)*

education: and brotherly bond, 136–37; and flesh slicing, 73, 76; regarding filial piety, 28–29, 36–37, 58; in stories of moral exemplars, 21, 173n52
Erke Pai'an jingqi. See *Slapping the Table in Amazement, Second Collection (Erke Pai'an jingqi)*
Er Pai (Two Slaps), 5, 16, 32–33. See also *Slapping the Table in Amazement (Pai'an jingqi)*; *Slapping the Table in Amazement, Second Collection (Erke Pai'an jingqi)*
Ershisi xiao. See *Twenty-Four Filial Exemplars (Ershisi xiao)*

"Eulogy for Overcoming and Exterminating the Great Iniquity," 101
eunuch, 6, 37–40, 98
excess, 3
exemplarity, 4, 161–62; ambiguous, 52–53; "crisis of," 77–78; in *Exemplary Words*, 21–22; male chastity and, 157; in "A Slice of Liver for Grandma," 72; in women, 69, 105–107, 116, 121, 124, 125–26. *See also* chastity
Exemplary Women (*Lienü zhuan*), 22, 105, 111
Exemplary Words for the World (*Xingshi yan*), 3, 9, 10, 11, 12; adoptive relationships in, 32; *bao* in, 24, 173n60; coherence in, 160–61; depiction of hardship in, 41–42, 176n43; father in, 41–44; filial piety in, 32–33; friendship in, 144, 146–47; ironsmiths and goldsmiths in, 66, 180n48; missing fascicle of, 13; models of loyalty in, 84; pairing structure of, 4–5, 170n14; paratextual apparati of, 7; provenance of, 4–5; social-historical concerns of, 46, 159–60; structure of, 13; text and authorship of, 165–66, 168, 205n6; virtue in, 24. *See also* "Cheng Ji and the Jianwen Emperor"; commentaries; "Faithful Widows of the Xiao Family, The"; "Filial Quest of Wang Yuan, The"; "Heroic Woman and Her Mother, The"; "Injustice to Tang Guimei"; "Mother Comes First"; prefaces; "Qin Zhu the New Liuxia Hui"; "Slice of Liver for Grandma, A"; "Tie Xuan and His Daughters"; "Wang Mian the Exemplary Friend"; "Wang Shiming the Filial Avenger"; "Yao Brothers, The"

"Faithful Widows of the Xiao Family, The," 107–108, 123–25
father, 40–44. *See also* filial piety
father and son, 128–29, 200n17. *See also* filial piety
Feng Menglong, 1, 15, 19. *See also San Yan*
filial dilemmas, 49–50; "feminization" of, 49; murder, 57–69, 179n38; regarding mother and wife, 51–55, 178n7
filial or graveside huts (*lumu*), 30–31, 56, 198n31
filial piety (*xiao*), 161–62, 174n7; in *Bell in the Still Night*, 20; conflict with political duty, 84, 104; contrasted to friendship, 71; in *Exemplary Words*, 20; female, 69–81, 114, 121; and gender, 34, 69–70; Lu Yunlong on, 182n75; the making of, 36–40; narratives of, 25; official discourse regarding, 29; religious dimension of, 30, 34, 175n28; and social status, 34; as a social value, 80–81; traditional discourse of, 28–31; in vernacular stories, 31–33. *See also* body; filial dilemmas; flesh slicing; loyalty; nature vs. nurture
filial quest, 27–28; narratives of, 33–34, 47–48; obliviousness during, 37, 176n38; reworkings of, 177n54. *See also* "Filial Quest of Wang Yuan, The"; "Wang Benli Searches for his Father at the Far End of the Empire"
"Filial Quest of Wang Yuan, The," 33–36, 38–40, 43–44, 46
Filial Records (*Xiaoji*), 28–29
firearms, 93, 188–89n41
Five Cardinal Relationships (*wu lun*), 4, 17–21, 26, 159–60, 173n50; in *Exemplary Words*, 20–21; friendship and, 140–41, 149; in *Illusion*, 16;

Five Cardinal Relationships (*wu lun*) (continued)
  reordering of, 18–19, 141–43, 172n35. *See also* brotherly bond; father and son; filial dilemmas; friendship (*you*); husband and wife; ruler and subject
Five Constant Norms (*wuchang*), 18–19
flesh slicing (*gegu*), 31, 56; in "Cheng Ji and the Jianwen Emperor," 95–96; in *Classic of Filial Piety*, 29, 73, 182n76; debates about, 30; Han Yu on, 182n79, 182n80; a Jesuit perspective on, 74–75; understood as "filial cannibalism," 183n84. *See also* "Slice of Liver for Grandma, A"
forbearance (*ren*), 137–38, 198–99n31
"Fratricide in the Rear Garden," 65, 134–38
friendship (*you*), 26, 139–41; Aristotle on, 199n6; brotherly bond and, 128, 197n10; contrasted to filial piety, 71, 152–53; death and, 201n30; European interest in, 144, 200n22; late Ming discourse of, 141–47; primacy of, 19–20; problems with translation as, 199n1. *See also* "Wang Mian the Exemplary Friend"

gegu. *See* flesh slicing (*gegu*)
Gong'an school, 6
Great Rite Controversy, 30, 32, 38
Gu Dashao, 19, 71, 142
Gukuangsheng. *See Sobering Stone (Zuixing shi)*
Guo Ju, 49, 51, 177–78n1, 178n3

hero: "deflation of heroism," 101–102, 190n70; moral heroism, 103; shaping of, 4. *See also* heroine
"Heroic Woman and Her Mother, The," 107–108, 118–23

heroine, 25–26, 107–108, 114
heroism. *See* hero; heroine
He Xinyin, 141–42
Hongwu emperor, 1, 28–29, 31, 34–35, 128. *See also Sacred Edict in Six Maxims (Shengyu liuyu)*
Hongzhi emperor, 30
Huang Guan, 87–88, 186n15, 189n45
Huang Ming shiliu mingjia xiaopin. *See Informal Essays by Sixteen Eminent Authors of the August Ming (Huang Ming shiliu mingjia xiaopin)*
Huanying. *See Illusion (Huanying)*
Hu Guang, 87, 185n12
Hu Run, 87–88, 186n15; daughter of, 92–93
husband and wife: in "Against Autopsy," 69; in "Chongzhen's Loyal Minister and His Wife," 102–103; in "Cui Jian the Filial Boy," 59–60; primacy of, 18–19, 172n41; in "Wang Shiming the Filial Avenger," 69

Idle Talk under the Bean Arbor (Doupeng xianhua), 4, 161–63
Illusion (Huanying), 166, 205n4; brothers in, 127, 129; as example of pairing, 171n14; preface of, 13–16. *See also* Confucianism; Five Cardinal Relationships
Illustrious Words to Instruct the World (Yushi mingyan): friendship stories in, 145. *See also* "Chicken-and-Millet Dinner for Fan Juqing, Friend in Life and Death, The"; "Magistrate Teng Solves the Case of Disputed Inheritance with Ghostly Cleverness"; "Shen Xiaoxia Encounters the Expedition Memorial"; "Wu Bao'an Abandons His Family to Ransom His Friend"; "Yang Jiao'ai Lays Down His Life for the Sake of Friendship"

Index

Imitatio and *mimesis*, 77–78, 183n91
Informal Essays by Sixteen Eminent Authors of the August Ming (*Huang Ming shiliu mingjia xiaopin*), 5–6, 194n36
Injustice to Dou E (*Dou E yuan*), 18, 109, 112
"Injustice to Tang Guimei," 107–108, 108–17; characterization in, 111–13; filial dilemmas in, 54–55; literacy in, 111–12; texts related to, 109–11, 193n16

Jiajing emperor, 30, 57, 194n30
Jianwen emperor, 29, 85–87, 89–90, 184n5, 184n7. See also "Cheng Ji and the Jianwen Emperor"; Jianwen-Yongle transition
Jianwen-Yongle transition, 84–87, 184n5, 184n7, 184n8, 185–86n15, 186n20; in *West Lake Stories, Second Collection* (*Xihu erji*), 189n45, 189n45. See also "Cheng Ji and the Jianwen Emperor"; "Tie Xuan and His Daughters"
jie. See chastity
"Jin Chao," 56–57
Jingshi tongyan. See *Common Words to Warn the World* (*Jingshi tongyan*)
Jingu qiguan. See *Remarkable Spectacles Past and Present* (*Jingu qiguan*)
Jizi, 100, 187n35, 190n63

Kangxi. See *Sixteen Maxims*

Langxian, 32, 40, 176n42. See also *Constant Words to Awaken the World* (*Xingshi hengyan*); *Rocks Nod Their Heads* (*Shi diantou*)
Liaohai danzhong lu. See *Record of Fervent Loyalty in the Liaodong Peninsula, A* (*Liaohai danzhong lu*)
Lienü zhuan. See *Exemplary Women* (*Lienü zhuan*)

Li Jinglong, 88, 186n20
Ling Mengchu, 1. See also *Er Pai* (*Two Slaps*)
Li Qing, 167–68
Li Shishi, 87, 185n12
literati: civilizing efforts of, 23; corrupt, 161; debate on flesh slicing by, 31; and fame, 133; and friendship, 139, 144–45, 149–50, 157, 159; political situation of, 140–41; virtuous, 47; writing about women, 106, 111, 116, 123
Li Yu, 206n20. See also "Nativity Room"
Li Zhi, 2, 18–20, 139, 142, 172n6. See also *Sequel to a Book to Hide* (*Xu Cangshu*)
Lodge of Lofty Clouds. See Zhengxiaoguan (Lodge of Lofty Clouds)
loyalty (*zhong*), 83; analogy between male and female, 106, 192n7; and filial piety, 73–74; in *Idle Talk under the Bean Arbor* (*Doupeng xianhua*), 162–63; in Jianwen-Yongle transition, 87–88; martial models of, 86, 185n11; and reciprocity, 96, 186n18; See also "Cheng Ji and the Jianwen Emperor"; "Chongzhen's Loyal Minister and His Wife"; "Divine Instructor Warned Him Three Times, The Director of Grain Transport Did Not Escape Death, The"; "Eulogy for Overcoming and Exterminating the Great Iniquity"; "Shen Xiaoxia Encounters the Expedition Memorial"; *Story of Wei Zhongxian: A Book of Indictment, The* (*Wei Zhongxian xiaoshuo chijian shu*); "Tie Xuan and His Daughters"
"Loyalty and Filial Piety Are Assembled in One Family," 33–35
Lü Kun, 142
"Lu Mengxian Looks for His Wife on the Yangzi River," 120

Lu Minshu, 7, 167–68
lumu. See filial or graveside huts (*lumu*)
Lunhui xingshi. See *Samsara Tales to Awaken the World* (*Lunhui xingshi*)
Lu Renlong, 6–7, 168, 170n7. See also *Bell in the Still Night* (*Qingye zhong*); *Exemplary Words for the World* (*Xingshi yan*)
Lu Yunlong, 5–7, 167–68, 170n7. See also *Bell in the Still Night* (*Qingye zhong*); "Eulogy for Overcoming and Exterminating the Great Iniquity"; *Exemplary Words for the World* (*Xingshi yan*); *Story of Wei Zhongxian: A Book of Indictment, The* (*Wei Zhongxian xiaoshuo chijian shu*)

"Magistrate Teng Solves the Case of Disputed Inheritance with Ghostly Cleverness," 133–34
Mao Wenlong, 6, 93
martyrdom, 103, 191n72. See also "Cheng Ji and the Jianwen Emperor"; "Chongzhen's Loyal Minister and His Wife"; Jianwen-Yongle transition; loyalty; "Tie Xuan and His Daughters"
May Fourth movement, 28, 170n4
Mencius (Mengzi), 26, 29, 127, 161–62, 190n64
Mengzi. See Mencius
metaphor, 17, 55, 75, 84, 119, 134
mimesis. See *imitatio* and *mimesis*
Mingshi, 190n70
monastery, 42–44, 56, 70, 141. See also nunnery
monk. See "Cheng Ji and the Jianwen Emperor"; monastery
morality: "conventional," 2–4, 159; filiality and, 53; "*gang*," 146; as organizing principle, 5; private vs. public, 50, 62; reader response and, 7; reality's dissonance with, 26, 48;
relationships as condition for, 36; "supermoral," 66, 180n49
morality books, 22, 156
mother, 40–41, 44–47, 58–60. See also filial dilemmas
"Mother Comes First," 50–56, 80, 160
mourning: by daughters, 86, 93; and filial dilemmas, 56, 62; and filial piety, 31, 33, 37, 41, 154
murder. See filial dilemmas

"Nativity Room," 177n54
nature vs. nurture, 4, 21–22, 36–37, 176n36
neighbors, 56
nun. See nunnery
nunnery, 70, 76

On Friendship, 144, 148, 153, 200n20, 200n21, 200–201n23, 203n48

Pai'an jingqi. See *Slapping the Table in Amazement*
paired stories, 4, 80, 170–71n14
prefaces 6, 7; in *Bell in the Still Night*, 5, 167; compared, 13–17; to "Eulogy for Overcoming and Exterminating the Great Iniquity," 101; to *Exemplary Words*, 8, 9, 10, 11, 160–61, 165–66; to *History of Love*, 19; to "Injustice to Tang Guimei," 111–12, 115; by Ling Mengchu, 68; to "Lu Mengxian Looks for His Wife on the Yangzi River," 123; by Lu Yunlong, 126; to "Mother Comes First," 53–54; to "Qin Zhu the New Liuxia Hui," 156; to *San Yan*, 103; to "A Slice of Liver for Grandma," 72, 80; to "Tie Xuan and His Daughters," 88; in *True Cases of Filial Piety*, 29; to "Wang Mian the Exemplary Friend," 147; to "Wang Shiming the Filial Avenger," 66–67; to "The Yao Brothers," 132

property, 62, 128–38, 153, 197n7
Qi'shi er chao renwu yanyi. See *Stories of Figures from the Seventy-Two Domains (Qi'shi er chao renwu yanyi)*
"Qin Zhu the New Liuxia Hui," 154–57
qing (love, feelings, emotions), 19, 30, 40, 117; and "cult of feelings," 2
Qingye zhong. See *Bell in the Still Night (Qingye zhong)*

reader response, 7
Recent Words by Cuiyuge (Cuiyuge Jinyan), 6
recognition, 42–43, 176n45
Record of Fervent Loyalty in the Liaodong Peninsula, A (Liaohai danzhong lu), 6, 168
Record of Rites (Liji), 17, 19, 20, 63, 175n25, 191n2
Remarkable Spectacles Past and Present (Jingu qiguan), 166
remonstrance, 105, 191n2
ren. See forbearance (*ren*)
retribution. See *bao*
Ricci, Matteo, 144. See also *On Friendship*
Rocks Nod Their Heads (Shi diantou), 32–33, 41–42. See also "Lu Mengxian Looks for His Wife on the Yangzi River"; "Wang Benli Searches for his Father at the Far End of the Empire"
ruler and subject, 27, 83–84, 187n27. *See also* loyalty (*zhong*)

Sacred Edict in Six Maxims (Shengyu liuyu), 1, 3, 29, 169n1, 169n2
Samsara Tales to Awaken the World (Lunhui xingshi), 129, 184–85n10, 197n12, 198n22
Sanke Pai'an jingqi. See *Slapping the Table in Amazement, Third Collection (Sanke Pai'an jingqi)*

San Yan (Three Words), 3; cautionary tales in, 5; filial piety in, 31; friendship stories in, 145–47, 156; paired stories in, 4, 170n14; prefaces of, 15–16. See also *Common Words to Warn the World (Jingshi tongyan)*; *Constant Words to Awaken the World (Xingshi hengyan)*; *Illustrious Words to Instruct the World (Yushi mingyan)*; "Shen Xiaoxia Encounters the Expedition Memorial"
"self-containment," 3
semantic shift, 105–106, 191n4, 191–92n5
Sequel to a Book to Hide (Xu Cangshu), 58, 95
Shen Lian, 94–95, 189n46
"Shen Xiaoxia Encounters the Expedition Memorial," 94–95
Shengyu liuyu. See *Sacred Edict in Six Maxims (Shengyu liuyu)*
Shi diantou. See *Rocks Nod Their Heads (Shi diantou)*
Sixteen Maxims, 170n2
Slapping the Table in Amazement (Pai'an jingqi), 170n14
Slapping the Table in Amazement, Second Collection (Erke Pai'an jingqi), 68, 180–81n61. See also "Against Autopsy"; "Deceitful Accomplice, The"
Slapping the Table in Amazement, Third Collection (Sanke Pai'an jingqi), 166, 205n4, 205n6
"Slice of Liver for Grandma, A" 31, 70–73, 75–80, 79, 160
Sobering Stone (Zuixing shi), 3, 20, 171n21, 194n36, 201n31
Song Lian, 70, 73–75
Song Maocheng, 50, 51, 56, 178n13
state reward system, 28, 31, 42, 72, 81, 110, 116, 121–22, 144, 160
"steaming the bones" (*zhenggu*), 64–65, 179–80n41

Stories of Figures from the Seventy-Two Domains (Qi'shi er chao renwu yanyi), 3
Story of Wei Zhongxian: A Book of Indictment, The (Wei Zhongxian xiaoshuo chijian shu), 6
suicide, 117–24, 195n46, 196n54
Sun Sui, 87, 185n12
supernatural, 5, 34, 40, 46, 80, 103–104, 156, 189n45

Taizhou school, 2, 141
Tang Xianzu, 2
Taoism, 16
"Three Devoted Brothers Win Honor by Yielding Family Property to One Another," 132–33
Three Words. See *San Yan (Three Words)*
Tianran chisou. See Langxian
"Tie Xuan and His Daughters," 84–95, 186n22, 101, 104, 150; compared to "Cheng Ji and the Jianwen Emperor," 97; daughters in, 91–94, 188n37, 188n38; Gao Xianning in, 90–91; sources for, 187n28
True Cases of Filial Piety (Xiaoshun shishi), 29
Twenty-Four Filial Exemplars (Ershisi xiao), 28–29, 34, 49, 163, 175n28, 198n17
Two Slaps. See *Er Pai (Two Slaps)*

Unofficial History of the Scholars, 46–47

Vagnone, Alfonso, 144, 172n35, 197n8
violence: displacement of, 189n45; implemented by Ming emperors, 182–83n82; military, 14; ruler and subject and, 187n27; whitewashing of, 93. See also Jianwen-Yongle transition
virtue, 4, 22–24; female, 105–106, 191n4, 191–92n5

"Wang Benli Searches for his Father at the Far End of the Empire," 33–36; eunuch episode in, 37–38; inception of journey in, 39–40; irony in, 40; mother in, 45–46
"Wang Mian the Exemplary Friend," 147–54, 160, 202n35, 203n44
"Wang Shiming the Filial Avenger," 62–68
Wang Shuying, 87–88, 185n15
Wang Yangming, 2, 30, 141
Wei Zhongxian xiaoshuo chijian shu. See *Story of Wei Zhongxian: A Book of Indictment, The (Wei Zhongxian xiaoshuo chijian shu)*
West Lake Stories, Second Collection (Xihu erji), 3; *bao* in, 23–24; filial piety in, 33; Wang Yuan's story in, 33, 35; Yongle in, 189n45, 189n45. See also "Loyalty and Filial Piety Are Assembled in One Family"
women. See chastity; filial piety: female; husband and wife; mother; virtue
"Wu Bao'an Abandons His Family to Ransom His Friend," 145, 147, 151–52, 203n46
wuchang. See Five Constant Norms (*wuchang*)
wu lun. See Five Cardinal Relationships (*wu lun*)

xia, 65–66, 67, 69
xiao. See filial piety
Xiaoji. See *Filial Records (Xiaoji)*
Xiaojing. See *Classic of Filial Piety (Xiaojing)*
Xiaoshun shishi. See *True Cases of Filial Piety (Xiaoshun shishi)*
Xihu erji. See *West Lake Stories, Second Collection (Xihu erji)*
Xingshi hengyan. See *Constant Words to Awaken the World (Xingshi hengyan)*

Xingshi yan. See *Exemplary Words for the World* (*Xingshi yan*)
Xu Cangshu. See *Sequel to a Book to Hide* (*Xu Cangshu*)
Xu Kui, 87, 185n12
Xu You, 100, 190n64

yan or *yanyi*, 7
Yang Jisheng, 119, 155, 195n46, 203n51
"Yang Jiao'ai Lays Down His Life for the Sake of Friendship," 145–46
Yang Lian, 101–102, 155, 190n67
Yang Shen, 109, 111, 113–14, 116, 123
"Yao Brothers, The" 129–32
Yongle emperor, 29, 85, 89, 186n20, 189n45. *See also* Jianwen-Yongle transition; "Tie Xuan and His Daughters"; *True Cases of Filial Piety* (*Xiaoshun shishi*)
Yongzheng, 170n2

you. See friendship (*you*)
Yushi mingyan. See *Illustrious Words to Instruct the World* (*Yushi mingyan*)

zhen. See chastity
zhenggu. See "steaming the bones" (*zhenggu*)
Zhengxiaoguan (Lodge of Lofty Clouds), 5–7, 167–68
zhong. See loyalty
Zhou Ji. See *West Lake Stories, Second Collection* (*Xihu erji*)
zhuan, 7
Zhu Di. *See* Yongle emperor
Zhu Xi, 169n2
Zhu Youjian. *See* Chongzhen emperor
Zhu Yuanzhang. *See* Hongwu emperor
Zhu Yunwen. *See* Jianwen emperor
Zuixing shi. See *Sobering Stone* (*Zuixing shi*)
Zuozhuan, 52, 97–98

www.ingramcontent.com/pod-product-compliance
Lightning Source LLC
Chambersburg PA
CBHW030646230426
43665CB00011B/979